Lecture I. Religion And Neurology.

It is with no small amount of trepidation that I take my place behind this desk, and face this learned audience. To us Americans, the experience of receiving instruction from the living voice, as well as from the books, of European scholars, is very familiar. At my own University of Harvard, not a winter passes without its harvest, large or small, of lectures from Scottish, English, French, or German representatives of the science or literature of their respective countries whom we have either induced to cross the ocean to address us, or captured on the wing as they were visiting our land. It seems the natural thing for us to listen whilst the Europeans talk. The contrary habit, of talking whilst the Europeans listen, we have not yet acquired; and in him who first makes the adventure it begets a certain sense of apology being due for so presumptuous an act. Particularly must this be the case on a soil as sacred to the American imagination as that of Edinburgh. The glories of the philosophic chair of this university were deeply impressed on my imagination in boyhood. Professor Fraser's Essays in Philosophy, then just published, was the first philosophic book I ever looked into, and I well remember the awe-struck feeling I received from the account of Sir William [pg 002] Hamilton's class-room therein contained. Hamilton's own lectures were the first philosophic writings I ever forced myself to study, and after that I was immersed in Dugald Stewart and Thomas Brown. Such juvenile emotions of reverence never get outgrown; and I confess that to find my humble self promoted from my native wilderness to be actually for the time an official here, and transmuted into a colleague of these illustrious names, carries with it a sense of dreamland quite as much as of reality.

But since I have received the honor of this appointment I have felt that it would never do to decline. The academic career also has its heroic obligations, so I stand here without further deprecatory words. Let me say only this, that now that the current, here and at Aberdeen, has begun to run from west to east, I hope it may continue to do so. As the years go by, I hope that many of my countrymen may be asked to lecture in the Scottish universities, changing places with Scotsmen lecturing in the United States; I hope that our people may become in all these higher matters even as one people; and that the peculiar philosophic temperament, as well as the peculiar political temperament, that goes with our English speech may more and more pervade and influence the world.

As regards the manner in which I shall have to administer this lectureship, I am neither a theologian, nor a scholar learned in the history of religions, nor an anthropologist. Psychology is the only branch of learning in which I am particularly versed. To the psychologist the religious propensities of man must be at least as interesting as any other of the facts pertaining to his mental constitution. It would seem, therefore, that, as a psychologist, [pg 003] the natural thing for me would be to invite you to a descriptive survey of those religious propensities.

If the inquiry be psychological, not religious institutions, but rather religious feelings and religious impulses must be its subject, and I must confine myself to those more developed subjective phenomena recorded in literature produced by articulate and fully self-conscious men, in works of piety and autobiography. Interesting as the origins and early stages of a subject always are, yet when one seeks earnestly for its full significance, one must always look to its more completely evolved and perfect forms. It follows from this that the documents that will most concern us will be those of the men who were most accomplished in the religious life and best able to give an intelligible account of their ideas and motives. These men, of course, are either comparatively modern writers, or else such earlier ones as have become religious classics. The *documents humains* which we shall find most instructive need not then be sought for in the haunts of special erudition—they lie along the beaten highway; and this circumstance, which flows so naturally from the character of our problem, suits admirably also your lecturer's lack of special theological learning. I may take my citations, my sentences and paragraphs of personal confession, from books that most of you at some time will have had already in your hands, and yet this will be no detriment to the value of my conclusions. It is true that some more adventurous reader and investigator, lecturing here in future, may unearth from the shelves of libraries documents that will make a more delectable and curious entertainment to listen to than mine. Yet I doubt whether he will necessarily, by his control of so much more out-of-the-way material, get much closer to the essence of the matter in hand.

[pg 004]
The question, What are the religious propensities? and the question, What is their philosophic significance? are two entirely different orders of question from the logical point of view; and, as a failure to recognize this fact distinctly may breed confusion, I wish to insist upon the point a little before we enter into the documents and materials to which I have referred.

In recent books on logic, distinction is made between two orders of inquiry concerning anything. First, what is the nature of it? how did it come about? what is its constitution, origin, and history? And second, What is its importance, meaning, or significance, now that it is once here? The answer to the one question is given in an *existential judgment* or proposition. The answer to the other is a *proposition of value,* what the Germans call a *Werthurtheil,* or what we may, if we like, denominate a *spiritual judgment.* Neither judgment can be deduced immediately from the other. They proceed from diverse intellectual preoccupations, and the mind combines them only by making them first separately, and then adding them together.

In the matter of religions it is particularly easy to distinguish the two orders of question. Every religious phenomenon has its history and its derivation from natural antecedents. What is nowadays called the higher criticism of the Bible is only a study of the Bible from this existential point of view, neglected too much by the earlier church. Under just what biographic conditions did the sacred writers bring forth their various contributions to the holy volume? And what had they exactly in their several individual minds, when they delivered their utterances? These are manifestly questions of historical fact, and one does not see how the answer to them can decide offhand the still further question: of what use [pg 005] should such a volume, with its manner of coming into existence so defined, be to us as a guide to life and a revelation? To answer this other question we must have already in our mind some sort of a general theory as to what the peculiarities in a thing should be which give it value for purposes of revelation; and this theory itself would be what I just called a spiritual judgment. Combining it with our existential judgment, we might indeed deduce another spiritual judgment as to the Bible's worth. Thus if our theory of revelation-value were to affirm that any book, to possess it, must have been composed automatically or not by the free caprice of the writer, or that it must exhibit no scientific and historic errors and express no local or personal passions, the Bible would probably fare ill at our hands. But if, on the other hand, our theory should allow that a book may well be a revelation in spite of errors and passions and deliberate human composition, if only it be a true record of the inner experiences of great-souled persons wrestling with the crises of their fate, then the verdict would be much more favorable. You see that the existential facts by themselves are insufficient for determining the value; and the best adepts of the higher criticism accordingly never confound the existential with the spiritual problem. With the same conclusions of fact before them, some take one view, and some another, of the Bible's value as a revelation, according as their spiritual judgment as to the foundation of values differs.

I make these general remarks about the two sorts of judgment, because there are many religious persons—some of you now present, possibly, are among them—who do not yet make a working use of the distinction, and who may therefore feel at first a little startled at [pg 006] the purely existential point of view from which in the following lectures the phenomena of religious experience must be considered. When I handle them biologically and psychologically as if they were mere curious facts of individual history, some of you may think it a degradation of so sublime a subject, and may even suspect me, until my purpose gets more fully expressed, of deliberately seeking to discredit the religious side of life.

Such a result is of course absolutely alien to my intention; and since such a prejudice on your part would seriously obstruct the due effect of much of what I have to relate, I will devote a few more words to the point.

There can be no doubt that as a matter of fact a religious life, exclusively pursued, does tend to make the person exceptional and eccentric. I speak not now of your ordinary religious believer, who follows the conventional observances of his country, whether it be Buddhist, Christian, or Mohammedan. His religion has been made for him by others, communicated to him by tradition, determined to fixed forms by imitation, and retained by habit. It would profit us little to study this second-hand religious life. We must make search rather for the original experiences which were the pattern-setters to all this mass of suggested feeling and imitated conduct. These experiences we can only find in individuals for whom religion exists not as a dull habit, but as an acute fever rather. But such individuals are "geniuses" in the religious line; and like many other geniuses who have brought forth fruits effective enough for commemoration in the pages of biography, such religious geniuses have often shown symptoms of nervous instability. Even more perhaps than other kinds of genius, religious leaders have been subject to abnormal psychical visitations. Invariably they have been creatures of exalted emotional sensibility. [pg 007] Often they have led a discordant inner life, and had melancholy during a part of their career. They have known no measure, been liable to obsessions and fixed ideas; and frequently they have fallen into trances, heard voices, seen visions, and presented all sorts of peculiarities which are ordinarily classed as pathological. Often, moreover, these pathological features in their career have helped to give them their religious authority and influence.

If you ask for a concrete example, there can be no better one than is furnished by the person of George Fox. The Quaker religion which he founded is something which it is impossible to overpraise. In a day of shams, it was a religion of veracity rooted in spiritual inwardness, and a return to something more like the original gospel truth than men had ever known in England. So far as our Christian sects to-day are evolving into liberality, they are simply reverting in essence to the position which Fox and the early Quakers so long ago assumed. No one can pretend for a moment that in point of spiritual sagacity and capacity, Fox's mind was unsound. Every one who confronted him personally, from Oliver Cromwell down to county magistrates and jailers, seems to have acknowledged his superior power. Yet from the point of view of his nervous constitution, Fox was a psychopath or *détraqué* of the deepest dye. His Journal abounds in entries of this sort:—

> "As I was walking with several friends, I lifted up my head, and saw three steeple-house spires, and they struck at my life. I asked them what place that was? They said, Lichfield. Immediately the word of the Lord came to me, that I must go thither. Being come to the house we were going to, I wished the friends to walk into the house, saying nothing to them of whither I was to go. As soon as they were gone I stept away, [pg 008]and went by my eye over hedge and ditch till I came within a mile of Lichfield; where, in a great field, shepherds were keeping their sheep. Then was I commanded by the Lord to pull off my shoes. I stood still, for it was winter: but the word of the Lord was like a fire in me. So I put off my shoes, and left them with the shepherds; and the poor shepherds trembled, and were astonished. Then I walked on about a mile, and as soon as I was got within the city, the word of the Lord came to me again, saying: Cry, 'Wo to the bloody city of Lichfield!' So I went up and down the streets, crying with a loud voice, Wo to the bloody city of Lichfield! It being market day, I went into the market-place, and to and fro in the several parts of it, and made stands, crying as before, Wo to the bloody city of Lichfield! And no one laid hands on me. As I went thus crying through the streets, there seemed to me to be a channel of blood running down the streets, and the market-place appeared like a pool of blood. When I had declared what was upon me, and felt myself clear, I went out of the town in peace; and returning to the shepherds gave them some money, and took my shoes of them again. But the fire of the Lord was so on my feet, and all over me, that I did not matter to put on my shoes again, and was at a stand whether I should or no, till I felt freedom from the Lord so to do: then, after I had washed my feet, I put on my shoes again. After this a deep consideration came upon me, for what reason I should be sent to cry against that city, and call it The bloody city! For though the parliament had the minister one while, and the king another, and much blood had been shed in the town during the wars between them, yet there was no more than had befallen many other places. But afterwards I came to understand, that in the Emperor Diocletian's time a thousand Christians were martyr'd in Lichfield. So I was to go, without my shoes, through the channel of their blood, and into the pool of their blood in the market-place, that I might raise up the memorial of the blood of those martyrs, which had been shed above a

thousand years before, and lay cold in their streets. So the sense of this blood was upon me, and I obeyed the word of the Lord."

[pg 009]
Bent as we are on studying religion's existential conditions, we cannot possibly ignore these pathological aspects of the subject. We must describe and name them just as if they occurred in non-religious men. It is true that we instinctively recoil from seeing an object to which our emotions and affections are committed handled by the intellect as any other object is handled. The first thing the intellect does with an object is to class it along with something else. But any object that is infinitely important to us and awakens our devotion feels to us also as if it must be *sui generis* and unique. Probably a crab would be filled with a sense of personal outrage if it could hear us class it without ado or apology as a crustacean, and thus dispose of it. "I am no such thing," it would say; "I am MYSELF, MYSELF alone."

The next thing the intellect does is to lay bare the causes in which the thing originates. Spinoza says: "I will analyze the actions and appetites of men as if it were a question of lines, of planes, and of solids." And elsewhere he remarks that he will consider our passions and their properties with the same eye with which he looks on all other natural things, since the consequences of our affections flow from their nature with the same necessity as it results from the nature of a triangle that its three angles should be equal to two right angles. Similarly M. Taine, in the introduction to his history of English literature, has written: "Whether facts be moral or physical, it makes no matter. They always have their causes. There are causes for ambition, courage, veracity, just as there are for digestion, muscular movement, animal heat. Vice and virtue are products like vitriol and sugar." When we read such proclamations of the intellect bent on showing the existential conditions of absolutely [pg 010] everything, we feel—quite apart from our legitimate impatience at the somewhat ridiculous swagger of the program, in view of what the authors are actually able to perform—menaced and negated in the springs of our innermost life. Such cold-blooded assimilations threaten, we think, to undo our soul's vital secrets, as if the same breath which should succeed in explaining their origin would simultaneously explain away their significance, and make them appear of no more preciousness, either, than the useful groceries of which M. Taine speaks.

Perhaps the commonest expression of this assumption that spiritual value is undone if lowly origin be asserted is seen in those comments which unsentimental people so often pass on their more sentimental acquaintances. Alfred believes in immortality so strongly because his temperament is so emotional. Fanny's extraordinary conscientiousness is merely a matter of over-instigated nerves. William's melancholy about the universe is due to bad digestion—probably his liver is torpid. Eliza's delight in her church is a symptom of her hysterical constitution. Peter would be less troubled about his soul if he would take more exercise in the open air, etc. A more fully developed example of the same kind of reasoning is the fashion, quite common nowadays among certain writers, of criticising the religious emotions by showing a connection between them and the sexual life. Conversion is a crisis of puberty and adolescence. The macerations of saints, and the devotion of missionaries, are only instances of the parental instinct of self-sacrifice gone astray. For the hysterical nun, starving for natural life, Christ is but an imaginary substitute for a more earthly object of affection. And the like.[1]

[pg 011]
We are surely all familiar in a general way with this method of discrediting states of mind for which we have [pg 012] an antipathy. We all use it to some degree in criticising persons whose states of mind we regard as overstrained. But when other people criticise our own more exalted soul-flights by calling them "nothing but" expressions of our organic disposition, we feel outraged and hurt, for we know that, whatever be our organism's peculiarities, our mental states have their substantive value as revelations [pg 013] of the living truth; and we wish that all this medical materialism could be made to hold its tongue.

Medical materialism seems indeed a good appellation for the too simple-minded system of thought which we are considering. Medical materialism finishes up Saint Paul by calling his vision on the road to Damascus a discharging lesion of the occipital cortex, he being an epileptic. It snuffs out Saint Teresa as an hysteric, Saint Francis of Assisi as an hereditary degenerate. George Fox's discontent with the shams of his age, and his pining for spiritual veracity, it treats as a symptom of a disordered colon. Carlyle's organ-tones of misery it accounts for by a gastro-duodenal catarrh. All such mental over-tensions, it says, are, when you come to the bottom of the matter, mere affairs of diathesis (auto-intoxications most probably), due to the perverted action of various glands which physiology will yet discover.

And medical materialism then thinks that the spiritual authority of all such personages is successfully undermined.[2]

Let us ourselves look at the matter in the largest possible way. Modern psychology, finding definite psycho-physical connections to hold good, assumes as a convenient hypothesis that the dependence of mental states upon bodily conditions must be thorough-going and complete. If we adopt the assumption, then of course what medical materialism insists on must be true in a general way, if not in every detail: Saint Paul certainly had once an epileptoid, if not an epileptic seizure; George Fox was an hereditary degenerate; Carlyle was undoubtedly auto-intoxicated by some organ or other, no matter which,—and [pg 014] the rest. But now, I ask you, how can such an existential account of facts of mental history decide in one way or another upon their spiritual significance? According to the general postulate of psychology just referred to, there is not a single one of our states of mind, high or low, healthy or morbid, that has not some organic process as its condition. Scientific theories are organically conditioned just as much as religious emotions are; and if we only knew the facts intimately enough, we should doubtless see "the liver" determining the dicta of the sturdy atheist as decisively as it does those of the Methodist under conviction anxious about his soul. When it alters in one way the blood that percolates it, we get the methodist, when in another way, we get the atheist form of mind. So of all our raptures and our drynesses, our longings and pantings, our questions and beliefs. They are equally organically founded, be they of religious or of non-religious content.

To plead the organic causation of a religious state of mind, then, in refutation of its claim to possess superior spiritual value, is quite illogical and arbitrary, unless one have already worked out in advance some psycho-physical theory connecting spiritual values in general with determinate sorts of physiological change. Otherwise none of our thoughts and feelings, not even our scientific doctrines, not even our *dis*-beliefs, could retain any value as revelations of the truth, for every one of them without exception flows from the state of their possessor's body at the time.

It is needless to say that medical materialism draws in point of fact no such sweeping skeptical conclusion. It is sure, just as every simple man is sure, that some states of mind are inwardly superior to others, and reveal to us more truth, and in this it simply makes use of an ordinary [pg 015] spiritual judgment. It has no physiological theory of the production of these its favorite states, by which it may accredit them; and its attempt to discredit the states which it dislikes, by vaguely associating them with nerves and liver, and connecting them with names connoting bodily affliction, is altogether illogical and inconsistent.

Let us play fair in this whole matter, and be quite candid with ourselves and with the facts. When we think certain states of mind superior to others, is it ever because of what we know concerning their organic antecedents? No! it is always for two entirely different reasons. It is either because we take an immediate delight in them; or else it is because we believe them to bring us good consequential fruits for life. When we speak disparagingly of "feverish fancies," surely the fever-process as such is not the ground of our disesteem—for aught we know to the contrary, 103° or 104° Fahrenheit might be a much more favorable temperature for truths to germinate and sprout in, than the more ordinary blood-heat of 97 or 98 degrees. It is either the disagreeableness itself of the fancies, or their inability to bear the criticisms of the convalescent hour. When we praise the thoughts which health brings, health's peculiar chemical metabolisms have nothing to do with determining our judgment. We know in fact almost nothing about these metabolisms. It is the character of inner happiness in the thoughts which stamps them as good, or else their consistency with our other opinions and their serviceability for our needs, which make them pass for true in our esteem.

Now the more intrinsic and the more remote of these criteria do not always hang together. Inner happiness and serviceability do not always agree. What immediately feels most "good" is not always most "true," when [pg 016] measured by the verdict of the rest of experience. The difference between Philip drunk and Philip sober is the classic instance in corroboration. If merely "feeling good" could decide, drunkenness would be the supremely valid human experience. But its revelations, however acutely satisfying at the moment, are inserted into an environment which refuses to bear them out for any length of time. The consequence of this discrepancy of the two criteria is the uncertainty which still prevails over so many of our spiritual judgments. There are moments of sentimental and mystical experience—we shall hereafter hear much of them—that carry an enormous sense of inner authority and illumination with them when they come. But they come seldom, and they do not come to every one; and the rest of life makes either no connection with them, or tends to contradict them more than it confirms them. Some persons follow more the voice of the moment in these cases, some prefer to be guided by the average results. Hence the sad discordancy of so many of the spiritual judgments of human beings; a discordancy which will be brought home to us acutely enough before these lectures end.

It is, however, a discordancy that can never be resolved by any merely medical test. A good example of the impossibility of holding strictly to the medical tests is seen in the theory of the pathological causation of genius promulgated by recent authors. "Genius," said Dr. Moreau, "is but one of the many branches of the neuropathic tree." "Genius," says Dr. Lombroso, "is a symptom of hereditary degeneration of the epileptoid variety, and is allied to moral insanity." "Whenever a man's life," writes Mr. Nisbet, "is at once sufficiently illustrious and recorded with sufficient fullness to be a subject of profitable [pg 017] study, he inevitably falls into the morbid category.... And it is worthy of remark that, as a rule, the greater the genius, the greater the unsoundness."[3]

Now do these authors, after having succeeded in establishing to their own satisfaction that the works of genius are fruits of disease, consistently proceed thereupon to impugn the *value* of the fruits? Do they deduce a new spiritual judgment from their new doctrine of existential conditions? Do they frankly forbid us to admire the productions of genius from now onwards? and say outright that no neuropath can ever be a revealer of new truth?

No! their immediate spiritual instincts are too strong for them here, and hold their own against inferences which, in mere love of logical consistency, medical materialism ought to be only too glad to draw. One disciple of the school, indeed, has striven to impugn the value of works of genius in a wholesale way (such works of contemporary art, namely, as he himself is unable to enjoy, and they are many) by using medical arguments.[4] But for the most part the masterpieces are left unchallenged; and the medical line of attack either confines itself to such secular productions as every one admits to be intrinsically eccentric, or else addresses itself exclusively to religious manifestations. And then it is because the religious manifestations have been already condemned because the critic dislikes them on internal or spiritual grounds.

In the natural sciences and industrial arts it never occurs to any one to try to refute opinions by showing up their author's neurotic constitution. Opinions here are invariably tested by logic and by experiment, no [pg 018] matter what may be their author's neurological type. It should be no otherwise with religious opinions. Their value can only be ascertained by spiritual judgments directly passed upon them, judgments based on our own immediate feeling primarily; and secondarily on what we can ascertan of their experiential relations to our moral needs and to the rest of what we hold as true.

Immediateluminousness , in short, *philosophicalr easonableness*, and *moral helpfulness* are the only available criteria. Saint Teresa might have had the nervous system of the placidest cow, and it would not now save her theology, if the trial of the theology by these other tests should show it to be contemptible. And conversely if her theology can stand these other tests, it will make no difference how hysterical or nervously off her balance Saint Teresa may have been when she was with us here below.

You see that at bottom we are thrown back upon the general principles by which the empirical philosophy has always contended that we must be guided in our search for truth. Dogmatic philosophies have sought for tests for truth which might dispense us from appealing to the future. Some direct mark, by noting which we can be protected immediately and absolutely, now and forever, against all mistake—such has been the darling dream of philosophic dogmatists. It is clear that the *origin* of the truth would be an admirable criterion of this sort, if only the various origins could be discriminated from one another from this point of view, and the history of dogmatic opinion shows that origin has always been a favorite test. Origin in immediate intuition; origin in pontifical authority; origin in supernatural revelation, as by vision, hearing, or unaccountable impression; origin in direct [pg 019] possession by a higher spirit, expressing itself in prophecy and warning; origin in automatic utterance generally,—these origins have been stock warrants for the truth of one opinion after another which we find represented in religious history. The medical materialists are therefore only so many belated dogmatists, neatly turning the tables on their predecessors by using the criterion of origin in a destructive instead of an accreditive way.

They are effective with their talk of pathological origin only so long as supernatural origin is pleaded by the other side, and nothing but the argument from origin is under discussion. But the argument from origin has seldom been used alone, for it is too obviously insufficient. Dr. Maudsley is perhaps the cleverest of the rebutters of supernatural religion on grounds of origin. Yet he finds himself forced to write:—

"What right have we to believe Nature under any obligation to do her work by means of complete minds only? She may find an incomplete mind a more suitable instrument for a particular purpose. It is the work that is done, and the quality in the worker by which it was done, that is alone of moment; and it may be no great matter from a cosmical standpoint, if in other qualities of character he was singularly defective—if indeed he were hypocrite, adulterer, eccentric, or lunatic.... Home we come again, then, to the old and last resort of certitude,—namely the common assent of mankind, or of the competent by instruction and training among mankind."[5]

In other words, not its origin, but *the way in which it works on the whole*, is Dr. Maudsley's final test of a belief. This is our own empiricist criterion; and this criterion [pg 020] the stoutest insisters on supernatural origin have also been forced to use in the end. Among the visions and messages some have always been too patently silly, among the trances and convulsive seizures some have been too fruitless for conduct and character, to pass themselves off as significant, still less as divine. In the history of Christian mysticism the problem how to discriminate between such messages and experiences as were really divine miracles, and such others as the demon in his malice was able to counterfeit, thus making the religious person twofold more the child of hell he was before, has always been a difficult one to solve, needing all the sagacity and experience of the best directors of conscience. In the end it had to come to our empiricist criterion: By their fruits ye shall know them, not by their roots, Jonathan Edwards's Treatise on Religious Affections is an elaborate working out of this thesis. The *roots* of a man's virtue are inaccessible to us. No appearances whatever are infallible proofs of grace. Our practice is the only sure evidence, even to ourselves, that we are genuinely Christians.

> "In forming a judgment of ourselves now," Edwards writes, "we should certainly adopt that evidence which our supreme Judge will chiefly make use of when we come to stand before him at the last day.... There is not one grace of the Spirit of God, of the existence of which, in any professor of religion, Christian practice is not the most decisive evidence.... The degree in which our experience is productive of practice shows the degree in which our experience is spiritual and divine."

Catholic writers are equally emphatic. The good dispositions which a vision, or voice, or other apparent heavenly favor leave behind them are the only marks by which we may be sure they are not possible deceptions of the tempter. Says Saint Teresa:—

[pg 021]

> "Like imperfect sleep which, instead of giving more strength to the head, doth but leave it the more exhausted, the result of mere operations of the imagination is but to weaken the soul. Instead of nourishment and energy she reaps only lassitude and disgust: whereas a genuine heavenly vision yields to

> her a harvest of ineffable spiritual riches, and an admirable renewal of bodily strength. I alleged these reasons to those who so often accused my visions of being the work of the enemy of mankind and the sport of my imagination.... I showed them the jewels which the divine hand had left with me:—they were my actual dispositions. All those who knew me saw that I was changed; my confessor bore witness to the fact; this improvement, palpable in all respects, far from being hidden, was brilliantly evident to all men. As for myself, it was impossible to believe that if the demon were its author, he could have used, in order to lose me and lead me to hell, an expedient so contrary to his own interests as that of uprooting my vices, and filling me with masculine courage and other virtues instead, for I saw clearly that a single one of these visions was enough to enrich me with all that wealth."[6]

I fear I may have made a longer excursus than was necessary, and that fewer words would have dispelled the uneasiness which may have arisen among some of you as I announced my pathological programme. At any rate you must all be ready now to judge the religious life by its results exclusively, and I shall assume that the bugaboo of morbid origin will scandalize your piety no more.

Still, you may ask me, if its results are to be the ground of our final spiritual estimate of a religious phenomenon, why threaten us at all with so much existential study of its conditions? Why not simply leave pathological questions out?

To this I reply in two ways: First, I say, irrepressible curiosity imperiously leads one on; and I say, secondly, [pg 022] that it always leads to a better understanding of a thing's significance to consider its exaggerations and perversions, its equivalents and substitutes and nearest relatives elsewhere. Not that we may thereby swamp the thing in the wholesale condemnation which we pass on its inferior congeners, but rather that we may by contrast ascertain the more precisely in what its merits consist, by learning at the same time to what particular dangers of corruption it may also be exposed.

Insane conditions have this advantage, that they isolate special factors of the mental life, and enable us to inspect them unmasked by their more usual surroundings. They play the part in mental anatomy which the scalpel and the microscope play in the anatomy of the body. To understand a thing rightly we need to see it both out of its environment and in it, and to have acquaintance with the whole range of its variations. The study of hallucinations has in this way been for psychologists the key to their comprehension of normal sensation, that of illusions has been the key to the right comprehension of perception. Morbid impulses and imperative conceptions, "fixed ideas," so called, have thrown a flood of light on the psychology of the normal will; and obsessions and delusions have performed the same service for that of the normal faculty of belief.

Similarly, the nature of genius has been illuminated by the attempts, of which I already made mention, to class it with psychopathical phenomena. Borderland insanity, crankiness, insane temperament, loss of mental balance, psychopathic degeneration (to use a few of the many synonyms by which it has been called), has certain peculiarities and liabilities which, when combined with a superior quality of intellect in an individual, make it more probable that he will make his mark and affect his [pg 023] age, than if his temperament were less neurotic. There is of course no special affinity between crankiness as such and superior intellect,[7] for most psychopaths have feeble intellects, and superior intellects more commonly have normal nervous systems. But the psychopathic temperament, whatever be the intellect with which it finds itself paired, often brings with it ardor and excitability of character. The cranky person has extraordinary emotional susceptibility. He is liable to fixed ideas and obsessions. His conceptions tend to pass immediately into belief and action; and when he gets a new idea, he has no rest till he proclaims it, or in some way "works it off." "What shall I think of it?" a common person says to himself about a vexed question; but in a "cranky" mind "What must I do about it?" is the form the question tends to take. In the autobiography of that high-souled woman, Mrs. Annie Besant, I read the following passage: "Plenty of people wish well to any good cause, but very few care to exert themselves to help it, and still fewer will risk anything in its support. 'Some one ought to do it, but why should I?' is the ever reëchoed phrase of weak-kneed amiability. 'Some one ought to do it, so why not I?' is the cry of some earnest servant of man, eagerly forward springing to face some perilous duty. Between these two sentences lie whole centuries of moral evolution." True enough! and between these two sentences lie also the different destinies of the ordinary sluggard and the psychopathic man. Thus, when a superior intellect and a psychopathic temperament coalesce—as in the endless permutations and combinations of human faculty, they are bound to coalesce often enough—in the same individual, we have [pg 024] the best possible condition for the kind of effective genius that gets into the biographical dictionaries. Such men do not remain mere critics and understanders with their intellect. Their ideas possess them, they inflict them, for better or worse, upon their companions or their age. It is they who get counted when Messrs Lombroso, Nisbet, and others invoke statistics to defend their paradox.

To pass now to religious phenomena, take the melancholy which, as we shall see, constitutes an essential moment in every complete religious evolution. Take the happiness which achieved religious belief confers. Take the trance-like states of insight into truth which all religious mystics report.[8] These are each and all of them special cases of kinds of human experience of much wider scope. Religious melancholy, whatever peculiarities it may have *quâ* religious, is at any rate melancholy. Religious happiness is happiness. Religious trance is trance. And the moment we renounce the absurd notion that a thing is exploded away as soon as it is classed with others, or its origin is shown; the moment we agree to stand by experimental results and inner quality, in judging of values,—who does not see that we are likely to ascertain the distinctive significance of religious melancholy and happiness, or of religious trances, far better by comparing them as conscientiously as we can with other varieties of melancholy, happiness, and trance, than by refusing to consider their place in any more general series, and treating them as if they were outside of nature's order altogether?

I hope that the course of these lectures will confirm us in this supposition. As regards the psychopathic origin of so many religious phenomena, that would not be [pg 025] in the least surprising or disconcerting, even were such phenomena certified from on high to be the most precious of human experiences. No one organism can possibly yield to its owner the whole body of truth. Few of us are not in some way infirm, or even diseased; and our very infirmities help us unexpectedly. In the psychopathic temperament we have the emotionality which is the *sinequânon* of moral perception; we have the intensity and tendency to emphasis which are the essence of practical moral vigor; and we have the love of metaphysics and mysticism which carry one's interests beyond the surface of the sensible world. What, then, is more natural than that this temperament should introduce one to regions of religious truth, to corners of the universe, which your robust Philistine type of nervous system, forever offering its biceps to be felt, thumping its breast, and thanking Heaven that it hasn't a single morbid fibre in its composition, would be sure to hide forever from its self-satisfied possessors?

If there were such a thing as inspiration from a higher realm, it might well be that the neurotic temperament would furnish the chief condition of the requisite receptivity. And having said thus much, I think that I may let the matter of religion and neuroticism drop.

The mass of collateral phenomena, morbid or healthy, with which the various religious phenomena must be compared in order to understand them better, forms what in the slang of pedagogics is termed "the apperceiving mass" by which we comprehend them. The only novelty that I can imagine this course of lectures to possess lies in the breadth of the apperceiving mass. I may succeed in discussing religious experiences in a wider context than has been usual in university courses.

Lecture II. Circumscription of the Topic.

Most books on the philosophy of religion try to begin with a precise definition of what its essence consists of. Some of these would-be definitions may possibly come before us in later portions of this course, and I shall not be pedantic enough to enumerate any of them to you now. Meanwhile the very fact that they are so many and so different from one another is enough to prove that the word "religion" cannot stand for any single principle or essence, but is rather a collective name. The theorizing mind tends always to the over-simplification of its materials. This is the root of all that absolutism and one-sided dogmatism by which both philosophy and religion have been infested. Let us not fall immediately into a one-sided view of our subject, but let us rather admit freely at the outset that we may very likely find no one essence, but many characters which may alternately be equally important in religion. If we should inquire for the essence of "government," for example, one man might tell us it was authority, another submission, another police, another an army, another an assembly, another a system of laws; yet all the while it would be true that no concrete government can exist without all these things, one of which is more important at one moment and others at another. The man who knows governments most completely is he who troubles himself least about a definition which shall give their essence. Enjoying an intimate acquaintance with all their particularities [pg 027] in turn, he would naturally regard an abstract conception in which these were unified as a thing more misleading than enlightening. And why may not religion be a conception equally complex?[9]

Consider also the "religious sentiment" which we see referred to in so many books, as if it were a single sort of mental entity.

In the psychologies and in the philosophies of religion, we find the authors attempting to specify just what entity it is. One man allies it to the feeling of dependence; one makes it a derivative from fear; others connect it with the sexual life; others still identify it with the feeling of the infinite; and so on. Such different ways of conceiving it ought of themselves to arouse doubt as to whether it possibly can be one specific thing; and the moment we are willing to treat the term "religious sentiment" as a collective name for the many sentiments which religious objects may arouse in alternation, we see that it probably contains nothing whatever of a psychologically specific nature. There is religious fear, religious love, religious awe, religious joy, and so forth. But religious love is only man's natural emotion of love directed to a religious object; religious fear is only the ordinary fear of commerce, so to speak, the common quaking of the human breast, in so far as the notion of divine retribution may arouse it; religious awe is the same organic thrill which we feel in a forest at twilight, or in a mountain gorge; only this time it comes over us at the thought of our supernatural relations; and similarly of all the various sentiments which may be called into play in the lives of [pg 028] religious persons. As concrete states of mind, made up of a feeling *plus* a specific sort of object, religious emotions of course are psychic entities distinguishable from other concrete emotions; but there is no ground for assuming a simple abstract "religious emotion" to exist as a distinct elementary mental affection by itself, present in every religious experience without exception.

As there thus seems to be no one elementary religious emotion, but only a common storehouse of emotions upon which religious objects may draw, so there might conceivably also prove to be no one specific and essential kind of religious object, and no one specific and essential kind of religious act.

The field of religion being as wide as this, it is manifestly impossible that I should pretend to cover it. My lectures must be limited to a fraction of the subject. And, although it would indeed be foolish to set up an abstract definition of religion's essence, and then proceed to defend that definition against all comers, yet this need not prevent me from taking my own narrow view of what religion shall consist in *for the purpose of these lectures*, or, out of the many meanings of the word, from choosing the one meaning in which I wish to interest you particularly, and proclaiming arbitrarily that when I say "religion" I mean *that*. This, in fact, is what I must do, and I will now preliminarily seek to mark out the field I choose.

One way to mark it out easily is to say what aspects of the subject we leave out. At the outset we are struck by one great partition which divides the religious field. On the one side of it lies institutional, on the other personal religion. As M. P. Sabatier says, one branch of religion keeps the divinity, another keeps man most in [pg 029] view. Worship and sacrifice, procedures for working on the dispositions of the deity, theology and ceremony and ecclesiastical organization, are the essentials of religion in the institutional branch. Were we to limit our view to it, we should have to define religion as an external art, the art of winning the favor of the gods. In the more personal branch of religion it is on the contrary the inner dispositions of man himself which form the centre of interest, his conscience, his deserts, his helplessness, his incompleteness. And although the favor of the God, as forfeited or gained, is still an essential feature of the story, and theology plays a vital part therein, yet the acts to which this sort of religion prompts are personal not ritual acts, the individual transacts the business by himself alone, and the ecclesiastical organization, with its priests and sacraments and other go-betweens, sinks to an altogether secondary place. The relation goes direct from heart to heart, from soul to soul, between man and his maker.

Now in these lectures I propose to ignore the institutional branch entirely, to say nothing of the ecclesiastical organization, to consider as little as possible the systematic theology and the ideas about the gods themselves, and to confine myself as far as I can to personal religion pure and simple. To some of you personal religion, thus nakedly considered, will no doubt seem too incomplete a thing to wear the general name. "It is a part of religion," you will say, "but only its unorganized rudiment; if we are to name it by itself, we had better call it man's conscience or morality than his religion. The name 'religion' should be reserved for the fully organized system of feeling, thought, and institution, for the Church, in short, of which this personal religion, so called, is but a fractional element."

[pg 030]
But if you say this, it will only show the more plainly how much the question of definition tends to become a dispute about names. Rather than prolong such a dispute, I am willing to accept almost any name for the personal religion of which I propose to treat. Call it conscience or morality, if you yourselves prefer, and not religion—under either name it will be equally worthy of our study. As for myself, I think it will prove to contain some elements which morality pure and simple does not contain, and these elements I shall soon seek to point out; so I will myself continue to apply the word "religion" to it; and in the last lecture of all, I will bring in the theologies and the ecclesiasticisms, and say something of its relation to them.

In one sense at least the personal religion will prove itself more fundamental than either theology or ecclesiasticism. Churches, when once established, live at second-hand upon tradition; but the *founders* of every church owed their power originally to the fact of their direct personal communion with the divine. Not only the superhuman founders, the Christ, the Buddha, Mahomet, but all the originators of Christian sects have been in this case;—so personal religion should still seem the primordial thing, even to those who continue to esteem it incomplete.

There are, it is true, other things in religion chronologically more primordial than personal devoutness in the moral sense. Fetishism and magic seem to have preceded inward piety historically—at least our records of inward piety do not reach back so far. And if fetishism and magic be regarded as stages of religion, one may say that personal religion in the inward sense and the genuinely spiritual ecclesiasticisms which it founds are phenomena of secondary or even tertiary order. But, quite [pg 031] apart from the fact that many anthropologists—for instance, Jevons and Frazer—expressly oppose "religion" and "magic" to each other, it is certain that the whole system of thought which leads to magic, fetishism, and the lower superstitions may just as well be called primitive science as called primitive religion. The question thus becomes a verbal one again; and our knowledge of all these early stages of thought and feeling is in any case so conjectural and imperfect that farther discussion would not be worth while.

Religion, therefore, as I now ask you arbitrarily to take it, shall mean for us *the feelings, acts, and experiences of individual men in their solitude, so far as they apprehend themselves to stand in relation to whatever they may consider the divine.* Since the relation may be either moral, physical, or ritual, it is evident that out of religion in the sense in which we take it, theologies, philosophies, and ecclesiastical organizations may secondarily grow. In these lectures, however, as I have already said, the immediate personal experiences will amply fill our time, and we shall hardly consider theology or ecclesiasticism at all.

We escape much controversial matter by this arbitrary definition of our field. But, still, a chance of controversy comes up over the word "divine" if we take it in the definition in too narrow a sense. There are systems of thought which the world usually calls religious, and yet which do not positively assume a God. Buddhism is in this case. Popularly, of course, the Buddha himself stands in place of a God; but in strictness the Buddhistic system is atheistic. Modern transcendental idealism, Emersonianism, for instance, also seems to let God evaporate into abstract Ideality. Not a deity *in concreto*, not a superhuman person, but the immanent divinity in [pg 032] things, the essentially spiritual structure of the universe, is the object of the transcendentalist cult. In that address to the graduating class at Divinity College in 1838 which made Emerson famous, the frank expression of this worship of mere abstract laws was what made the scandal of the performance.

> "These laws," said the speaker, "execute themselves. They are out of time, out of space, and not subject to circumstance: Thus, in the soul of man there is a justice whose retributions are instant and entire. He who does a good deed is instantly ennobled. He who does a mean deed is by the action itself contracted. He who puts off impurity thereby puts on purity. If a man is at heart just, then in so far is he God; the safety of God, the immortality of God, the majesty of God, do enter into that man with justice. If a man dissemble, deceive, he deceives himself, and goes out of acquaintance with his own being. Character is always known. Thefts never enrich; alms never impoverish; murder will speak out of stone walls. The least admixture of a lie —for example, the taint of vanity, any attempt to make a good impression, a favorable appearance—will instantly vitiate the effect. But speak the truth,

and all things alive or brute are vouchers, and the very roots of the grass underground there do seem to stir and move to bear your witness. For all things proceed out of the same spirit, which is differently named love, justice, temperance, in its different applications, just as the ocean receives different names on the several shores which it washes. In so far as he roves from these ends, a man bereaves himself of power, of auxiliaries. His being shrinks ... he becomes less and less, a mote, a point, until absolute badness is absolute death. The perception of this law awakens in the mind a sentiment which we call the religious sentiment, and which makes our highest happiness. Wonderful is its power to charm and to command. It is a mountain air. It is the embalmer of the world. It makes the sky and the hills sublime, and the silent song of the stars is it. It is the beatitude of man. It makes him illimitable. When he says 'I ought'; when love warns him; when he chooses, [pg 033]warned from on high, the good and great deed; then, deep melodies wander through his soul from supreme wisdom. Then he can worship, and be enlarged by his worship; for he can never go behind this sentiment. All the expressions of this sentiment are sacred and permanent in proportion to their purity. [They] affect us more than all other compositions. The sentences of the olden time, which ejaculate this piety, are still fresh and fragrant. And the unique impression of Jesus upon mankind, whose name is not so much written as ploughed into the history of this world, is proof of the subtle virtue of this infusion."[10]

Such is the Emersonian religion. The universe has a divine soul of order, which soul is moral, being also the soul within the soul of man. But whether this soul of the universe be a mere quality like the eye's brilliancy or the skin's softness, or whether it be a self-conscious life like the eye's seeing or the skin's feeling, is a decision that never unmistakably appears in Emerson's pages. It quivers on the boundary of these things, sometimes leaning one way, sometimes the other, to suit the literary rather than the philosophic need. Whatever it is, though, it is active. As much as if it were a God, we can trust it to protect all ideal interests and keep the world's balance straight. The sentences in which Emerson, to the very end, gave utterance to this faith are as fine as anything in literature: "If you love and serve men, you cannot by any hiding or stratagem escape the remuneration. Secret retributions are always restoring the level, when disturbed, of the divine justice. It is impossible to tilt the beam. All the tyrants and proprietors and monopolists of the world in vain set their shoulders to heave the bar. Settles forevermore the ponderous equator to its line, and man and mote, and star and sun, must range to it, or be pulverized by the recoil."[11]

[pg 034]

Now it would be too absurd to say that the inner experiences that underlie such expressions of faith as this and impel the writer to their utterance are quite unworthy to be called religious experiences. The sort of appeal that Emersonian optimism, on the one hand, and Buddhistic pessimism, on the other, make to the individual and the sort of response which he makes to them in his life are in fact indistinguishable from, and in many respects identical with, the best Christian appeal and response. We must therefore, from the experiential point of view, call these godless or quasi-godless creeds "religions"; and accordingly when in our definition of religion we speak of the individual's relation to "what he considers the divine," we must interpret the term "divine" very broadly, as denoting any object that is god*like*, whether it be a concrete deity or not.

But the term "godlike," if thus treated as a floating general quality, becomes exceedingly vague, for many gods have flourished in religious history, and their attributes have been discrepant enough. What then is that essentially godlike quality—be it embodied in a concrete deity or not—our relation to which determines our character as religious men? It will repay us to seek some answer to this question before we proceed farther.

For one thing, gods are conceived to be first things in the way of being and power. They overarch and envelop, and from them there is no escape. What relates to them is the first and last word in the way of truth. Whatever then were most primal and enveloping and deeply true might at this rate be treated as godlike, and a man's religion might thus be identified with his attitude, whatever it might be, towards what he felt to be the primal truth.

[pg 035]
Such a definition as this would in a way be defensible. Religion, whatever it is, is a man's total reaction upon life, so why not say that any total reaction upon life is a religion? Total reactions are different from casual reactions, and total attitudes are different from usual or professional attitudes. To get at them you must go behind the foreground of existence and reach down to that curious sense of the whole residual cosmos as an everlasting presence, intimate or alien, terrible or amusing, lovable or odious, which in some

degree every one possesses. This sense of the world's presence, appealing as it does to our peculiar individual temperament, makes us either strenuous or careless, devout or blasphemous, gloomy or exultant, about life at large; and our reaction, involuntary and inarticulate and often half unconscious as it is, is the completest of all our answers to the question, "What is the character of this universe in which we dwell?" It expresses our individual sense of it in the most definite way. Why then not call these reactions our religion, no matter what specific character they may have? Non-religious as some of these reactions may be, in one sense of the word "religious," they yet belong to *the general sphere of the religious life*, and so should generically be classed as religious reactions. "He believes in No-God, and he worships him," said a colleague of mine of a student who was manifesting a fine atheistic ardor; and the more fervent opponents of Christian doctrine have often enough shown a temper which, psychologically considered, is indistinguishable from religious zeal.

But so very broad a use of the word "religion" would be inconvenient, however defensible it might remain on logical grounds. There are trifling, sneering attitudes even towards the whole of life; and in some men these [pg 036] attitudes are final and systematic. It would strain the ordinary use of language too much to call such attitudes religious, even though, from the point of view of an unbiased critical philosophy, they might conceivably be perfectly reasonable ways of looking upon life. Voltaire, for example, writes thus to a friend, at the age of seventy-three: "As for myself," he says, "weak as I am, I carry on the war to the last moment, I get a hundred pike-thrusts, I return two hundred, and I laugh. I see near my door Geneva on fire with quarrels over nothing, and I laugh again; and, thank God, I can look upon the world as a farce even when it becomes as tragic as it sometimes does. All comes out even at the end of the day, and all comes out still more even when all the days are over."

Much as we may admire such a robust old gamecock spirit in a valetudinarian, to call it a religious spirit would be odd. Yet it is for the moment Voltaire's reaction on the whole of life. *Je m'en fiche* is the vulgar French equivalent for our English ejaculation "Who cares?" And the happy term *je m'en fichisme* recently has been invented to designate the systematic determination not to take anything in life too solemnly. "All is vanity" is the relieving word in all difficult crises for this mode of thought, which that exquisite literary genius Renan took pleasure, in his later days of sweet decay, in putting into coquettishly sacrilegious forms which remain to us as excellent expressions of the "all is vanity" state of mind. Take the following passage, for example,—we must hold to duty, even against the evidence, Renan says,—but he then goes on:—

> "There are many chances that the world may be nothing but a fairy pantomime of which no God has care. We must therefore arrange ourselves so that on neither hypothesis we shall be [pg 037]completely wrong. We must listen to the superior voices, but in such a way that if the second hypothesis were true we should not have been too completely duped. If in effect the world be not a serious thing, it is the dogmatic people who will be the shallow ones, and the worldly minded whom the theologians now call frivolous will be those who are really wise.
>
> "*In utrumque paratus*, then. Be ready for anything—that perhaps is wisdom. Give ourselves up, according to the hour, to confidence, to skepticism, to optimism, to irony, and we may be sure that at certain moments at least we shall be with the truth.... Good-humor is a philosophic state of mind; it seems to say to Nature that we take her no more seriously than she takes us. I maintain that one should always talk of philosophy with a smile. We owe it to the Eternal to be virtuous; but we have the right to add to this tribute our irony as a sort of personal reprisal. In this way we return to the right quarter jest for jest; we play the trick that has been played on us. Saint Augustine's phrase: *Lord, if we are deceived, it is by thee!* remains a fine one, well suited to our modern feeling. Only we wish the Eternal to know that if we accept the fraud, we accept it knowingly and willingly. We are resigned in advance to losing the interest on our investments of virtue, but we wish not to appear ridiculous by having counted on them too securely."[12]

Surely all the usual associations of the word "religion" would have to be stripped away if such a systematic *parti pris* of irony were also to be denoted by the name. For common men "religion," whatever more special meanings it may have, signifies always a *serious* state of mind. If any one phrase could gather its universal message, that phrase would be, "All is *not* vanity in this Universe, whatever the appearances may suggest." If it can stop anything, religion as commonly apprehended can stop just such chaffing talk as Renan's. It favors gravity, not pertness; it says "hush" to all vain chatter and smart wit.

[pg 038]
But if hostile to light irony, religion is equally hostile to heavy grumbling and complaint. The world appears tragic enough in some religions, but the tragedy is realized as purging, and a way of deliverance is held to exist. We shall see enough of the religious melancholy in a future lecture; but melancholy, according to our ordinary use of language, forfeits all title to be called religious when, in Marcus Aurelius's racy words, the sufferer simply lies kicking and screaming after the fashion of a sacrificed pig. The mood of a Schopenhauer or a Nietzsche,—and in a less degree one may sometimes say the same of our own sad Carlyle,—though often an ennobling sadness, is almost as often only peevishness running away with the bit between its teeth. The sallies of the two German authors remind one, half the time, of the sick shriekings of two dying rats. They lack the purgatorial note which religious sadness gives forth.

There must be something solemn, serious, and tender about any attitude which we denominate religious. If glad, it must not grin or snicker; if sad, it must not scream or curse. It is precisely as being *solemn* experiences that I wish to interest you in religious experiences. So I propose—arbitrarily again, if you please—to narrow our definition once more by saying that the word "divine," as employed therein, shall mean for us not merely the primal and enveloping and real, for that meaning if taken without restriction might well prove too broad. The divine shall mean for us only such a primal reality as the individual feels impelled to respond to solemnly and gravely, and neither by a curse nor a jest.

But solemnity, and gravity, and all such emotional attributes, admit of various shades; and, do what we will with our defining, the truth must at last be confronted [pg 039] that we are dealing with a field of experience where there is not a single conception that can be sharply drawn. The pretension, under such conditions, to be rigorously "scientific" or "exact" in our terms would only stamp us as lacking in understanding of our task. Things are more or less divine, states of mind are more or less religious, reactions are more or less total, but the boundaries are always misty, and it is everywhere a question of amount and degree. Nevertheless, at their extreme of development, there can never be any question as to what experiences are religious. The divinity of the object and the solemnity of the reaction are too well marked for doubt. Hesitation as to whether a state of mind is "religious," or "irreligious," or "moral," or "philosophical," is only likely to arise when the state of mind is weakly characterized, but in that case it will be hardly worthy of our study at all. With states that can only by courtesy be called religious we need have nothing to do, our only profitable business being with what nobody can possibly feel tempted to call anything else. I said in my former lecture that we learn most about a thing when we view it under a microscope, as it were, or in its most exaggerated form. This is as true of religious phenomena as of any other kind of fact. The only cases likely to be profitable enough to repay our attention will therefore be cases where the religious spirit is unmistakable and extreme. Its fainter manifestations we may tranquilly pass by. Here, for example, is the total reaction upon life of Frederick Locker Lampson, whose autobiography, entitled "Confidences," proves him to have been a most amiable man.

> "I am so far resigned to my lot that I feel small pain at the thought of having to part from what has been called the pleasant habit of existence, the sweet fable of life. I would not [pg 040]care to live my wasted life over again, and so to prolong my span. Strange to say, I have but little wish to be younger. I submit with a chill at my heart. I humbly submit because it is the Divine Will, and my appointed destiny. I dread the increase of infirmities that will make me a burden to those around me, those dear to me. No! let me slip away as quietly and comfortably as I can. Let the end come, if peace come with it.
>
> "I do not know that there is a great deal to be said for this world, or our sojourn here upon it; but it has pleased God so to place us, and it must please me also. I ask you, what is human life? Is not it a maimed happiness—care and weariness, weariness and care, with the baseless expectation, the strange cozenage of a brighter to-morrow? At best it is but a froward child, that must be played with and humored, to keep it quiet till it falls asleep, and then the care is over."[13]

This is a complex, a tender, a submissive, and a graceful state of mind. For myself, I should have no objection to calling it on the whole a religious state of mind, although I dare say that to many of you it may seem too listless and half-hearted to merit so good a name. But what matters it in the end whether we call such a state of mind religious or not? It is too insignificant for our instruction in any case; and its very possessor wrote it down in terms which he would not have used unless he had been thinking of more energetically religious moods in others, with which he found himself unable to compete. It is with these more energetic states that our sole business lies, and we can perfectly well afford to let the minor notes and the uncertain border go.

It was the extremer cases that I had in mind a little while ago when I said that personal religion, even without theology or ritual, would prove to embody some elements that morality pure and simple does not contain. You may remember that I promised shortly to point out [pg 041] what those elements were. In a general way I can now say what I had in mind.

"I accept the universe" is reported to have been a favorite utterance of our New England transcendentalist, Margaret Fuller; and when some one repeated this phrase to Thomas Carlyle, his sardonic comment is said to have been: "Gad! she'd better!" At bottom the whole concern of both morality and religion is with the manner of our acceptance of the universe. Do we accept it only in part and grudgingly, or heartily and altogether? Shall our protests against certain things in it be radical and unforgiving, or shall we think that, even with evil, there are ways of living that must lead to good? If we accept the whole, shall we do so as if stunned into submission, —as Carlyle would have us—"Gad! we'd better!"—or shall we do so with enthusiastic assent? Morality pure and simple accepts the law of the whole which it finds reigning, so far as to acknowledge and obey it, but it may obey it with the heaviest and coldest heart, and never cease to feel it as a yoke. But for religion, in its strong and fully developed manifestations, the service of the highest never is felt as a yoke. Dull submission is left far behind, and a mood of welcome, which may fill any place on the scale between cheerful serenity and enthusiastic gladness, has taken its place.

It makes a tremendous emotional and practical difference to one whether one accept the universe in the drab discolored way of stoic resignation to necessity, or with the passionate happiness of Christian saints. The difference is as great as that between passivity and activity, as that between the defensive and the aggressive mood. Gradual as are the steps by which an individual may [pg 042] grow from one state into the other, many as are the intermediate stages which different individuals represent, yet when you place the typical extremes beside each other for comparison, you feel that two discontinuous psychological universes confront you, and that in passing from one to the other a "critical point" has been overcome.

If we compare stoic with Christian ejaculations we see much more than a difference of doctrine; rather is it a difference of emotional mood that parts them. When Marcus Aurelius reflects on the eternal reason that has ordered things, there is a frosty chill about his words which you rarely find in a Jewish, and never in a Christian piece of religious writing. The universe is "accepted" by all these writers; but how devoid of passion or exultation the spirit of the Roman Emperor is! Compare his fine sentence: "If gods care not for me or my children, here is a reason for it," with Job's cry: "Though he slay me, yet will I trust in him!" and you immediately see the difference I mean. The *anima mundi*, to whose disposal of his own personal destiny the Stoic consents, is there to be respected and submitted to, but the Christian God is there to be loved; and the difference of emotional atmosphere is like that between an arctic climate and the tropics, though the outcome in the way of accepting actual conditions uncomplainingly may seem in abstract terms to be much the same.

> "It is a man's duty," says Marcus Aurelius, "to comfort himself and wait for the natural dissolution, and not to be vexed, but to find refreshment solely in these thoughts—first that nothing will happen to me which is not conformable to the nature of the universe; and secondly that I need do nothing contrary to the God and deity within me; for there is no man who can compel me to transgress.[14] He is an abscess on the [pg 043]universe who withdraws and separates himself from the reason of our common nature, through being displeased with the things which happen. For the same nature produces these, and has produced thee too. And so accept everything which happens, even if it seem disagreeable, because it leads to this, the health of the universe and to the prosperity and felicity of Zeus. For he would not have brought on any man what he has brought, if it were not useful for the whole. The integrity of the whole is mutilated if thou cuttest off anything. And thou dost cut off, as far as it is in thy power, when thou art dissatisfied, and in a manner triest to put anything out of the way."[15]

Compare now this mood with that of the old Christian author of the Theologia Germanica:—

> "Where men are enlightened with the true light, they renounce all desire and choice, and commit and commend themselves and all things to the eternal Goodness, so that every enlightened man could say: 'I would fain be to the Eternal Goodness what his own hand is to a man.' Such men are in a state of freedom, because they have lost the fear of pain or hell, and the hope of reward or heaven, and are living in pure submission to the eternal Goodness, in the perfect freedom of fervent love. When a man truly perceiveth and considereth himself, who and what he is, and findeth himself utterly vile and wicked and unworthy, he falleth into such a deep abasement that it seemeth to him reasonable that all creatures in heaven and earth should rise up against him. And therefore he will not and dare not desire any consolation and release; but he is willing to be unconsoled and unreleased; and he doth not grieve over his sufferings, for they are right in his eyes, and he hath nothing to say against them. This is what is meant by true repentance for sin; and he who in this present time entereth into this hell, none may console him. Now God hath not forsaken a man in this hell, but He is laying his hand upon him, that the man may not desire nor regard anything but the eternal Good only. And then, when the man neither careth for nor desireth anything but the eternal Good alone, and seeketh [pg 044] not himself nor his own things, but the honour of God only, he is made a partaker of all manner of joy, bliss, peace, rest, and consolation, and so the man is henceforth in the kingdom of heaven. This hell and this heaven are two good safe ways for a man, and happy is he who truly findeth them."[16]

How much more active and positive the impulse of the Christian writer to accept his place in the universe is! Marcus Aurelius agrees *to* the scheme—the German theologian agrees *with* it. He literally *abounds* in agreement, he runs out to embrace the divine decrees.

Occasionally, it is true, the Stoic rises to something like a Christian warmth of sentiment, as in the often quoted passage of Marcus Aurelius:—

> "Everything harmonizes with me which is harmonious to thee, O Universe. Nothing for me is too early nor too late, which is in due time for thee. Everything is fruit to me which thy seasons bring, O Nature: from thee are all things, in thee are all things, to thee all things return. The poet says, Dear City of Cecrops; and wilt thou not say, Dear City of Zeus?"[17]

But compare even as devout a passage as this with a genuine Christian outpouring, and it seems a little cold. Turn, for instance, to the Imitation of Christ:—

"Lord, thou knowest what is best; let this or that be according as thou wilt. Give what thou wilt, so much as thou wilt, when thou wilt. Do with me as thou knowest best, and as shall be most to thine honour. Place me where thou wilt, and freely work thy will with me in all things.... When could it be evil when thou wert near? I had rather be poor for thy sake than rich without thee. I choose rather to be a pilgrim upon the earth with thee, than without thee to possess heaven. Where thou art, there is heaven; and where thou art not, behold there death and hell."[18]

[pg 045]
It is a good rule in physiology, when we are studying the meaning of an organ, to ask after its most peculiar and characteristic sort of performance, and to seek its office in that one of its functions which no other organ can possibly exert. Surely the same maxim holds good in our present quest. The essence of religious experiences, the thing by which we finally must judge them, must be that element or quality in them which we can meet nowhere else. And such a quality will be of course most prominent and easy to notice in those religious experiences which are most one-sided, exaggerated, and intense.

Now when we compare these intenser experiences with the experiences of tamer minds, so cool and reasonable that we are tempted to call them philosophical rather than religious, we find a character that is perfectly distinct. That character, it seems to me, should be regarded as the practically important *differentia* of religion for our purpose; and just what it is can easily be brought out by comparing the mind of an abstractly conceived Christian with that of a moralist similarly conceived.

A life is manly, stoical, moral, or philosophical, we say, in proportion as it is less swayed by paltry personal considerations and more by objective ends that call for energy, even though that energy bring personal loss and pain. This is the good side of war, in so far as it calls for "volunteers." And for morality life is a war, and the service of the highest is a sort of cosmic patriotism which also calls for volunteers. Even a sick man, unable to be militant outwardly, can carry on the moral warfare. He can willfully turn his attention away from his own [pg 046] future, whether in this world or the next. He can train himself to indifference to his present drawbacks and immerse himself in whatever objective interests still remain accessible. He can follow public news, and sympathize with other people's affairs. He can cultivate cheerful manners, and be silent about his miseries. He can contemplate whatever ideal aspects of existence his philosophy is able to present to him, and practice whatever duties, such as patience, resignation, trust, his ethical system requires. Such a man lives on his loftiest, largest plane. He is a high-hearted freeman and no pining slave. And yet he lacks something which the Christian *par excellence*, the mystic and ascetic saint, for example, has in abundant measure, and which makes of him a human being of an altogether different denomination.

The Christian also spurns the pinched and mumping sick-room attitude, and the lives of saints are full of a kind of callousness to diseased conditions of body which probably no other human records show. But whereas the merely moralistic spurning takes an effort of volition, the Christian spurning is the result of the excitement of a higher kind of emotion, in the presence of which no exertion of volition is required. The moralist must hold his breath and keep his muscles tense; and so long as this athletic attitude is possible all goes well—morality suffices. But the athletic attitude tends ever to break down, and it inevitably does break down even in the most stalwart when the organism begins to decay, or when morbid fears invade the mind. To suggest personal will and effort to one all sicklied o'er with the sense of irremediable impotence is to suggest the most impossible of things. What he craves is to be consoled in his very powerlessness, to feel that the spirit of the universe recognizes and secures him, all decaying and failing as he [pg 047] is. Well, we are all such helpless failures in the last resort. The sanest and best of us are of one clay with lunatics and prison inmates, and death finally runs the robustest of us down. And whenever we feel this, such a sense of the vanity and provisionality of our voluntary career comes over us that all our morality appears but as a plaster hiding a sore it can never cure, and all our well-doing as the hollowest substitute for that well-*being* that our lives ought to be grounded in, but, alas! are not.

And here religion comes to our rescue and takes our fate into her hands. There is a state of mind, known to religious men, but to no others, in which the will to assert ourselves and hold our own has been displaced by a willingness to close our mouths and be as nothing in the floods and waterspouts of God. In this state of mind, what we most dreaded has become the habitation of our safety, and the hour of our moral death has turned into our spiritual birthday. The time for tension in our soul is over, and that of happy relaxation, of calm deep breathing, of an eternal present, with no discordant future to be anxious about, has arrived. Fear is not held in abeyance as it is by mere morality, it is positively expunged and washed away.

We shall see abundant examples of this happy state of mind in later lectures of this course. We shall see how infinitely passionate a thing religion at its highest flights can be. Like love, like wrath, like hope, ambition, jealousy, like every other instinctive eagerness and impulse, it adds to life an enchantment which is not rationally or logically deducible from anything else. This enchantment, coming as a gift when it does come,—a gift of our organism, the physiologists will tell us, a gift of God's grace, the theologians say,—is either there or not there for us, and there are persons who can no more become [pg 048] possessed by it than they can fall in love with a given woman by mere word of command. Religious feeling is thus an absolute addition to the Subject's range of life. It gives him a new sphere of power. When the outward battle is lost, and the outer world disowns him, it redeems and vivifies an interior world which otherwise would be an empty waste.

If religion is to mean anything definite for us, it seems to me that we ought to take it as meaning this added dimension of emotion, this enthusiastic temper of espousal, in regions where morality strictly so called can at best but bow its head and acquiesce. It ought to mean nothing short of this new reach of freedom for us, with the struggle over, the keynote of the universe sounding in our ears, and everlasting possession spread before our eyes.[19]

This sort of happiness in the absolute and everlasting is what we find nowhere but in religion. It is parted off from all mere animal happiness, all mere enjoyment of the present, by that element of solemnity of which I have already made so much account. Solemnity is a hard thing to define abstractly, but certain of its marks are patent enough. A solemn state of mind is never crude or simple—it seems to contain a certain measure of its own opposite in solution. A solemn joy preserves a sort of bitter in its sweetness; a solemn sorrow is one to which we intimately consent. But there are writers who, realizing that happiness of a supreme sort is the prerogative of religion, forget this complication, and call all happiness, as such, religious. Mr. Havelock Ellis, for example, [pg 049] identifies religion with the entire field of the soul's liberation from oppressive moods.

> "The simplest functions of physiological life," he writes, "may be its ministers. Every one who is at all acquainted with the Persian mystics knows how wine may be regarded as an instrument of religion. Indeed, in all countries and in all ages, some form of physical enlargement—singing, dancing, drinking, sexual excitement—has been intimately associated with worship. Even the momentary expansion of the soul in laughter is, to however slight an extent, a religious exercise.... Whenever an impulse from the world strikes against the organism, and the resultant is not discomfort or pain, not even the muscular contraction of strenuous manhood, but a joyous expansion or aspiration of the whole soul—there is religion. It is the infinite for which we hunger, and we ride gladly on every little wave that promises to bear us towards it."[20]

But such a straight identification of religion with any and every form of happiness leaves the essential peculiarity of religious happiness out. The more commonplace happinesses which we get are "reliefs," occasioned by our momentary escapes from evils either experienced or threatened. But in its most characteristic embodiments, religious happiness is no mere feeling of escape. It cares no longer to escape. It consents to the evil outwardly as a form of sacrifice—inwardly it knows it to be permanently overcome. If you ask *how* religion thus falls on the thorns and faces death, and in the very act annuls annihilation, I cannot explain the matter, for it is religion's secret, and to understand it you must yourself have been a religious man of the extremer type. In our future examples, even of the simplest and healthiest-minded type of religious consciousness, we shall find this complex sacrificial constitution, in which a higher happiness holds a lower unhappiness in check. In the Louvre there is a [pg 050] picture, by Guido Reni, of St. Michael with his foot on Satan's neck. The richness of the picture is in large part due to the fiend's figure being there. The richness of its allegorical meaning also is due to his being there—that is, the world is all the richer for having a devil in it, *so long as we keep our foot upon his neck.* In the religious consciousness, that is just the position in which the fiend, the negative or tragic principle, is found; and for that very reason the religious consciousness is so rich from the emotional point of view.[21] We shall see how in certain men and women it takes on a monstrously ascetic form. There are saints who have literally fed on the negative principle, on humiliation and privation, and the thought of suffering and death,—their souls growing in happiness just in proportion as their outward state grew more intolerable. No other emotion than religious emotion can bring a man to this peculiar pass. And it is for that reason that when we ask our question about the value of religion for human life, I think we ought to look for the answer among these violenter examples rather than among those of a more moderate hue.

Having the phenomenon of our study in its acutest possible form to start with, we can shade down as much as we please later. And if in these cases, repulsive as they are to our ordinary worldly way of judging, we find ourselves compelled to acknowledge religion's value and treat it with respect, it will have proved in some way its value for life at large. By subtracting and toning down extravagances we may thereupon proceed to trace the boundaries of its legitimate sway.

To be sure, it makes our task difficult to have to deal so much with eccentricities and extremes. "How *can* [pg 051] religion on the whole be the most important of all human functions," you may ask, "if every several manifestation of it in turn have to be corrected and sobered down and pruned away?" Such a thesis seems a paradox impossible to sustain reasonably,—yet I believe that something like it will have to be our final contention. That personal attitude which the individual finds himself impelled to take up towards what he apprehends to be the divine—and you will remember that this was our definition—will prove to be both a helpless and a sacrificial attitude. That is, we shall have to confess to at least some amount of dependence on sheer mercy, and to practice some amount of renunciation, great or small, to save our souls alive. The constitution of the world we live in requires it:—

> "Entbehren sollst du! sollst entbehren!
> Das ist der ewige Gesang
> Der jedem an die Ohren klingt,
> Den, unser ganzes Leben lang
> Uns heiser jede Stunde singt."

For when all is said and done, we are in the end absolutely dependent on the universe; and into sacrifices and surrenders of some sort, deliberately looked at and accepted, we are drawn and pressed as into our only permanent positions of repose. Now in those states of mind which fall short of religion, the surrender is submitted to as an imposition of necessity, and the sacrifice is undergone at the very best without complaint. In the religious life, on the contrary, surrender and sacrifice are positively espoused: even unnecessary givings-up are added in order that the happiness may increase. *Religion thus makes easy and felicitous what in any case is necessary*; and if it be the only agency that can accomplish this result, its vital importance as a human faculty [pg 052] stands vindicated beyond dispute. It becomes an essential organ of our life, performing a function which no other portion of our nature can so successfully fulfill. From the merely biological point of view, so to call it, this is a conclusion to which, so far as I can now see, we shall inevitably be led, and led moreover by following the purely empirical method of demonstration which I sketched to you in the first lecture. Of the farther office of religion as a metaphysical revelation I will say nothing now.

But to foreshadow the terminus of one's investigations is one thing, and to arrive there safely is another. In the next lecture, abandoning the extreme generalities which have engrossed us hitherto, I propose that we begin our actual journey by addressing ourselves directly to the concrete facts.

Lecture III. The Reality Of The Unseen.

Were one asked to characterize the life of religion in the broadest and most general terms possible, one might say that it consists of the belief that there is an unseen order, and that our supreme good lies in harmoniously adjusting ourselves thereto. This belief and this adjustment are the religious attitude in the soul. I wish during this hour to call your attention to some of the psychological peculiarities of such an attitude as this, of belief in an object which we cannot see. All our attitudes, moral, practical, or emotional, as well as religious, are due to the "objects" of our consciousness, the things which we believe to exist, whether really or ideally, along with ourselves. Such objects may be present to our senses, or they may be present only to our thought. In either case they elicit from us a *reaction*; and the reaction due to things of thought is notoriously in many cases as strong as that due to sensible presences. It may be even stronger. The memory of an insult may make us angrier than the insult did when we received it. We are frequently more ashamed of our blunders afterwards than we were at the moment of making them; and in general our whole higher prudential and moral life is based on the fact that material sensations actually present may have a weaker influence on our action than ideas of remoter facts.

The more concrete objects of most men's religion, the deities whom they worship, are known to them only in [pg 054] idea. It has been vouchsafed, for example, to very few Christian believers to have had a sensible vision of their Saviour; though enough appearances of this sort are on record, by way of miraculous exception, to merit our attention later. The whole force of the Christian religion, therefore, so far as belief in the divine personages determines the prevalent attitude of the believer, is in general exerted by the instrumentality of pure ideas, of which nothing in the individual's past experience directly serves as a model.

But in addition to these ideas of the more concrete religious objects, religion is full of abstract objects which prove to have an equal power. God's attributes as such, his holiness, his justice, his mercy, his absoluteness, his infinity, his omniscience, his tri-unity, the various mysteries of the redemptive process, the operation of the sacraments, etc., have proved fertile wells of inspiring meditation for Christian believers.[22] We shall see later that the absence of definite sensible images is positively insisted on by the mystical authorities in all religions as the *sine qua non* of a successful orison, or contemplation of the higher divine truths. Such contemplations are expected (and abundantly verify the expectation, as we shall also see) to influence the believer's subsequent attitude very powerfully for good.

Immanuel Kant held a curious doctrine about such objects of belief as God, the design of creation, the soul, its freedom, and the life hereafter. These things, he said, [pg 055] are properly not objects of knowledge at all. Our conceptions always require a sense-content to work with, and as the words "soul," "God," "immortality," cover no distinctive sense-content whatever, it follows that theoretically speaking they are words devoid of any significance. Yet strangely enough they have a definite meaning *for our practice*. We can act *as if* there were a God; feel *as if* we were free; consider Nature *as if* she were full of special designs; lay plans *as if* we were to be immortal; and we find then that these words do make a genuine difference in our moral life. Our faith *that* these unintelligible objects actually exist proves thus to be a full equivalent in *praktischer Hinsicht*, as Kant calls it, or from the point of view of our action, for a knowledge of *what* they might be, in case we were permitted positively to conceive them. So we have the strange phenomenon, as Kant assures us, of a mind believing with all its strength in the real presence of a set of things of no one of which it can form any notion whatsoever.

My object in thus recalling Kant's doctrine to your mind is not to express any opinion as to the accuracy of this particularly uncouth part of his philosophy, but only to illustrate the characteristic of human nature which we are considering, by an example so classical in its exaggeration. The sentiment of reality can indeed attach itself so strongly to our object of belief that our whole life is polarized through and through, so to speak, by its sense of the existence of the thing believed in, and yet that thing, for purpose of definite description, can hardly be said to be present to our mind at all. It is as if a bar of iron, without touch or sight, with no representative faculty whatever, might nevertheless be strongly endowed with an inner capacity for magnetic feeling; and as if, through the various arousals of its magnetism by magnets coming [pg 056] and going in its neighborhood, it might be consciously determined to different attitudes and tendencies. Such a bar of iron could never give you an outward description of the agencies that had the power of stirring it so strongly; yet of their presence, and of their significance for its life, it would be intensely aware through every fibre of its being.

It is not only the Ideas of pure Reason, as Kant styled them, that have this power of making us vitally feel presences that we are impotent articulately to describe. All sorts of higher abstractions bring with them the same kind of impalpable appeal. Remember those passages from Emerson which I read at my last lecture. The whole universe of concrete objects, as we know them, swims, not only for such a transcendentalist writer, but for all of us, in a wider and higher universe of abstract ideas, that lend it its significance. As time, space, and the ether soak through all things, so (we feel) do abstract and essential goodness, beauty, strength, significance, justice, soak through all things good, strong, significant, and just.

Such ideas, and others equally abstract, form the background for all our facts, the fountain-head of all the possibilities we conceive of. They give its "nature," as we call it, to every special thing. Everything we know is "what" it is by sharing in the nature of one of these abstractions. We can never look directly at them, for they are bodiless and featureless and footless, but we grasp all other things by their means, and in handling the real world we should be stricken with helplessness in just so far forth as we might lose these mental objects, these adjectives and adverbs and predicates and heads of classification and conception.

This absolute determinability of our mind by abstractions [pg 057] is one of the cardinal facts in our human constitution. Polarizing and magnetizing us as they do, we turn towards them and from them, we seek them, hold them, hate them, bless them, just as if they were so many concrete beings. And beings they are, beings as real in the realm which they inhabit as the changing things of sense are in the realm of space.

Plato gave so brilliant and impressive a defense of this common human feeling, that the doctrine of the reality of abstract objects has been known as the platonic theory of ideas ever since. Abstract Beauty, for example, is for Plato a perfectly definite individual being, of which the intellect is aware as of something additional to all the perishing beauties of the earth. "The true order of going," he says, in the often quoted passage in his "Banquet," "is to use the beauties of earth as steps along which one mounts upwards for the sake of that other Beauty, going from one to two, and from two to all fair forms, and from fair forms to fair actions, and from fair actions to fair notions, until from fair notions he arrives at the notion of absolute Beauty, and at last knows what the essence of Beauty is."[23] In our last lecture we had a glimpse of the way in which a platonizing writer like Emerson may treat the abstract divineness of things, the moral structure of the universe, as a fact worthy of worship. In those various churches without a God which to-day are spreading through the world under the name of ethical societies, we have a similar worship of the abstract divine, the moral law believed in as an ultimate object. "Science" in many minds is genuinely taking the place of a religion. Where this is so, the scientist treats the "Laws of Nature" as objective facts to be revered. A brilliant school of interpretation of Greek mythology [pg 058] would have it that in their origin the Greek gods were only half-metaphoric personifications of those great spheres of abstract law and order into which the natural world falls apart—the sky-sphere, the ocean-sphere, the earth-sphere, and the like; just as even now we may speak of the smile of the morning, the kiss of the breeze, or the bite of the cold, without really meaning that these phenomena of nature actually wear a human face.[24]

As regards the origin of the Greek gods, we need not at present seek an opinion. But the whole array of our instances leads to a conclusion something like this: It is as if there were in the human consciousness a *sense of reality, a feeling of objective presence, a perception* of what we may call *"something there,"* more deep and more general than any of the special and particular "senses" by which the current psychology supposes existent realities to be originally revealed. If this were so, we might suppose the senses to waken our attitudes and conduct as they so habitually do, by first exciting this sense of reality; but anything else, any idea, for example, that might similarly excite it, would have that same prerogative of appearing real which objects of sense normally possess. So far as religious conceptions were able to touch this reality-feeling, they would be believed in in spite of criticism, even though they might be so vague and remote as to be almost unimaginable, even though they might be such non-entities in point of *whatness*, as Kant makes the objects of his moral theology to be.

The most curious proofs of the existence of such an undifferentiated sense of reality as this are found in experiences of hallucination. It often happens that an [pg 059] hallucination is imperfectly developed: the person affected will feel a "presence" in the room, definitely localized, facing in one particular way, real in the most emphatic sense of the word, often coming suddenly, and as suddenly gone; and yet neither seen, heard, touched, nor cognized in any of the usual "sensible" ways. Let me give you an example of this, before I pass to the objects with whose presence religion is more peculiarly concerned.

An intimate friend of mine, one of the keenest intellects I know, has had several experiences of this sort. He writes as follows in response to my inquiries:—

> "I have several times within the past few years felt the so-called 'consciousness of a presence.' The experiences which I have in mind are clearly distinguishable from another kind of experience which I have had very frequently, and which I fancy many persons would also call the 'consciousness of a presence.' But the difference for me between the two sets of experience is as great as the difference between feeling a slight warmth originating I know not where, and standing in the midst of a conflagration with all the ordinary senses alert.
>
> "It was about September, 1884, when I had the first experience. On the previous night I had had, after getting into bed at my rooms in College, a vivid tactile hallucination of being grasped by the arm, which made me get up and search the room for an intruder; but the sense of presence properly so

called came on the next night. After I had got into bed and blown out the candle, I lay awake awhile thinking on the previous night's experience, when suddenly I *felt* something come into the room and stay close to my bed. It remained only a minute or two. I did not recognize it by any ordinary sense, and yet there was a horribly unpleasant 'sensation' connected with it. It stirred something more at the roots of my being than any ordinary perception. The feeling had something of the quality of a very large tearing vital pain spreading chiefly over the chest, but within the organism—and yet the feeling [pg 060] was not *pain* so much as *abhorrence*. At all events, something was present with me, and I knew its presence far more surely than I have ever known the presence of any fleshly living creature. I was conscious of its departure as of its coming: an almost instantaneously swift going through the door, and the 'horrible sensation' disappeared.

"On the third night when I retired my mind was absorbed in some lectures which I was preparing, and I was still absorbed in these when I became aware of the actual presence (though not of the *coming*) of the thing that was there the night before, and of the 'horrible sensation.' I then mentally concentrated all my effort to charge this 'thing,' if it was evil, to depart, if it was *not* evil, to tell me who or what it was, and if it could not explain itself, to go, and that I would compel it to go. It went as on the previous night, and my body quickly recovered its normal state.

"On two other occasions in my life I have had precisely the same 'horrible sensation.' Once it lasted a full quarter of an hour. In all three instances the certainty that there in outward space there stood *something* was indescribably *stronger* than the ordinary certainty of companionship when we are in the close presence of ordinary living people. The something seemed close to me, and intensely more real than any ordinary perception. Although I felt it to be like unto myself, so to speak, or finite, small, and distressful, as it were, I didn't recognize it as any individual being or person."

Of course such an experience as this does not connect itself with the religious sphere. Yet it may upon occasion do so; and the same correspondent informs me that at more than one other conjuncture he had the sense of presence developed with equal intensity and abruptness, only then it was filled with a quality of joy.

"There was not a mere consciousness of something there, but fused in the central happiness of it, a startling awareness of some ineffable good. Not vague either, not like the emotional effect of some poem, or scene, or blossom, of music, but the sure knowledge of the close presence of a sort of mighty person, and [pg 061]after it went, the memory persisted as the one perception of reality. Everything else might be a dream, but not that."

My friend, as it oddly happens, does not interpret these latter experiences theistically, as signifying the presence of God. But it would clearly not have been unnatural to interpret them as a revelation of the deity's existence. When we reach the subject of mysticism, we shall have much more to say upon this head.

Lest the oddity of these phenomena should disconcert you, I will venture to read you a couple of similar narratives, much shorter, merely to show that we are dealing with a well-marked natural kind of fact. In the first case, which I take from the Journal of the Society for Psychical Research, the sense of presence developed in a few moments into a distinctly visualized hallucination,—but I leave that part of the story out.

> "I had read," the narrator says, "some twenty minutes or so, was thoroughly absorbed in the book, my mind was perfectly quiet, and for the time being my friends were quite forgotten, when suddenly without a moment's warning my whole being seemed roused to the highest state of tension or aliveness, and I was aware, with an intenseness not easily imagined by those who had never experienced it, that another being or presence was not only in the room, but quite close to me. I put my book down, and although my excitement was great, I felt quite collected, and not conscious of any sense of fear. Without changing my position, and looking straight at the fire, I knew somehow that my friend A. H. was standing at my left elbow, but so far behind me as to be hidden by the armchair in which I was leaning back. Moving my eyes round slightly without otherwise changing my position, the lower portion of one leg became visible, and I instantly recognized the gray-blue material of trousers he often wore, but the stuff appeared semi-transparent, reminding me of tobacco smoke in consistency,"[25]—and hereupon the visual hallucination came.

[pg 062]
Another informant writes:—

> "Quite early in the night I was awakened.... I felt as if I had been aroused intentionally, and at first thought some one was breaking into the house.... I then turned on my side to go to sleep again, and immediately felt a consciousness of a presence in the room, and singular to state, it was not the

consciousness of a live person, but of a spiritual presence. This may provoke a smile, but I can only tell you the facts as they occurred to me. I do not know how to better describe my sensations than by simply stating that I felt a consciousness of a spiritual presence.... I felt also at the same time a strong feeling of superstitious dread, as if something strange and fearful were about to happen."[26]

Professor Flournoy of Geneva gives me the following testimony of a friend of his, a lady, who has the gift of automatic or involuntary writing:—

"Whenever I practice automatic writing, what makes me feel that it is not due to a subconscious self is the feeling I always have of a foreign presence, external to my body. It is sometimes so definitely characterized that I could point to its exact position. This impression of presence is impossible to describe. It varies in intensity and clearness according to the personality from whom the writing professes to come. If it is some one whom I love, I feel it immediately, before any writing has come. My heart seems to recognize it."

In an earlier book of mine I have cited at full length a curious case of presence felt by a blind man. The presence was that of the figure of a gray-bearded man dressed in a pepper and salt suit, squeezing himself under the crack of the door and moving across the floor of the room towards a sofa. The blind subject of this quasi-hallucination is an exceptionally intelligent reporter. He is entirely without internal visual imagery and cannot represent light or colors to himself, and is positive that [pg 063] his other senses, hearing, etc., were not involved in this false perception. It seems to have been an abstract conception rather, with the feelings of reality and spatial outwardness directly attached to it—in other words, a fully objectified and exteriorized *idea*.

Such cases, taken along with others which would be too tedious for quotation, seem sufficiently to prove the existence in our mental machinery of a sense of present reality more diffused and general than that which our special senses yield. For the psychologists the tracing of the organic seat of such a feeling would form a pretty problem—nothing could be more natural than to connect it with the muscular sense, with the feeling that our muscles were innervating themselves for action. Whatsoever thus innervated our activity, or "made our flesh creep,"—our senses are what do so oftenest,—might then appear real and present, even though it were but an abstract idea.

But with such vague conjectures we have no concern at present, for our interest lies with the faculty rather than with its organic seat.

Like all positive affections of consciousness, the sense of reality has its negative counterpart in the shape of a feeling of unreality by which persons may be haunted, and of which one sometimes hears complaint:—

> "When I reflect on the fact that I have made my appearance by accident upon a globe itself whirled through space as the sport of the catastrophes of the heavens," says Madame Ackermann; "when I see myself surrounded by beings as ephemeral and incomprehensible as I am myself, and all excitedly pursuing pure chimeras, I experience a strange feeling of being in a dream. It seems to me as if I have loved and suffered and that erelong I shall die, in a dream. My last word will be, 'I have been dreaming.' "[27]

[pg 064]
In another lecture we shall see how in morbid melancholy this sense of the unreality of things may become a carking pain, and even lead to suicide.

We may now lay it down as certain that in the distinctively religious sphere of experience, many persons (how many we cannot tell) possess the objects of their belief, not in the form of mere conceptions which their intellect accepts as true, but rather in the form of quasi-sensible realities directly apprehended. As his sense of the real presence of these objects fluctuates, so the believer alternates between warmth and coldness in his faith. Other examples will bring this home to one better than abstract description, so I proceed immediately to cite some. The first example is a negative one, deploring the loss of the sense in question. I have extracted it from an account given me by a scientific man of my acquaintance, of his religious life. It seems to me to show clearly that the feeling of reality may be something more like a sensation than an intellectual operation properly so-called.

> "Between twenty and thirty I gradually became more and more agnostic and irreligious, yet I cannot say that I ever lost that 'indefinite consciousness' which Herbert Spencer describes so well, of an Absolute Reality behind phenomena. For me this Reality was not the pure Unknowable of Spencer's philosophy, for although I had ceased my childish prayers to God, and never

prayed to *It* in a formal manner, yet my more recent experience shows me to have been in a relation to *It* which practically was the same thing as prayer. Whenever I had any trouble, especially when I had conflict with other people, either domestically or in the way of business, or when I was depressed in spirits or anxious about affairs, I now recognize that I used to fall back for support upon this curious relation I felt myself to be in to this fundamental cosmical *It*. It was on my side, or I was on Its side, however you please to term it, in the particular [pg 065]trouble, and it always strengthened me and seemed to give me endless vitality to feel its underlying and supporting presence. In fact, it was an unfailing fountain of living justice, truth, and strength, to which I instinctively turned at times of weakness, and it always brought me out. I know now that it was a personal relation I was in to it, because of late years the power of communicating with it has left me, and I am conscious of a perfectly definite loss. I used never to fail to find it when I turned to it. Then came a set of years when sometimes I found it, and then again I would be wholly unable to make connection with it. I remember many occasions on which at night in bed, I would be unable to get to sleep on account of worry. I turned this way and that in the darkness, and groped mentally for the familiar sense of that higher mind of my mind which had always seemed to be close at hand as it were, closing the passage, and yielding support, but there was no electric current. A blank was there instead of *It*: I couldn't find anything. Now, at the age of nearly fifty, my power of getting into connection with it has entirely left me; and I have to confess that a great help has gone out of my life. Life has become curiously dead and indifferent; and I can now see that my old experience was probably exactly the same thing as the prayers of the orthodox, only I did not call them by that name. What I have spoken of as 'It' was practically not Spencer's Unknowable, but just my own instinctive and individual God, whom I relied upon for higher sympathy, but whom somehow I have lost."

Nothing is more common in the pages of religious biography than the way in which seasons of lively and of difficult faith are described as alternating. Probably every religious person has the recollection of particular crises in which a directer vision of the truth, a direct perception, perhaps, of a living God's existence, swept in and overwhelmed the languor of the more ordinary belief. In James Russell Lowell's correspondence there is a brief memorandum of an experience of this kind:—

[pg 066]

"I had a revelation last Friday evening. I was at Mary's, and happening to say something of the presence of spirits (of whom, I said, I was often dimly aware), Mr. Putnam entered into an argument with me on spiritual matters.

As I was speaking, the whole system rose up before me like a vague destiny looming from the Abyss. I never before so clearly felt the Spirit of God in me and around me. The whole room seemed to me full of God. The air seemed to waver to and fro with the presence of Something I knew not what. I spoke with the calmness and clearness of a prophet. I cannot tell you what this revelation was. I have not yet studied it enough. But I shall perfect it one day, and then you shall hear it and acknowledge its grandeur."[28]

Here is a longer and more developed experience from a manuscript communication by a clergyman,—I take it from Starbuck's manuscript collection:—

"I remember the night, and almost the very spot on the hilltop, where my soul opened out, as it were, into the Infinite, and there was a rushing together of the two worlds, the inner and the outer. It was deep calling unto deep,—the deep that my own struggle had opened up within being answered by the unfathomable deep without, reaching beyond the stars. I stood alone with Him who had made me, and all the beauty of the world, and love, and sorrow, and even temptation. I did not seek Him, but felt the perfect unison of my spirit with His. The ordinary sense of things around me faded. For the moment nothing but an ineffable joy and exaltation remained. It is impossible fully to describe the experience. It was like the effect of some great orchestra when all the separate notes have melted into one swelling harmony that leaves the listener conscious of nothing save that his soul is being wafted upwards, and almost bursting with its own emotion. The perfect stillness of the night was thrilled by a more solemn silence. The darkness held a presence that was all the more felt because it was not seen. I could not any more have doubted that *He* was [pg 067]there than that I was. Indeed, I felt myself to be, if possible, the less real of the two.

"My highest faith in God and truest idea of him were then born in me. I have stood upon the Mount of Vision since, and felt the Eternal round about me. But never since has there come quite the same stirring of the heart. Then, if ever, I believe, I stood face to face with God, and was born anew of his spirit. There was, as I recall it, no sudden change of thought or of belief, except that my early crude conception had, as it were, burst into flower. There was no destruction of the old, but a rapid, wonderful unfolding. Since that time no discussion that I have heard of the proofs of God's existence has been able to shake my faith. Having once felt the presence of God's spirit, I have never lost it again for long. My most assuring evidence of his existence is deeply rooted in that hour of vision, in the memory of that supreme experience, and in the conviction, gained from reading and reflection, that something the same has come to all who have found God. I am aware that it may justly be called mystical. I am not enough acquainted with philosophy to defend it from that or any other charge. I feel that in writing of it I have overlaid it with words rather than put it clearly to your thought. But, such as it is, I have described it as carefully as I now am able to do."

Here is another document, even more definite in character, which, the writer being a Swiss, I translate from the French original.[29]

"I was in perfect health: we were on our sixth day of tramping, and in good training. We had come the day before from Sixt to Trient by Buet. I felt neither fatigue, hunger, nor thirst, and my state of mind was equally healthy. I had had at Forlaz good news from home; I was subject to no anxiety, either near or remote, for we had a good guide, and there was not a shadow of uncertainty about the road we should follow. I can best describe the condition in which I was by calling it a [pg 068]state of equilibrium. When all at once I experienced a feeling of being raised above myself, I felt the presence of God—I tell of the thing just as I was conscious of it—as if his goodness and his power were penetrating me altogether. The throb of emotion was so violent that I could barely tell the boys to pass on and not wait for me. I then sat down on a stone, unable to stand any longer, and my eyes overflowed with tears. I thanked God that in the course of my life he had taught me to know him, that he sustained my life and took pity both on the insignificant creature and on the sinner that I was. I begged him ardently that my life might be consecrated to the doing of his will. I felt his reply, which was that I should do his will from day to day, in humility and poverty, leaving him, the Almighty God, to be judge of whether I should some time be called to bear witness more conspicuously. Then, slowly, the ecstasy left my heart; that is, I felt that God had withdrawn the communion which he had granted, and I was able to walk on, but very slowly, so strongly was I still possessed by the interior emotion. Besides, I had wept uninterruptedly for several minutes, my eyes were swollen, and I did not wish my companions to see me. The state of ecstasy may have lasted four or five minutes, although it seemed at the time to last much longer. My comrades waited for me ten minutes at the cross of Barine, but I took about twenty-five or thirty minutes to join them, for as well as I can remember, they said that I had kept them back for about half an hour. The impression had been so profound that in climbing slowly the slope I asked myself if it were possible that Moses on Sinai could have had a more intimate communication with God. I think it well to add that in this ecstasy of mine God had neither form, color, odor, nor taste; moreover, that the feeling of his presence was accompanied with no determinate localization. It was rather as if my personality had been transformed by the presence of a *spiritual spirit*. But the more I seek words to express this intimate intercourse, the more I feel the impossibility of describing the thing by any of our usual images. At bottom the expression most apt to render what I felt is this: God was present, though invisible; he fell under no one of my senses, yet my consciousness perceived him."

The adjective "mystical" is technically applied, most often, to states that are of brief duration. Of course such hours of rapture as the last two persons describe are mystical experiences, of which in a later lecture I shall have much to say. Meanwhile here is the abridged record of another mystical or semi-mystical experience, in a mind evidently framed by nature for ardent piety. I owe it to Starbuck's collection. The lady who gives the account is the daughter of a man well known in his time as a writer against Christianity. The suddenness of her conversion shows well how native the sense of God's presence must be to certain minds. She relates that she was brought up in entire ignorance of Christian doctrine, but, when in Germany, after being talked to by Christian friends, she read the Bible and prayed, and finally the plan of salvation flashed upon her like a stream of light.

> "To this day," she writes, "I cannot understand dallying with religion and the commands of God. The very instant I heard my Father's cry calling unto me, my heart bounded in recognition. I ran, I stretched forth my arms, I cried aloud, 'Here, here I am, my Father.' Oh, happy child, what should I do?
>
> 'Love me,' answered my God. 'I do, I do,' I cried passionately. 'Come unto me,' called my Father. 'I will,' my heart panted. Did I stop to ask a single question? Not one. It never occurred to me to ask whether I was good enough, or to hesitate over my unfitness, or to find out what I thought of his church, or ... to wait until I should be satisfied. Satisfied! I was satisfied. Had I not found my God and my Father? Did he not love me? Had he not called me? Was there not a Church into which I might enter?... Since then I have had direct answers to prayer—so significant as to be almost like talking with God and hearing his answer. The idea of God's reality has never left me for one moment."

Here is still another case, the writer being a man aged [pg 070] twenty-seven, in which the experience, probably almost as characteristic, is less vividly described:—

> "I have on a number of occasions felt that I had enjoyed a period of intimate communion with the divine. These meetings came unasked and unexpected, and seemed to consist merely in the temporary obliteration of the conventionalities which usually surround and cover my life.... Once it was when from the summit of a high mountain I looked over a gashed and corrugated landscape extending to a long convex of ocean that ascended to the horizon, and again from the same point when I could see nothing beneath me but a boundless expanse of white cloud, on the blown surface of which a

few high peaks, including the one I was on, seemed plunging about as if they were dragging their anchors. What I felt on these occasions was a temporary loss of my own identity, accompanied by an illumination which revealed to me a deeper significance than I had been wont to attach to life. It is in this that I find my justification for saying that I have enjoyed communication with God. Of course the absence of such a being as this would be chaos. I cannot conceive of life without its presence."

Of the more habitual and so to speak chronic sense of God's presence the following sample from Professor Starbuck's manuscript collection may serve to give an idea. It is from a man aged forty-nine,—probably thousands of unpretending Christians would write an almost identical account.

"God is more real to me than any thought or thing or person. I feel his presence positively, and the more as I live in closer harmony with his laws as written in my body and mind. I feel him in the sunshine or rain; and awe mingled with a delicious restfulness most nearly describes my feelings. I talk to him as to a companion in prayer and praise, and our communion is delightful. He answers me again and again, often in words so clearly spoken that it seems my outer ear must have carried the tone, but generally in strong mental impressions. Usually a text of Scripture, unfolding some new view [pg 071]of him and his love for me, and care for my safety. I could give hundreds of instances, in school matters, social problems, financial difficulties, etc. That he is mine and I am his never leaves me, it is an abiding joy. Without it life would be a blank, a desert, a shoreless, trackless waste."

I subjoin some more examples from writers of different ages and sexes. They are also from Professor Starbuck's collection, and their number might be greatly multiplied. The first is from a man twenty-seven years old:—

"God is quite real to me. I talk to him and often get answers. Thoughts sudden and distinct from any I have been entertaining come to my mind after asking God for his direction. Something over a year ago I was for some weeks in the direst perplexity. When the trouble first appeared before me I was dazed, but before long (two or three hours) I could hear distinctly a passage of Scripture: 'My grace is sufficient for thee.' Every time my thoughts turned to the trouble I could hear this quotation. I don't think I ever doubted the existence of God, or had him drop out of my consciousness. God has frequently stepped into my affairs very perceptibly, and I feel that he directs many little details all the time. But on two or three occasions he has ordered ways for me very contrary to my ambitions and plans."

Another statement (none the less valuable psychologically for being so decidedly childish) is that of a boy of seventeen:—

> "Sometimes as I go to church, I sit down, join in the service, and before I go out I feel as if God was with me, right side of me, singing and reading the Psalms with me.... And then again I feel as if I could sit beside him, and put my arms around him, kiss him, etc. When I am taking Holy Communion at the altar, I try to get with him and generally feel his presence."

I let a few other cases follow at random:—

> "God surrounds me like the physical atmosphere. He is [pg 072]closer to me than my own breath. In him literally I live and move and have my being."—

> "There are times when I seem to stand, in his very presence, to talk with him. Answers to prayer have come, sometimes direct and overwhelming in their revelation of his presence and powers. There are times when God seems far off, but this is always my own fault."—

> "I have the sense of a presence, strong, and at the same time soothing, which hovers over me. Sometimes it seems to enwrap me with sustaining arms."

Such is the human ontological imagination, and such is the convincingness of what it brings to birth. Unpicturable beings are realized, and realized with an intensity almost like that of an hallucination. They determine our vital attitude as decisively as the vital attitude of lovers is determined by the habitual sense, by which each is haunted, of the other being in the world. A lover has notoriously this sense of the continuous being of his idol, even when his attention is addressed to other matters and he no longer represents her features. He cannot forget her; she uninterruptedly affects him through and through.

I spoke of the convincingness of these feelings of reality, and I must dwell a moment longer on that point. They are as convincing to those who have them as any direct sensible experiences can be, and they are, as a rule, much more convincing than results established by mere logic ever are. One may indeed be entirely without them; probably more than one of you here present is without them in any marked degree; but if you do have them, and have them at all strongly, the probability is that you cannot help regarding them as genuine perceptions of truth, as revelations of a kind of reality which no adverse argument, however unanswerable by you in [pg 073] words, can expel from your belief. The opinion opposed to mysticism in philosophy is sometimes spoken of as *rationalism*. Rationalism insists that all our beliefs ought ultimately to find for themselves articulate grounds. Such grounds, for rationalism, must consist of four things: (1) definitely statable abstract principles; (2) definite facts of sensation; (3) definite hypotheses based on such facts; and (4) definite inferences logically drawn. Vague impressions of something indefinable have no place in the rationalistic system, which on its positive side is surely a splendid intellectual tendency, for not only are all our philosophies fruits of it, but physical science (amongst other good things) is its result.

Nevertheless, if we look on man's whole mental life as it exists, on the life of men that lies in them apart from their learning and science, and that they inwardly and privately follow, we have to confess that the part of it of which rationalism can give an account is relatively superficial. It is the part that has the *prestige* undoubtedly, for it has the loquacity, it can challenge you for proofs, and chop logic, and put you down with words. But it will fail to convince or convert you all the same, if your dumb intuitions are opposed to its conclusions. If you have intuitions at all, they come from a deeper level of your nature than the loquacious level which rationalism inhabits. Your whole subconscious life, your impulses, your faiths, your needs, your divinations, have prepared the premises, of which your consciousness now feels the weight of the result; and something in you absolutely *knows* that that result must be truer than any logic-chopping rationalistic talk, however clever, that may contradict it. This inferiority of the rationalistic level in founding belief is just as manifest when rationalism argues for religion as when it argues against it. That [pg 074] vast literature of proofs of God's existence drawn from the order of nature, which a century ago seemed so overwhelmingly convincing, to-day does little more than gather dust in libraries, for the simple reason that our generation has ceased to believe in the kind of God it argued for. Whatever sort of a being God may be, we *know* to-day that he is nevermore that mere external inventor of "contrivances" intended to make manifest his "glory" in which our great-grandfathers took such satisfaction, though just how we know this we cannot possibly make clear by words either to others or to ourselves. I defy any of you here fully to account for your persuasion that if a God exist he must be a more cosmic and tragic personage than that Being.

The truth is that in the metaphysical and religious sphere, articulate reasons are cogent for us only when our inarticulate feelings of reality have already been impressed in favor of the same conclusion. Then, indeed, our intuitions and our reason work together, and great world-ruling systems, like that of the Buddhist or of the Catholic philosophy, may grow up. Our impulsive belief is here always what sets up the original body of truth, and our articulately verbalized philosophy is but its showy translation into formulas. The unreasoned and immediate assurance is the deep thing in us, the reasoned argument is but a surface exhibition. Instinct leads, intelligence does but follow. If a person feels the presence of a living God after the fashion shown by my quotations, your critical arguments, be they never so superior, will vainly set themselves to change his faith.

Please observe, however, that I do not yet say that it is *better* that the subconscious and non-rational should thus hold primacy in the religious realm. I confine myself to simply pointing out that they do so hold it as a matter of fact.

[pg 075]
So much for our sense of the reality of the religious objects. Let me now say a brief word more about the attitudes they characteristically awaken.

We have already agreed that they are *solemn*; and we have seen reason to think that the most distinctive of them is the sort of joy which may result in extreme cases from absolute self-surrender. The sense of the kind of object to which the surrender is made has much to do with determining the precise complexion of the joy; and the whole phenomenon is more complex than any simple formula allows. In the literature of the subject, sadness and gladness have each been emphasized in turn. The ancient saying that the first maker of the Gods was fear receives voluminous corroboration from every age of religious history; but none the less does religious history show the part which joy has evermore tended to play. Sometimes the joy has been primary; sometimes secondary, being the gladness of deliverance from the fear. This latter state of things, being the more complex, is also the more complete; and as we proceed, I think we shall have abundant reason for refusing to leave out either the sadness or the gladness, if we look at religion with the breadth of view which it demands. Stated in the completest possible terms, a man's religion involves both moods of contraction and moods of expansion of his being. But the quantitative mixture and order of these moods vary so much from one age of the world, from one system of thought, and from one individual to another, that you may insist either on the dread and the submission, or on the peace and the freedom as the essence of the matter, and still remain materially within the limits of the truth. The constitutionally sombre and the constitutionally sanguine onlooker are bound to emphasize opposite aspects of what lies before their eyes.

[pg 076]
The constitutionally sombre religious person makes even of his religious peace a very sober thing. Danger still hovers in the air about it. Flexion and contraction are not wholly checked. It were sparrowlike and childish after our deliverance to explode into twittering laughter and caper-cutting, and utterly to forget the imminent hawk on bough. Lie low, rather, lie low; for you are in the hands of a living God. In the Book of Job, for example, the impotence of man and the omnipotence of God is the exclusive burden of its author's mind. "It is as high as heaven; what canst thou do?—deeper than hell; what canst thou know?" There is an astringent relish about the truth of this conviction which some men can feel, and which for them is as near an approach as can be made to the feeling of religious joy.

> "In Job," says that coldly truthful writer, the author of Mark Rutherford, "God reminds us that man is not the measure of his creation. The world is immense, constructed on no plan or theory which the intellect of man can grasp. It is *transcendent* everywhere. This is the burden of every verse, and is the secret, if there be one, of the poem. Sufficient or insufficient, there is nothing more.... God is great, we know not his ways. He takes from us all we have, but yet if we possess our souls in patience, we *may* pass the valley of the shadow, and come out in sunlight again. We may or we may not!... What more have we to say now than God said from the whirlwind over two thousand five hundred years ago?"[30]

If we turn to the sanguine onlooker, on the other hand, we find that deliverance is felt as incomplete unless the burden be altogether overcome and the danger forgotten. Such onlookers give us definitions that seem to the sombre minds of whom we have just been speaking to leave out all the solemnity that makes religious peace so different from merely animal joys. In the opinion of some [pg 077] writers an attitude might be called religious, though no touch were left in it of sacrifice or submission, no tendency to flexion, no bowing of the head. Any "habitual and regulated admiration," says Professor J. R. Seeley,[31] "is worthy to be called a religion"; and accordingly he thinks that our Music, our Science, and our so-called "Civilization," as these things are now organized and admiringly believed in, form the more genuine religions of our time. Certainly the unhesitating and unreasoning way in which we feel that we must inflict our civilization upon "lower" races, by means of Hotchkiss guns, etc., reminds one of nothing so much as of the early spirit of Islam spreading its religion by the sword.

In my last lecture I quoted to you the ultra-radical opinion of Mr. Havelock Ellis, that laughter of any sort may be considered a religious exercise, for it bears witness to the soul's emancipation. I quoted this opinion in order to deny its adequacy. But we must now settle our scores more carefully with this whole optimistic way of thinking. It is far too complex to be decided off-hand. I propose accordingly that we make of religious optimism the theme of the next two lectures.

[pg 078]

Lectures IV and V. The Religion Of Healthy-Mindedness.

If we were to ask the question: "What is human life's chief concern?" one of the answers we should receive would be: "It is happiness." How to gain, how to keep, how to recover happiness, is in fact for most men at all times the secret motive of all they do, and of all they are willing to endure. The hedonistic school in ethics deduces the moral life wholly from the experiences of happiness and unhappiness which different kinds of conduct bring; and, even more in the religious life than in the moral life, happiness and unhappiness seem to be the poles round which the interest revolves. We need not go so far as to say with the author whom I lately quoted that any persistent enthusiasm is, as such, religion, nor need we call mere laughter a religious exercise; but we must admit that any persistent enjoyment may *produce* the sort of religion which consists in a grateful admiration of the gift of so happy an existence; and we must also acknowledge that the more complex ways of experiencing religion are new manners of producing happiness, wonderful inner paths to a supernatural kind of happiness, when the first gift of natural existence is unhappy, as it so often proves itself to be.

With such relations between religion and happiness, it is perhaps not surprising that men come to regard the happiness which a religious belief affords as a proof of its truth. If a creed makes a man feel happy, he almost inevitably adopts it. Such a belief ought to be true; [pg 079] therefore it is true—such, rightly or wrongly, is one of the "immediate inferences" of the religious logic used by ordinary men.

> "The near presence of God's spirit," says a German writer,[32] "may be experienced in its reality—indeed *only* experienced. And the mark by which the spirit's existence and nearness are made irrefutably clear to those who have ever had the experience is the utterly incomparable *feeling of happiness* which is connected with the nearness, and which is therefore not only a possible and altogether proper feeling for us to have here below, but is the best and most indispensable proof of God's reality. No other proof is equally convincing, and therefore happiness is the point from which every efficacious new theology should start."

In the hour immediately before us, I shall invite you to consider the simpler kinds of religious happiness, leaving the more complex sorts to be treated on a later day.

In many persons, happiness is congenital and irreclaimable. "Cosmic emotion" inevitably takes in them the form of enthusiasm and freedom. I speak not only of those who are animally happy. I mean those who, when unhappiness is offered or proposed to them, positively refuse to feel it, as if it were something mean and wrong. We find such persons in every age, passionately flinging themselves upon their sense of the goodness of life, in spite of the hardships of their own condition, and in spite of the sinister theologies into which they may be born. From the outset their religion is one of union with the divine. The heretics who went before the reformation are lavishly accused by the church writers of antinomian practices, just as the first Christians were accused of indulgence in orgies by the Romans. It is probable that there never has been a century in which the deliberate refusal to think ill of life has not been idealized [pg 080] by a sufficient number of persons to form sects, open or secret, who claimed all natural things to be permitted. Saint Augustine's maxim, *Dilige et quod vis fac*,—if you but love [God], you may do as you incline,—is morally one of the profoundest of observations, yet it is pregnant, for such persons, with passports beyond the bounds of conventional morality. According to their characters they have been refined or gross; but their belief has been at all times systematic enough to constitute a definite religious attitude. God was for them a giver of freedom, and the sting of evil was overcome. Saint Francis and his immediate disciples were, on the whole, of this company of spirits, of which there are of course infinite varieties. Rousseau in the earlier years of his writing, Diderot, B. de Saint Pierre, and many of the leaders of the eighteenth century anti-christian movement were of this optimistic type. They owed their influence to a certain authoritativeness in their feeling that Nature, if you will only trust her sufficiently, is absolutely good.

It is to be hoped that we all have some friend, perhaps more often feminine than masculine, and young than old, whose soul is of this sky-blue tint, whose affinities are rather with flowers and birds and all enchanting innocencies than with dark human passions, who can think no ill of man or God, and in whom religious gladness, being in possession from the outset, needs no deliverance from any antecedent burden.

> "God has two families of children on this earth," says Francis W. Newman,[33] "*the once-born* and *the twice-born*," and the once-born he describes as follows: "They see God, not as a strict Judge, not as a Glorious Potentate; but as the animating Spirit of a beautiful harmonious world, Beneficent and Kind, Merciful as well as Pure. The same characters generally have [pg 081]no metaphysical tendencies: they do not look back into themselves. Hence they are not distressed by their own imperfections: yet it would be absurd to call them self-righteous; for they hardly think of themselves *at all*. This childlike quality of their nature makes the opening of religion very happy to them: for they no more shrink from God, than a child from an emperor, before whom the parent trembles: in fact, they have no vivid conception of *any* of the qualities in which the severer Majesty of God consists.[34] He is to them the impersonation of Kindness and Beauty. They read his character, not in the disordered world of man, but in romantic and harmonious nature. Of human sin they know perhaps little in their own hearts and not very much in the world; and human suffering does but melt them to tenderness. Thus, when they approach God, no inward disturbance ensues; and without being as yet spiritual, they have a certain complacency and perhaps romantic sense of excitement in their simple worship."

In the Romish Church such characters find a more congenial soil to grow in than in Protestantism, whose fashions of feeling have been set by minds of a decidedly pessimistic order. But even in Protestantism they have been abundant enough; and in its recent "liberal" developments of Unitarianism and latitudinarianism generally, minds of this order have played and still are playing leading and constructive parts. Emerson himself is an admirable example. Theodore Parker is another,—here are a couple of characteristic passages from Parker's correspondence.[35]

> "Orthodox scholars say: 'In the heathen classics you find no consciousness of sin.' It is very true—God be thanked for it. They were conscious of wrath, of cruelty, avarice, drunkenness, lust, sloth, cowardice, and other actual vices, and struggled and got rid of the deformities, but they were not conscious of [pg 082] 'enmity against God,' and didn't sit down and whine and groan against non-existent evil. I have done wrong things enough in my life, and do them now; I miss the mark, draw bow, and try again. But I am not conscious of hating God, or man, or right, or love, and I know there is much 'health in me'; and in my body, even now, there dwelleth many a good thing, spite of consumption and Saint Paul." In another letter Parker writes: "I have swum in clear sweet waters all my days; and if sometimes they were a little cold, and the stream ran adverse and something rough, it was never too strong to be breasted and swum through. From the days of earliest boyhood, when I went stumbling through the grass,... up to the gray-bearded manhood of this time, there is none but has left me honey in the hive of memory that I now feed on for present delight. When I recall the years ... I am filled with a sense of sweetness and wonder that such little things can make a mortal so exceedingly rich. But I must confess that the chiefest of all my delights is still the religious."

Another good expression of the "once-born" type of consciousness, developing straight and natural, with no element of morbid compunction or crisis, is contained in the answer of Dr. Edward Everett Hale, the eminent Unitarian preacher and writer, to one of Dr. Starbuck's circulars. I quote a part of it:—

> "I observe, with profound regret, the religious struggles which come into many biographies, as if almost essential to the formation of the hero. I ought to speak of these, to say that any man has an advantage, not to be estimated, who is born, as I was, into a family where the religion is simple and rational; who is trained in the theory of such a religion, so that he never knows, for an hour, what these religious or irreligious struggles are. I always knew God loved me, and I was always grateful to him for the world he placed me in. I always liked to tell him so, and was always glad to receive his suggestions to me.... I can remember perfectly that when I was coming to manhood, the half-philosophical novels of the time had a deal [pg 083] to say about the young men and maidens who were facing the 'problem of life.' I had no idea whatever what the problem of life was. To live with all my might seemed to me easy; to learn where there was so much to learn seemed pleasant and

almost of course; to lend a hand, if one had a chance, natural; and if one did this, why, he enjoyed life because he could not help it, and without proving to himself that he ought to enjoy it.... A child who is early taught that he is God's child, that he may live and move and have his being in God, and that he has, therefore, infinite strength at hand for the conquering of any difficulty, will take life more easily, and probably will make more of it, than one who is told that he is born the child of wrath and wholly incapable of good."[36]

One can but recognize in such writers as these the presence of a temperament organically weighted on the side of cheer and fatally forbidden to linger, as those of opposite temperament linger, over the darker aspects of the universe. In some individuals optimism may become quasi-pathological. The capacity for even a transient sadness or a momentary humility seems cut off from them as by a kind of congenital anæsthesia.[37]

[pg 084]
The supreme contemporary example of such an inability to feel evil is of course Walt Whitman.

"His favorite occupation," writes his disciple, Dr. Bucke, "seemed to be strolling or sauntering about outdoors by himself, looking at the grass, the trees, the flowers, the vistas of light, the varying aspects of the sky, and listening to the birds, the crickets, the tree frogs, and all the hundreds of natural sounds. It was evident that these things gave him a pleasure far beyond what they give to ordinary people. Until I knew the man," continues Dr. Bucke, "it had not occurred to me that any one could derive so much absolute happiness from these things as he did. He was very fond of flowers, either wild or cultivated; liked all sorts. I think he admired lilacs and sunflowers just as much as roses. Perhaps, indeed, no man who ever lived liked so many things and disliked so few as Walt Whitman. All natural objects seemed to have a charm for him. All sights and sounds seemed to please him. He appeared to like (and I believe he did like) all the men, women, and children he saw (though I never knew him to say that he liked any one), but each who knew him felt that he liked him or her, and that he liked others also. I never knew him to argue or dispute, and he never spoke about money. He always justified, sometimes playfully, sometimes quite seriously, those who spoke harshly of himself or his writings, and I often thought he even took pleasure in the opposition of enemies. When I first knew [him], I used to think that he watched himself, and would not allow his tongue to give expression to fretfulness, antipathy, complaint, and remonstrance. It did not occur to me as possible that these mental states could be absent in him. After long observation, however, I satisfied myself that such absence or unconsciousness was entirely real. He never spoke deprecatingly of any nationality or class of men, or time in the world's history, or against any trades or occupations—not even against any animals, insects, or inanimate things, nor any of the [pg 085]laws of nature, nor any of the results of those laws, such as illness, deformity, and death. He never complained or grumbled either at the weather, pain, illness, or anything else. He never swore. He could not very well, since he never spoke in anger and apparently never was angry. He never exhibited fear, and I do not believe he ever felt it."[38]

Walt Whitman owes his importance in literature to the systematic expulsion from his writings of all contractile elements. The only sentiments he allowed himself to express were of the expansive order; and he expressed these in the first person, not as your mere monstrously conceited individual might so express them, but vicariously for all men, so that a passionate and mystic ontological emotion suffuses his words, and ends by persuading the reader that men and women, life and death, and all things are divinely good.

Thus it has come about that many persons to-day regard Walt Whitman as the restorer of the eternal natural religion. He has infected them with his own love of comrades, with his own gladness that he and they exist. Societies are actually formed for his cult; a periodical organ exists for its propagation, in which the lines of orthodoxy and heterodoxy are already beginning to be drawn;[39] hymns are written by others in his peculiar prosody; and he is even explicitly compared with the founder of the Christian religion, not altogether to the advantage of the latter.

Whitman is often spoken of as a "pagan." The word nowadays means sometimes the mere natural animal man without a sense of sin; sometimes it means a Greek or Roman with his own peculiar religious consciousness. In [pg 086] neither of these senses does it fitly define this poet. He is more than your mere animal man who has not tasted of the tree of good and evil. He is aware enough of sin for a swagger to be present in his indifference towards it, a conscious pride in his freedom from flexions and contractions, which your genuine pagan in the first sense of the word would never show.

"I could turn and live with animals, they are so placid and self-contained,
I stand and look at them long and long;
They do not sweat and whine about their condition.

> They do not lie awake in the dark and weep for their sins.
> Not one is dissatisfied, not one is demented with the mania of owning things,
> Not one kneels to another, nor to his kind that lived thousands of years ago,
> Not one is respectable or unhappy over the whole earth."[40]

No natural pagan could have written these well-known lines. But on the other hand Whitman is less than a Greek or Roman; for their consciousness, even in Homeric times, was full to the brim of the sad mortality of this sunlit world, and such a consciousness Walt Whitman resolutely refuses to adopt. When, for example, Achilles, about to slay Lycaon, Priam's young son, hears him sue for mercy, he stops to say:—

> "Ah, friend, thou too must die: why thus lamentest thou? Patroclos too is dead, who was better far than thou.... Over me too hang death and forceful fate. There cometh morn or eve or some noonday when my life too some man shall take in battle, whether with spear he smite, or arrow from the string."[41]

Then Achilles savagely severs the poor boy's neck with his sword, heaves him by the foot into the Scamander, and calls to the fishes of the river to eat the white fat of Lycaon. Just as here the cruelty and the sympathy each [pg 087] ring true, and do not mix or interfere with one another, so did the Greeks and Romans keep all their sadnesses and gladnesses unmingled and entire. Instinctive good they did not reckon sin; nor had they any such desire to save the credit of the universe as to make them insist, as so many of *us* insist, that what immediately appears as evil must be "good in the making," or something equally ingenious. Good was good, and bad just bad, for the earlier Greeks. They neither denied the ills of nature,—Walt Whitman's verse, "What is called good is perfect and what is called bad is just as perfect," would have been mere silliness to them,—nor did they, in order to escape from those ills, invent "another and a better world" of the imagination, in which, along with the ills, the innocent goods of sense would also find no place. This integrity of the instinctive reactions, this freedom from all moral sophistry and strain, gives a pathetic dignity to ancient pagan feeling. And this quality Whitman's outpourings have not got. His optimism is too voluntary and defiant; his gospel has a touch of bravado and an affected twist,[42] and this diminishes its effect on many readers who yet are well disposed towards optimism, and on the whole quite willing to admit that in important respects Whitman is of the genuine lineage of the prophets.

If, then, we give the name of healthy-mindedness to the tendency which looks on all things and sees that they are good, we find that we must distinguish between a more involuntary and a more voluntary or systematic way of being healthy-minded. In its involuntary variety, healthy-mindedness [pg 088] is a way of feeling happy about things immediately. In its systematical variety, it is an abstract way of conceiving things as good. Every abstract way of conceiving things selects some one aspect of them as their essence for the time being, and disregards the other aspects. Systematic healthy-mindedness, conceiving good as the essential and universal aspect of being, deliberately excludes evil from its field of vision; and although, when thus nakedly stated, this might seem a difficult feat to perform for one who is intellectually sincere with himself and honest about facts, a little reflection shows that the situation is too complex to lie open to so simple a criticism.

In the first place, happiness, like every other emotional state, has blindness and insensibility to opposing facts given it as its instinctive weapon for self-protection against disturbance. When happiness is actually in possession, the thought of evil can no more acquire the feeling of reality than the thought of good can gain reality when melancholy rules. To the man actively happy, from whatever cause, evil simply cannot then and there be believed in. He must ignore it; and to the bystander he may then seem perversely to shut his eyes to it and hush it up.

But more than this: the hushing of it up may, in a perfectly candid and honest mind, grow into a deliberate religious policy, or *parti pris*. Much of what we call evil is due entirely to the way men take the phenomenon. It can so often be converted into a bracing and tonic good by a simple change of the sufferer's inner attitude from one of fear to one of fight; its sting so often departs and turns into a relish when, after vainly seeking to shun it, we agree to face about and bear it cheerfully, that a man is simply bound in honor, with reference to [pg 089] many of the facts that seem at first to disconcert his peace, to adopt this way of escape. Refuse to admit their badness; despise their power; ignore their presence; turn your attention the other way; and so far as you yourself are concerned at any rate, though the facts may still exist, their evil character exists no longer. Since you make them evil or good by your own thoughts about them, it is the ruling of your thoughts which proves to be your principal concern.

The deliberate adoption of an optimistic turn of mind thus makes its entrance into philosophy. And once in, it is hard to trace its lawful bounds. Not only does the human instinct for happiness, bent on self-protection by ignoring, keep working in its favor, but higher inner ideals have weighty words to say. The attitude of unhappiness is not only painful, it is mean and ugly. What can be more base and unworthy than the pining, puling, mumping mood, no matter by what outward ills it may have been engendered? What is more injurious to others? What less helpful as a way out of the difficulty? It but fastens and perpetuates the trouble which occasioned it, and increases the total evil of the situation. At all costs, then, we ought to reduce the sway of that mood; we ought to scout it in ourselves and others, and never show it tolerance. But it is impossible to carry on this discipline in the subjective sphere without zealously emphasizing the brighter and minimizing the darker aspects of the objective sphere of things at the same time. And thus our resolution not to indulge in misery, beginning at a comparatively small point within ourselves, may not stop until it has brought the entire frame of reality under a systematic conception optimistic enough to be congenial with its needs.

In all this I say nothing of any mystical insight or [pg 090] persuasion that the total frame of things absolutely must be good. Such mystical persuasion plays an enormous part in the history of the religious consciousness, and we must look at it later with some care. But we need not go so far at present. More ordinary non-mystical conditions of rapture suffice for my immediate contention. All invasive moral states and passionate enthusiasms make one feelingless to evil in some direction. The common penalties cease to deter the patriot, the usual prudences are flung by the lover to the winds. When the passion is extreme, suffering may actually be gloried in, provided it be for the ideal cause, death may lose its sting, the grave its victory. In these states, the ordinary contrast of good and ill seems to be swallowed up in a higher denomination, an omnipotent excitement which engulfs the evil, and which the human being welcomes as the crowning experience of his life. This, he says, is truly to live, and I exult in the heroic opportunity and adventure.

The systematic cultivation of healthy-mindedness as a religious attitude is therefore consonant with important currents in human nature, and is anything but absurd. In fact, we all do cultivate it more or less, even when our professed theology should in consistency forbid it. We divert our attention from disease and death as much as we can; and the slaughter-houses and indecencies without end on which our life is founded are huddled out of sight and never mentioned, so that the world we recognize officially in literature and in society is a poetic fiction far handsomer and cleaner and better than the world that really is.[43]

[pg 091]
The advance of liberalism, so-called, in Christianity, during the past fifty years, may fairly be called a victory of healthy-mindedness within the church over the morbidness with which the old hell-fire theology was more harmoniously related. We have now whole congregations whose preachers, far from magnifying our consciousness of sin, seem devoted rather to making little of it. They ignore, or even deny, eternal punishment, and insist on the dignity rather than on the depravity of man. They look at the continual preoccupation of the old-fashioned Christian with the salvation of his soul as something sickly and reprehensible rather than admirable; and a sanguine and "muscular" attitude, which to our forefathers would have seemed purely heathen, has become in their eyes an ideal element of Christian character. I am not asking whether or not they are right, I am only pointing out the change.

The persons to whom I refer have still retained for the most part their nominal connection with Christianity, in spite of their discarding of its more pessimistic theological elements. But in that "theory of evolution" which, gathering momentum for a century, has within the past twenty-five years swept so rapidly over Europe and America, we see the ground laid for a new sort of religion of Nature, which has entirely displaced Christianity from the thought of a large part of our generation. The idea of a universal evolution lends itself to a doctrine of general meliorism and progress which fits the religious needs of the healthy-minded so well that it seems almost as if it might have been created for their use. Accordingly we find "evolutionism" interpreted thus optimistically and [pg 092] embraced as a substitute for the religion they were born in, by a multitude of our contemporaries who have either been trained scientifically, or been fond of reading popular science, and who had already begun to be inwardly dissatisfied with what seemed to them the harshness and irrationality of the orthodox Christian scheme. As examples are better than descriptions, I will quote a document received in answer to Professor Starbuck's circular of questions. The writer's state of mind may by courtesy be called a religion, for it is his reaction on the whole nature of things, it is systematic and reflective, and it loyally binds him to certain inner ideals. I think you will recognize in him, coarse-meated and incapable of wounded spirit as he is, a sufficiently familiar contemporary type.

Q. *What does Religion mean to you?*

A. It means nothing; and it seems, so far as I can observe, useless to others. I am sixty-seven years of age and have resided in X. fifty years, and have been in business forty-five, consequently I have some little experience of life and men, and some women too, and I find that the most religious and pious people are as a rule those most lacking in uprightness and morality. The men who do not go to church or have any religious convictions are the best. Praying, singing of hymns, and sermonizing are pernicious—they teach us to rely on some supernatural power, when we ought to rely on ourselves. I *tee*totally disbelieve in a God. The God-idea was begotten in ignorance, fear, and a general lack of any knowledge of Nature. If I were to die now, being in a healthy condition for my age, both mentally and physically, I would just as lief, yes, rather, die with a hearty enjoyment of music, sport, or any other rational pastime. As a timepiece stops, we die—there being no immortality in either case.

Q. *What comes before your mind corresponding to the words God, Heaven, Angels, etc.?*

A. Nothing whatever. I am a man without a religion. These words mean so much mythic bosh.

[pg 093]
Q. *Have you had any experiences which appeared providential?*

A. None whatever. There is no agency of the superintending kind. A little judicious observation as well as knowledge of scientific law will convince any one of this fact.

Q. *What things work most strongly on your emotions?*

A. Lively songs and music; Pinafore instead of an Oratorio. I like Scott, Burns, Byron, Longfellow, especially Shakespeare, etc., etc. Of songs, the Star-spangled Banner, America, Marseillaise, and all moral and soul-stirring songs, but wishy-washy hymns are my detestation. I greatly enjoy nature, especially fine weather, and until within a few years used to walk Sundays into the country, twelve miles often, with no fatigue, and bicycle forty or fifty. I have dropped the bicycle. I never go to church, but attend lectures when there are any good ones. All of my thoughts and cogitations have been of a healthy and cheerful kind, for instead of doubts and fears I see things as they are, for I endeavor to adjust myself to my environment. This I regard as the deepest law. Mankind is a progressive animal. I am satisfied he will have made a great advance over his present status a thousand years hence.

Q. *What is your notion of sin?*

A. It seems to me that sin is a condition, a disease, incidental to man's development not being yet advanced enough. Morbidness over it increases the disease. We should think that a million of years hence equity, justice, and mental and physical good order will be so fixed and organized that no one will have any idea of evil or sin.

Q. *What is your temperament?*

A. Nervous, active, wide-awake, mentally and physically. Sorry that Nature compels us to sleep at all.

If we are in search of a broken and a contrite heart, clearly we need not look to this brother. His contentment with the finite incases him like a lobster-shell and shields him from all morbid repining at his distance from the Infinite. We have in him an excellent example of the optimism which may be encouraged by popular science.

[pg 094]
To my mind a current far more important and interesting religiously than that which sets in from natural science towards healthy-mindedness is that which has recently poured over America and seems to be gathering force every day,—I am ignorant what foothold it may yet have acquired in Great Britain,—and to which, for the sake of having a brief designation, I will

give the title of the "Mind-cure movement." There are various sects of this "New Thought," to use another of the names by which it calls itself; but their agreements are so profound that their differences may be neglected for my present purpose, and I will treat the movement, without apology, as if it were a simple thing.

It is a deliberately optimistic scheme of life, with both a speculative and a practical side. In its gradual development during the last quarter of a century, it has taken up into itself a number of contributory elements, and it must now be reckoned with as a genuine religious power. It has reached the stage, for example, when the demand for its literature is great enough for insincere stuff, mechanically produced for the market, to be to a certain extent supplied by publishers,—a phenomenon never observed, I imagine, until a religion has got well past its earliest insecure beginnings.

One of the doctrinal sources of Mind-cure is the four Gospels; another is Emersonianism or New England transcendentalism; another is Berkeleyan idealism; another is spiritism, with its messages of "law" and "progress" and "development"; another the optimistic popular science evolutionism of which I have recently spoken; and, finally, Hinduism has contributed a strain. But the most characteristic feature of the mind-cure movement is an inspiration much more direct. The leaders in this faith have had an intuitive belief in the all-saving power [pg 095] of healthy-minded attitudes as such, in the conquering efficacy of courage, hope, and trust, and a correlative contempt for doubt, fear, worry, and all nervously precautionary states of mind.[44] Their belief has in a general way been corroborated by the practical experience of their disciples; and this experience forms to-day a mass imposing in amount.

The blind have been made to see, the halt to walk; lifelong invalids have had their health restored. The moral fruits have been no less remarkable. The deliberate adoption of a healthy-minded attitude has proved possible to many who never supposed they had it in them; regeneration of character has gone on on an extensive scale; and cheerfulness has been restored to countless homes. The indirect influence of this has been great. The mind-cure principles are beginning so to pervade the air that one catches their spirit at second-hand. One hears of the "Gospel of Relaxation," of the

"Don't Worry Movement," of people who repeat to themselves, "Youth, health, vigor!" when dressing in the morning, as their motto for the day. Complaints of the weather are getting to be forbidden in many households; and more and more people are recognizing it to be bad form to speak of disagreeable sensations, or to make much of the ordinary inconveniences and ailments of life. These general tonic effects on public opinion would be good even if the more striking results were non-existent. But the latter abound so that we can afford to overlook the [pg 096] innumerable failures and self-deceptions that are mixed in with them (for in everything human failure is a matter of course), and we can also overlook the verbiage of a good deal of the mind-cure literature, some of which is so moonstruck with optimism and so vaguely expressed that an academically trained intellect finds it almost impossible to read it at all.

The plain fact remains that the spread of the movement has been due to practical fruits, and the extremely practical turn of character of the American people has never been better shown than by the fact that this, their only decidedly original contribution to the systematic philosophy of life, should be so intimately knit up with concrete therapeutics. To the importance of mind-cure the medical and clerical professions in the United States are beginning, though with much recalcitrancy and protesting, to open their eyes. It is evidently bound to develop still farther, both speculatively and practically, and its latest writers are far and away the ablest of the group.[45] It matters nothing that, just as there are hosts of persons who cannot pray, so there are greater hosts who cannot by any possibility be influenced by the mind-curers' ideas. For our immediate purpose, the important point is that so large a number should exist who *can* be so influenced. They form a psychic type to be studied with respect.[46]

[pg 097]
To come now to a little closer quarters with their creed. The fundamental pillar on which it rests is nothing more than the general basis of all religious experience, the fact that man has a dual nature, and is connected with two spheres of thought, a shallower and a profounder sphere, in either of which he may learn to live more habitually. The shallower and lower sphere is that of the fleshly sensations, instincts, and desires, of egotism, doubt, and the lower personal interests. But whereas Christian theology has always

considered *frowardness* [pg 098] to be the essential vice of this part of human nature, the mind-curers say that the mark of the beast in it is *fear*; and this is what gives such an entirely new religious turn to their persuasion.

> "Fear," to quote a writer of the school, "has had its uses in the evolutionary process, and seems to constitute the whole of forethought in most animals; but that it should remain any part of the mental equipment of human civilized life is an absurdity. I find that the fear element of forethought is not stimulating to those more civilized persons to whom duty and attraction are the natural motives, but is weakening and deterrent. As soon as it becomes unnecessary, fear becomes a positive deterrent, and should be entirely removed, as dead flesh is removed from living tissue. To assist in the analysis of fear, and in the denunciation of its expressions, I have coined the word *fearthought* to stand for the unprofitable element of forethought, and have defined the word 'worry' as *fearthought in contradistinction to forethought.* I have also defined fearthought as *the self-imposed or self-permitted suggestion of inferiority*, in order to place it where it really belongs, in the category of harmful, unnecessary, and therefore not respectable things."[47]

The "misery-habit," the "martyr-habit," engendered by the prevalent "fearthought," get pungent criticism from the mind-cure writers:—

> "Consider for a moment the habits of life into which we are born. There are certain social conventions or customs and alleged requirements, there is a theological bias, a general view of the world. There are conservative ideas in regard to our early training, our education, marriage, and occupation in life. Following close upon this, there is a long series of anticipations, namely, that we shall suffer certain children's diseases, diseases of middle life, and of old age; the thought that we shall grow [pg 099]old, lose our faculties, and again become childlike; while crowning all is the fear of death. Then there is a long line of particular fears and trouble-bearing expectations, such, for example, as ideas associated with certain articles of food, the dread of the east wind, the terrors of hot weather, the aches and pains associated with cold weather, the fear of catching cold if one sits in a draught, the coming of hay-fever upon the 14th of August in the middle of the day, and so on through a long list of fears, dreads, worriments, anxieties, anticipations, expectations, pessimisms, morbidities, and the whole ghostly train of fateful shapes which our fellow-men, and especially physicians, are ready to help us conjure up, an array worthy to rank with Bradley's 'unearthly ballet of bloodless categories.'

> "Yet this is not all. This vast array is swelled by innumerable volunteers from daily life,—the fear of accident, the possibility of calamity, the loss of property, the chance of robbery, of fire, or the outbreak of war. And it is not deemed sufficient to fear for ourselves. When a friend is taken ill, we must forthwith fear the worst and apprehend death. If one meets with sorrow ... sympathy means to enter into and increase the suffering."[48]

> "Man," to quote another writer, "often has fear stamped upon him before his entrance into the outer world; he is reared in fear; all his life is passed in bondage to fear of disease and death, and thus his whole mentality becomes cramped, limited, and depressed, and his body follows its shrunken pattern and specification.... Think of the millions of sensitive and responsive souls among our ancestors who have been under the dominion of such a perpetual nightmare! Is it not surprising that health exists at all? Nothing but the boundless divine love, exuberance, and vitality, constantly poured in, even though unconsciously to us, could in some degree neutralize such an ocean of morbidity."[49]

Although the disciples of the mind-cure often use Christian terminology, one sees from such quotations [pg 100] how widely their notion of the fall of man diverges from that of ordinary Christians.[50]

Their notion of man's higher nature is hardly less divergent, being decidedly pantheistic. The spiritual in man appears in the mind-cure philosophy as partly conscious, but chiefly subconscious; and through the subconscious part of it we are already one with the Divine without any miracle of grace, or abrupt creation of a new inner man. As this view is variously expressed by different writers, we find in it traces of Christian mysticism, of transcendental idealism, of vedantism, and of the modern psychology of the subliminal self. A quotation or two will put us at the central point of view:

"The great central fact of the universe is that spirit of infinite life and power that is back of all, that manifests itself in and through all. This spirit of infinite life and power that is back of all is what I call God. I care not what term you may use, be it Kindly Light, Providence, the Over-Soul, Omnipotence, [pg 101]or whatever term may be most convenient, so long as we are agreed in regard to the great central fact itself. God then fills the universe alone, so that all is from Him and in Him, and there is nothing that is outside. He is the life of our life, our very life itself. We are partakers of the life of God; and though we differ from Him in that we are individualized spirits, while He is the Infinite Spirit, including us, as well as all else beside, yet in essence the life of God and the life of man are identically the same, and so are one. They differ not in essence or quality; they differ in degree.

"The great central fact in human life is the coming into a conscious vital realization of our oneness with this Infinite Life, and the opening of ourselves fully to this divine inflow. In just the degree that we come into a conscious realization of our oneness with the Infinite Life, and open ourselves to this divine inflow, do we actualize in ourselves the qualities and powers of the Infinite Life, do we make ourselves channels through which the Infinite Intelligence and Power can work. In just the degree in which you realize your oneness with the Infinite Spirit, you will exchange dis-ease for ease, inharmony for harmony, suffering and pain for abounding health and strength. To recognize our own divinity, and our intimate relation to the Universal, is to attach the belts of our machinery to the powerhouse of the Universe. One need remain in hell no longer than one chooses to; we can rise to any heaven we ourselves choose; and when we choose so to rise, all the higher powers of the Universe combine to help us heavenward."[51]

Let me now pass from these abstracter statements to some more concrete accounts of experience with the mind-cure religion. I have many answers from correspondents—the only difficulty is to choose. The first two whom I shall quote are my personal friends. One of them, a woman, writing as follows, expresses well the feeling of continuity with the Infinite Power, by which all mind-cure disciples are inspired.

[pg 102]

"The first underlying cause of all sickness, weakness, or depression is the *human sense of separateness* from that Divine Energy which we call God. The soul which can feel and affirm in serene but jubilant confidence, as did the Nazarene: 'I and my Father are one,' has no further need of healer, or of healing. This is the whole truth in a nutshell, and other foundation for wholeness can no man lay than this fact of impregnable divine union. Disease can no longer attack one whose feet are planted on this rock, who feels hourly, momently, the influx of the Deific Breath. If one with Omnipotence, how can weariness enter the consciousness, how illness assail that indomitable spark?

"This possibility of annulling forever the law of fatigue has been abundantly proven in my own case; for my earlier life bears a record of many, many years of bedridden invalidism, with spine and lower limbs paralyzed. My thoughts were no more impure than they are to-day, although my belief in the necessity of illness was dense and unenlightened; but since my resurrection in the flesh, I have worked as a healer unceasingly for fourteen years without a vacation, and can truthfully assert that I have never known a moment of fatigue or pain, although coming in touch constantly with excessive weakness, illness, and disease of all kinds. For how can a conscious part of Deity be sick?—since 'Greater is he that is *with* us than all that can strive against us.' "

My second correspondent, also a woman, sends me the following statement:—

"Life seemed difficult to me at one time. I was always breaking down, and had several attacks of what is called nervous prostration, with terrible insomnia, being on the verge of insanity; besides having many other troubles, especially of the digestive organs. I had been sent away from home in charge of doctors, had taken all the narcotics, stopped all work, been fed up, and in fact knew all the doctors within reach. But I never recovered permanently till this New Thought took possession of me.

"I think that the one thing which impressed me most was [pg 103]learning the fact that we must be in absolutely constant relation or mental touch (this word is to me very expressive) with that essence of life which permeates all and which we call God. This is almost unrecognizable unless we live it into ourselves *actually*, that is, by a constant turning to the very innermost, deepest consciousness of our real selves or of God in us, for illumination from within, just as we turn to the sun for light, warmth, and invigoration without. When you do this consciously, realizing that to turn inward to the light within you is to live in the presence of God or your divine self, you soon discover the unreality of the objects to which you have hitherto been turning and which have engrossed you without.

"I have come to disregard the meaning of this attitude for bodily health *as such*, because that comes of itself, as an incidental result, and cannot be found by any special mental act or desire to have it, beyond that general attitude of mind I have referred to above. That which we usually make the object of life, those outer things we are all so wildly seeking, which we so often live and die for, but which then do not give us peace and happiness, they should all come of themselves as accessory, and as the mere outcome or natural result of a far higher life sunk deep in the bosom of the spirit. This life is the real seeking of the kingdom of God, the desire for his supremacy in our hearts, so that all else comes as that which shall be 'added unto you'—as quite incidental and as a surprise to us, perhaps; and yet it is the proof of the reality of the perfect poise in the very centre of our being.

"When I say that we commonly make the object of our life that which we should not work for primarily, I mean many things which the world considers praiseworthy and excellent, such as success in business, fame as author or artist, physician or lawyer, or renown in philanthropic undertakings. Such things should be results, not objects. I would also include pleasures of many kinds which seem harmless and good at the time, and are pursued because many accept them—I mean conventionalities, sociabilities, and fashions in their various development, these being mostly approved by the masses, although they may be unreal, and even unhealthy superfluities."

[pg 104]
Here is another case, more concrete, also that of a woman. I read you these cases without comment,—they express so many varieties of the state of mind we are studying.

"I had been a sufferer from my childhood till my fortieth year. [Details of ill-health are given which I omit.] I had been in Vermont several months hoping for good from the change of air, but steadily growing weaker, when one day during the latter part of October, while resting in the afternoon, I suddenly heard as it were these words: 'You will be healed and do a work you never dreamed of.' These words were impressed upon my mind with such power I said at once that only God could have put them there. I believed them in spite of myself and of my suffering and weakness, which continued until Christmas, when I returned to Boston. Within two days a young friend offered to take me to a mental healer (this was January 7, 1881). The healer said: 'There is nothing but Mind; we are expressions of the One Mind; body is only a mortal belief; as a man thinketh so is he.' I could not accept all she said, but I translated all that was there for *me* in this way: 'There is nothing but God; I am created by Him, and am absolutely dependent upon Him; mind is given me to use; and by just so much of it as I will put upon the thought of right action in body I shall be lifted out of bondage to my ignorance and fear and past experience.' That day I commenced accordingly to take a little of every food provided for the family, constantly saying to myself: 'The Power that created the stomach must take care of what I have eaten.' By holding these suggestions through the evening I went to bed and fell asleep, saying: 'I am soul, spirit, just one with God's Thought of me,' and slept all night without waking, for the first time in several years [the distress-turns had usually recurred about two o'clock in the night]. I felt the next day like an escaped prisoner, and believed I had found the secret that would in time give me perfect health. Within ten days I was able to eat anything provided for others, and after two weeks I began to have my own positive mental suggestions of Truth, [pg 105]which were to me like stepping-stones. I will note a few of them; they came about two weeks apart.

"1st. I am Soul, therefore it is well with me.

"2d. I am Soul, therefore I *am* well.

"3d. A sort of inner vision of myself as a four-footed beast with a protuberance on every part of my body where I had suffering, with my own face, begging me to acknowledge it as myself. I resolutely fixed my attention on being well, and refused to even look at my old self in this form.

"4th. Again the vision of the beast far in the background, with faint voice. Again refusal to acknowledge.

"5th. Once more the vision, but only of my eyes with the longing look; and again the refusal. Then came the conviction, the inner consciousness, that I was perfectly well and always had been, for I was Soul, an expression of God's Perfect Thought. That was to me the perfect and completed separation between what I was and what I appeared to be. I succeeded in never losing sight after this of my real being, by constantly affirming this truth, and by degrees (though it took me two years of hard work to get there) *I expressed health continuously throughout my whole body.*

"In my subsequent nineteen years' experience I have never known this Truth to fail when I applied it, though in my ignorance I have often failed to apply it, but through my failures I have learned the simplicity and trustfulness of the little child."

But I fear that I risk tiring you by so many examples, and I must lead you back to philosophic generalities again. You see already by such records of experience how impossible it is not to class mind-cure as primarily a religious movement. Its doctrine of the oneness of our life with God's life is in fact quite indistinguishable from an interpretation of Christ's message which in these very Gifford lectures has been defended by some of your very ablest Scottish religious philosophers.[52]

[pg 106]
But philosophers usually profess to give a quasi-logical explanation of the existence of evil, whereas of the general fact of evil in the world, the existence of the selfish, suffering, timorous finite consciousness, the mind-curers, so far as I am acquainted with them, profess to give no speculative explanation. Evil is empirically there for them as it is for everybody, but the practical point of view predominates, and it would ill agree with the spirit of their system to spend time in worrying over it as a "mystery" or "problem," or in "laying to heart" the lesson of its experience, after the manner of the Evangelicals. Don't reason about it, as Dante says, but give a glance and pass beyond! It is Avidhya, ignorance! something merely to be outgrown and left behind, transcended and forgotten. Christian Science so-called, the sect of Mrs. Eddy, is the most radical branch of mind-cure in its dealings with evil. For it evil is simply a *lie*, [pg 107] and any one who mentions it is a liar. The optimistic ideal of duty forbids us to pay it the compliment even of explicit attention. Of course, as our next lectures will show us, this is a bad speculative omission, but it is intimately linked with the practical merits of the system we are examining. Why regret a philosophy of evil, a mind-curer would ask us, if I can put you in possession of a life of good?

After all, it is the life that tells; and mind-cure has developed a living system of mental hygiene which may well claim to have thrown all previous literature of the *Diätetik der Seele* into the shade. This system is wholly and exclusively compacted of optimism: "Pessimism leads to weakness. Optimism leads to power." "Thoughts are things," as one of the most vigorous mind-cure writers prints in bold type at the bottom of each of his pages; and if your thoughts are of health, youth, vigor, and success, before you know it these things will also be your outward portion. No one can fail of the regenerative influence of optimistic thinking, pertinaciously pursued. Every man owns indefeasibly this inlet to the divine. Fear, on the contrary, and all the contracted and egoistic modes of thought, are inlets to destruction. Most mind-curers here bring in a doctrine that thoughts are "forces," and that, by virtue of a law that like attracts like, one man's thoughts draw to themselves as allies all the thoughts of the same character that exist the world over. Thus one gets, by one's thinking, reinforcements from elsewhere for the realization of one's desires; and the great point in the conduct of life is to get the heavenly forces on one's side by opening one's own mind to their influx.

On the whole, one is struck by a psychological similarity between the mind-cure movement and the Lutheran [pg 108] and Wesleyan movements. To the believer in moralism and works, with his anxious query, "What shall I do to be saved?" Luther and Wesley replied: "You are saved now, if you would but believe it." And the mind-curers come with precisely similar words of emancipation. They speak, it is true, to persons for whom the conception of salvation has lost its ancient theological meaning, but who labor nevertheless with the same eternal human difficulty. *Things are wrong with them*; and "What shall I do to be clear, right, sound, whole, well?" is the form of their question. And the answer is: "You *are* well, sound, and clear already, if you did but know it." "The whole matter may be summed up in one sentence," says one of the authors whom I have already quoted, "*God is well, and so are you*. You must awaken to the knowledge of your real being."

The adequacy of their message to the mental needs of a large fraction of mankind is what gave force to those earlier gospels. Exactly the same adequacy holds in the case of the mind-cure message, foolish as it may sound upon its surface; and seeing its rapid growth in influence, and its therapeutic triumphs, one is tempted to ask whether it may not be destined (probably by very reason of the crudity and extravagance of many of its manifestations[53]) to play a part almost as great in the evolution of the popular religion of the future as did those earlier movements in their day.

But I here fear that I may begin to "jar upon the nerves" of some of the members of this academic audience. Such contemporary vagaries, you may think, [pg 109] should hardly take so large a place in dignified Gifford lectures. I can only beseech you to have patience. The whole outcome of these lectures will, I imagine, be the emphasizing to your mind of the enormous diversities which the spiritual lives of different men exhibit. Their wants, their susceptibilities, and their capacities all vary and must be classed under different heads. The result is that we have really different types of religious experience; and, seeking in these lectures closer acquaintance with the healthy-minded type, we must take it where we find it in most radical form. The psychology of individual types of character has hardly begun even to be sketched as yet—our lectures may possibly serve as a crumb-like contribution to the structure. The first thing to bear in mind (especially if we ourselves belong to the clerico-academic-scientific type, the officially and conventionally "correct" type, "the deadly respectable" type, for which to ignore others is a besetting temptation) is that nothing can be more stupid than to bar out phenomena from our notice, merely because we are incapable of taking part in anything like them ourselves.

Now the history of Lutheran salvation by faith, of methodistic conversions, and of what I call the mind-cure movement seems to prove the existence of numerous persons in whom—at any rate at a certain stage in their development—a change of character for the better, so far from being facilitated by the rules laid down by official moralists, will take place all the more successfully if those rules be exactly reversed. Official moralists advise us never to relax our strenuousness. "Be vigilant, day and night," they adjure us; "hold your passive tendencies in check; shrink from no effort; keep your will like a bow always bent." But the persons I speak of find that all this conscious effort leads to nothing but failure [pg 110] and vexation in their hands, and only makes them two-fold more the children of hell they were before. The tense and voluntary attitude becomes in them an impossible fever and torment. Their machinery refuses to run at all when the bearings are made so hot and the belts so tight.

Under these circumstances the way to success, as vouched for by innumerable authentic personal narrations, is by an anti-moralistic method, by the "surrender" of which I spoke in my second lecture. Passivity, not activity; relaxation, not intentness, should be now the rule. Give up the feeling of responsibility, let go your hold, resign the care of your destiny to higher powers, be genuinely indifferent as to what becomes of it all, and you will find not only that you gain a perfect inward relief, but often also, in addition, the particular goods you sincerely thought you were renouncing.

This is the salvation through self-despair, the dying to be truly born, of Lutheran theology, the passage into *nothing* of which Jacob Behmen writes. To get to it, a critical point must usually be passed, a corner turned within one. Something must give way, a native hardness must break down and liquefy; and this event (as we shall abundantly see hereafter) is frequently sudden and automatic, and leaves on the Subject an impression that he has been wrought on by an external power.

Whatever its ultimate significance may prove to be, this is certainly one fundamental form of human experience. Some say that the capacity or incapacity for it is what divides the religious from the merely moralistic character. With those who undergo it in its fullness, no criticism avails to cast doubt on its reality. They *know*; for they have actually *felt* the higher powers, in giving up the tension of their personal will.

[pg 111]
A story which revivalist preachers often tell is that of a man who found himself at night slipping down the side of a precipice. At last he caught a branch which stopped his fall, and remained clinging to it in misery for hours. But finally his fingers had to loose their hold, and with a despairing farewell to life, he let himself drop. He fell just six inches. If he had given up the struggle earlier, his agony would have been spared. As the mother earth received him, so, the preachers tell us, will the everlasting arms receive *us* if we confide absolutely in them, and give up the hereditary habit of relying on our personal strength, with its precautions that cannot shelter and safeguards that never save.

The mind-curers have given the widest scope to this sort of experience. They have demonstrated that a form of regeneration by relaxing, by letting go, psychologically indistinguishable from the Lutheran justification by faith and the Wesleyan acceptance of free grace, is within the reach of persons who have no conviction of sin and care nothing for the Lutheran theology. It is but giving your little private convulsive self a rest, and finding that a greater Self is there. The results, slow or sudden, or great or small, of the combined optimism and expectancy, the regenerative phenomena which ensue on the abandonment of effort, remain firm facts of human nature, no matter whether we adopt a theistic, a pantheisticidealistic, or a medical-materialistic view of their ultimate causal explanation.[54]

[pg 112]
When we take up the phenomena of revivalistic conversion, we shall learn something more about all this. Meanwhile I will say a brief word about the mind-curer's *methods*.

They are of course largely suggestive. The suggestive influence of environment plays an enormous part in all spiritual education. But the word "suggestion," having acquired official status, is unfortunately already beginning to play in many quarters the part of a wet blanket upon investigation, being used to fend off all inquiry into the varying susceptibilities of individual cases. "Suggestion" is only another name for the power of ideas, *so far as they prove efficacious over belief and conduct*. Ideas efficacious over some people prove inefficacious over others. Ideas efficacious at some times and in some human surroundings are not so at other times and elsewhere. The ideas of Christian churches are not efficacious in the therapeutic direction to-day, whatever they may have been in earlier centuries; and when the whole question is as to why the salt has lost its savor here or gained it there, the mere blank waving of the word "suggestion" as if it were a banner gives no light. Dr. Goddard, whose candid psychological essay on Faith Cures ascribes them to nothing but ordinary suggestion, concludes by saying that "Religion [and by this he seems to mean our popular Christianity] has in it all there is in mental therapeutics, and has it in its best form. Living up to [our religious] ideas will do anything for us that can be done." And this in spite of the actual fact that the popular Christianity does absolutely [pg 113] *nothing*, or did nothing until mind-cure came to the rescue.[55]

An idea, to be suggestive, must come to the individual with the force of a revelation. The mind-cure with its gospel of healthy-mindedness has come as a revelation to many whose hearts the church Christianity had left hardened. It has let loose their springs of higher life. [pg 114] In what can the originality of any religious movement consist, save in finding a channel, until then sealed up, through which those springs may be set free in some group of human beings?

The force of personal faith, enthusiasm, and example, and above all the force of novelty, are always the prime suggestive agency in this kind of success. If mind-cure should ever become official, respectable, and intrenched, these elements of suggestive efficacy will be lost. In its acuter stages every religion must be a homeless Arab of the desert. The church knows this well enough, with its everlasting inner struggle of the acute religion of the few against the chronic religion of the many, indurated into an obstructiveness worse than that which irreligion opposes to the movings of the Spirit. "We may pray," says Jonathan Edwards, "concerning all those saints that are not lively Christians, that they may either be enlivened, or taken away; if that be true that is often said by some at this day, that these cold dead saints do more hurt than natural men, and lead more souls to hell, and that it would be well for mankind if they were all dead."[56]

The next condition of success is the apparent existence, in large numbers, of minds who unite healthy-mindedness with readiness for regeneration by letting go. Protestantism has been too pessimistic as regards the natural man, Catholicism has been too legalistic and moralistic, for either the one or the other to appeal in any generous way to the type of character formed of this peculiar mingling of elements. However few of us here present may belong to such a type, it is now evident that [pg 115] it forms a specific moral combination, well represented in the world.

Finally, mind-cure has made what in our protestant countries is an unprecedentedly great use of the subconscious life. To their reasoned advice and dogmatic assertion, its founders have added systematic exercise in passive relaxation, concentration, and meditation, and have even invoked something like hypnotic practice. I quote some passages at random:—

> "The value, the potency of ideals is the great practical truth on which the New Thought most strongly insists,—the development namely from within outward, from small to great.[57] Consequently one's thought should be centred on the ideal outcome, even though this trust be literally like a step in the dark.[58] To attain the ability thus effectively to direct the mind, the New Thought advises the practice of concentration, or in other words, the attainment of self-control. One is to learn to marshal the tendencies of the mind, so that they may be held together as a unit by the chosen ideal. To this end, one should set apart times for silent meditation, by one's self, preferably

> in a room where the surroundings are favorable to spiritual thought. In New Thought terms, this is called 'entering the silence.' "[59]
>
> "The time will come when in the busy office or on the noisy street you can enter into the silence by simply drawing the mantle of your own thoughts about you and realizing that there and everywhere the Spirit of Infinite Life, Love, Wisdom, Peace, Power, and Plenty is guiding, keeping, protecting, leading you. This is the spirit of continual prayer.[60] One of the most intuitive men we ever met had a desk at a city office where several other gentlemen were doing business constantly, and often talking loudly. Entirely undisturbed by the many various sounds about him, this self-centred faithful man would, [pg 116]in any moment of perplexity, draw the curtains of privacy so completely about him that he would be as fully inclosed in his own psychic aura, and thereby as effectually removed from all distractions, as though he were alone in some primeval wood. Taking his difficulty with him into the mystic silence in the form of a direct question, to which he expected a certain answer, he would remain utterly passive until the reply came, and never once through many years' experience did he find himself disappointed or misled."[61]

Wherein, I should like to know, does this *intrinsically* differ from the practice of "recollection" which plays so great a part in Catholic discipline? Otherwise called the practice of the presence of God (and so known among ourselves, as for instance in Jeremy Taylor), it is thus defined by the eminent teacher Alvarez de Paz in his work on Contemplation.

> "It is the recollection of God, the thought of God, which in all places and circumstances makes us see him present, lets us commune respectfully and lovingly with him, and fills us with desire and affection for him.... Would you escape from every ill? Never lose this recollection of God, neither in prosperity nor in adversity, nor on any occasion whichsoever it be. Invoke not, to excuse yourself from this duty, either the difficulty or the importance of your business, for you can always remember that God sees you, that you are under his eye. If a thousand times an hour you forget him, reanimate a thousand times the recollection. If you cannot practice this exercise continuously, at least make yourself as familiar with it as possible; and, like unto those who in a rigorous winter draw near the fire as often as they can, go as often as you can to that ardent fire which will warm your soul."[62]

All the external associations of the Catholic discipline are of course unlike anything in mind-cure thought, but the purely spiritual part of the exercise is identical in [pg 117] both communions, and in both communions those who urge it write with authority, for they have evidently experienced in their own persons that whereof they tell. Compare again some mind-cure utterances:—

> "High, healthful, pure thinking can be encouraged, promoted, and strengthened. Its current can be turned upon grand ideals until it forms a habit and wears a channel. By means of such discipline the mental horizon can be flooded with the sunshine of beauty, wholeness, and harmony. To inaugurate pure and lofty thinking may at first seem difficult, even almost mechanical, but perseverance will at length render it easy, then pleasant, and finally delightful.
>
> "The soul's real world is that which it has built of its thoughts, mental states, and imaginations. If we *will*, we can turn our backs upon the lower and sensuous plane, and lift ourselves into the realm of the spiritual and Real, and there gain a residence. The assumption of states of expectancy and receptivity will attract spiritual sunshine, and it will flow in as naturally as air inclines to a vacuum.... Whenever the thought is not occupied with one's daily duty or profession, it should be sent aloft into the spiritual atmosphere. There are quiet leisure moments by day, and wakeful hours at night, when this wholesome and delightful exercise may be engaged in to great advantage. If one who has never made any systematic effort to lift and control the thought-forces will, for a single month, earnestly pursue the course here suggested, he will be surprised and delighted at the result, and nothing will induce him to go back to careless, aimless, and superficial thinking. At such favorable seasons the outside world, with all its current of daily events, is barred out, and one goes into the silent sanctuary of the inner temple of soul to commune and aspire. The spiritual hearing becomes delicately sensitive, so that the 'still, small voice' is audible, the tumultuous waves of external sense are hushed, and there is a great calm. The ego gradually becomes conscious that it is face to face with the Divine Presence; that mighty, healing, loving, Fatherly life which is nearer to us than we are to ourselves. There is soul-contact [pg 118]with the Parent-Soul, and an influx of life, love, virtue, health, and happiness from the Inexhaustible Fountain."[63]

When we reach the subject of mysticism, you will undergo so deep an immersion into these exalted states of consciousness as to be wet all over, if I may so express myself; and the cold shiver of doubt with which this little sprinkling may affect you will have long since passed away—doubt, I mean, as to whether all such writing be not mere abstract talk and rhetoric set down *pour encourager les autres*. You will then be convinced, I trust, that these states of consciousness of "union" form a perfectly definite class of experiences, of which the soul may occasionally partake, and which certain persons may live by in a deeper sense than they live by anything else with which they have acquaintance. This brings me to a general philosophical reflection with which I should like to pass from the subject of healthy-mindedness, and close a topic which I fear is already only too long drawn out. It concerns the relation of all this systematized healthy-mindedness and mind-cure religion to scientific method and the scientific life.

In a later lecture I shall have to treat explicitly of the relation of religion to science on the one hand, and to primeval savage thought on the other. There are plenty of persons to-day—"scientists" or "positivists," they are fond of calling themselves—who will tell you that religious thought is a mere survival, an atavistic reversion to a type of consciousness which humanity in its more enlightened examples has long since left behind and outgrown. If you ask them to explain themselves more fully, they will probably say that for primitive thought [pg 119] everything is conceived of under the form of personality. The savage thinks that things operate by personal forces, and for the sake of individual ends. For him, even external nature obeys individual needs and claims, just as if these were so many elementary powers. Now science, on the other hand, these positivists say, has proved that personality, so far from being an elementary force in nature, is but a passive resultant of the really elementary forces, physical, chemical, physiological, and psycho-physical, which are all impersonal and general in character. Nothing individual accomplishes anything in the universe save in so far as it obeys and exemplifies some universal law. Should you then inquire of them by what means science has thus supplanted primitive thought, and discredited its personal way of looking at things, they would undoubtedly say it has been by the strict use of the method of experimental verification. Follow out science's conceptions practically, they will say, the conceptions that ignore personality altogether, and you will always be corroborated. The world is so made that all your expectations will be experientially verified so long, and only so long, as you keep the terms from which you infer them impersonal and universal.

But here we have mind-cure, with her diametrically opposite philosophy, setting up an exactly identical claim. Live as if I were true, she says, and every day will practically prove you right. That the controlling energies of nature are personal, that your own personal thoughts are forces, that the powers of the universe will directly respond to your individual appeals and needs, are propositions which your whole bodily and mental experience will verify. And that experience does largely verify these primeval religious ideas is proved by the fact that the mind-cure movement spreads as it does, not by proclamation [pg 120] and assertion simply, but by palpable experiential results. Here, in the very heyday of science's authority, it carries on an aggressive warfare against the scientific philosophy, and succeeds by using science's own peculiar methods and weapons. Believing that a higher power will take care of us in certain ways better than we can take care of ourselves, if we only genuinely throw ourselves upon it and consent to use it, it finds the belief, not only not impugned, but corroborated by its observation.

How conversions are thus made, and converts confirmed, is evident enough from the narratives which I have quoted. I will quote yet another couple of shorter ones to give the matter a perfectly concrete turn. Here is one:—

> "One of my first experiences in applying my teaching was two months after I first saw the healer. I fell, spraining my right ankle, which I had done once four years before, having then had to use a crutch and elastic anklet for some months, and carefully guarding it ever since. As soon as I was on my feet I made the positive suggestion (and felt it through all my being): 'There is nothing but God, all life comes from him perfectly. I cannot be sprained or hurt, I will let him take care of it.' Well, I never had a sensation in it, and I walked two miles that day."

The next case not only illustrates experiment and verification, but also the element of passivity and surrender of which awhile ago I made such account.

> "I went into town to do some shopping one morning, and I had not been gone long before I began to feel ill. The ill feeling increased rapidly, until I had pains in all my bones, nausea and faintness, headache, all the symptoms in short that precede an attack of influenza. I thought that I was going to have

the grippe, epidemic then in Boston, or something worse. The mind-cure teachings that I had been listening to all the winter [pg 121]thereupon came into my mind, and I thought that here was an opportunity to test myself. On my way home I met a friend, and I refrained with some effort from telling her how I felt. That was the first step gained. I went to bed immediately, and my husband wished to send for the doctor. But I told him that I would rather wait until morning and see how I felt. Then followed one of the most beautiful experiences of my life.

"I cannot express it in any other way than to say that I did 'lie down in the stream of life and let it flow over me.' I gave up all fear of any impending disease; I was perfectly willing and obedient. There was no intellectual effort, or train of thought. My dominant idea was: 'Behold the handmaid of the Lord: be it unto me even as thou wilt,' and a perfect confidence that all would be well, that all *was* well. The creative life was flowing into me every instant, and I felt myself allied with the Infinite, in harmony, and full of the peace that passeth understanding. There was no place in my mind for a jarring body. I had no consciousness of time or space or persons; but only of love and happiness and faith.

"I do not know how long this state lasted, nor when I fell asleep; but when I woke up in the morning, *I was well.*"

These are exceedingly trivial instances,[64] but in them, if we have anything at all, we have the method of experiment and verification. For the point I am driving at now, it makes no difference whether you consider the patients to be deluded victims of their imagination or not. That they seemed to *themselves* to have been cured by the experiments tried was enough to make them converts to the system. And although it is evident that one must be of a certain mental mould to get such results (for not every one can get thus cured to his own satisfaction any more than every one can be cured by the first regular practitioner whom he calls in), yet it would surely be pedantic and over-scrupulous for those who *can* get their savage and primitive philosophy of mental healing verified [pg 122] in such experimental ways as this, to give them up at word of command for more scientific therapeutics. What are we to think of all this? Has science made too wide a claim?

I believe that the claims of the sectarian scientist are, to say the least, premature. The experiences which we have been studying during this hour (and a great many other kinds of religious experiences are like them) plainly show the universe to be a more many-sided affair than any sect, even the scientific sect, allows for. What, in the end, are all our verifications but experiences that agree with more or less isolated systems of ideas (conceptual systems) that our minds have framed? But why in the name of common sense need we assume that only one such system of ideas can be true? The obvious outcome of our total experience is that the world can be handled according to many systems of ideas, and is so handled by different men, and will each time give some characteristic kind of profit, for which he cares, to the handler, while at the same time some other kind of profit has to be omitted or postponed. Science gives to all of us telegraphy, electric lighting, and diagnosis, and succeeds in preventing and curing a certain amount of disease. Religion in the shape of mind-cure gives to some of us serenity, moral poise, and happiness, and prevents certain forms of disease as well as science does, or even better in a certain class of persons. Evidently, then, the science and the religion are both of them genuine keys for unlocking the world's treasure-house to him who can use either of them practically. Just as evidently neither is exhaustive or exclusive of the other's simultaneous use. And why, after all, may not the world be so complex as to consist of many interpenetrating spheres of reality, which we can thus approach in alternation by using different [pg 123] conceptions and assuming different attitudes, just as mathematicians handle the same numerical and spatial facts by geometry, by analytical geometry, by algebra, by the calculus, or by quaternions, and each time come out right? On this view religion and science, each verified in its own way from hour to hour and from life to life, would be co-eternal. Primitive thought, with its belief in individualized personal forces, seems at any rate as far as ever from being driven by science from the field to-day. Numbers of educated people still find it the directest experimental channel by which to carry on their intercourse with reality.[65]

The case of mind-cure lay so ready to my hand that I could not resist the temptation of using it to bring these last truths home to your attention, but I must content myself to-day with this very brief indication. In a later lecture the relations of religion both to science and to primitive thought will have to receive much more explicit attention.

Appendix

(See note to p. 121.)

CASE I. "My own experience is this: I had long been ill, and one of the first results of my illness, a dozen years before, had been a diplopia which deprived me of the use of my eyes for reading and writing almost entirely, while a later one had been to shut me out from exercise of any kind under penalty of [pg 124]immediate and great exhaustion. I had been under the care of doctors of the highest standing both in Europe and America, men in whose power to help me I had had great faith, with no or ill result. Then, at a time when I seemed to be rather rapidly losing ground, I heard some things that gave me interest enough in mental healing to make me try it; I had no great hope of getting any good from it—it was a *chance* I tried, partly because my thought was interested by the new possibility it seemed to open, partly because it was the only chance I then could see. I went to X. in Boston, from whom some friends of mine had got, or thought that they had got, great help; the treatment was a silent one; little was said, and that little carried no conviction to my mind; whatever influence was exerted was that of another person's thought or feeling silently projected on to my unconscious mind, into my nervous system as it were, as we sat still together. I believed from the start in the *possibility* of such action, for I knew the power of the mind to shape, helping or hindering, the body's nerve-activities, and I thought telepathy probable, although unproved, but I had no belief in it as more than a possibility, and no strong conviction nor any mystic or religious faith connected with my thought of it that might have brought imagination strongly into play.

"I sat quietly with the healer for half an hour each day, at first with no result; then, after ten days or so, I became quite suddenly and swiftly conscious of a tide of new energy rising within me, a sense of power to pass beyond old halting-places, of power to break the bounds that, though often tried before, had long been veritable walls about my life, too high to climb. I began to read and walk as I had not done for years, and the change was sudden, marked, and unmistakable. This tide seemed to mount for some weeks, three or four perhaps, when, summer having come, I came away, taking the treatment up again a few months later. The lift I got proved permanent, and left me slowly gaining ground instead of losing it, but with this lift the influence seemed in a way to have spent itself, and, though my confidence in the reality of the power had gained immensely from this first experience, and should have helped me to make further gain in health and strength if my belief in [pg 125]it had been the potent factor there, I never after this got any result at all as striking or as clearly marked as this which came when I made trial of it first, with little faith and doubtful expectation. It is difficult to put all the evidence in such a matter into words, to gather up into a distinct statement all that one bases one's conclusions on, but I have always felt that I had abundant evidence to justify (to myself, at least) the conclusion that I came to then, and since have held to, that the physical change which came at that time was, first, the result of a change wrought within me by a change of mental state; and, secondly, that that change of mental state was not, save in a very secondary way, brought about through the influence of an excited imagination, or a *consciously* received suggestion of an hypnotic sort. Lastly, I believe that this change was the result of my receiving telepathically, and upon a mental stratum quite below the level of immediate consciousness, a healthier and more energetic attitude, receiving it from another person whose thought was directed upon me with the intention of impressing the idea of this attitude upon me. In my case the disease was distinctly what would be classed as nervous, not organic; but from such opportunities as I have had of observing, I have come to the conclusion that the dividing line that has been drawn is an arbitrary one, the nerves controlling the internal activities and the nutrition of the body throughout; and I believe that the central nervous system, by starting and inhibiting local centres, can exercise a vast influence upon disease of any kind, if it can be brought to bear. In my judgment the question is simply how to bring it to bear, and I think that the uncertainty and remarkable differences in the results obtained through mental healing do but show how ignorant we are as yet of the forces at work and of the means we should take to make them effective. That these results are not due to chance coincidences my observation of myself and others makes me sure; that the conscious mind, the imagination, enters into them as a factor in many cases is doubtless true, but in many others, and sometimes very extraordinary ones, it hardly seems to enter in at all. On the whole I am inclined to think that as the healing action, like the morbid one, springs from the plane [pg 126]of the normally *un*conscious mind, so the strongest and most effective impressions are those which *it* receives, in some as yet unknown, subtle way, *directly* from a healthier mind whose state, through a hidden law of sympathy, it reproduces."

Case II. "At the urgent request of friends, and with no faith and hardly any hope (possibly owing to a previous unsuccessful experience with a Christian Scientist), our little daughter was placed under the care of a healer, and cured of a trouble about which the physician had been very discouraging in his diagnosis. This interested me, and I began studying earnestly the method and philosophy of this method of healing. Gradually an inner peace and tranquillity came to me in so positive a way that my manner changed greatly. My children and friends noticed the change and commented upon it. All feelings of irritability disappeared. Even the expression of my face changed noticeably.

"I had been bigoted, aggressive, and intolerant in discussion, both in public and private. I grew broadly tolerant and receptive toward the views of others. I had been nervous and irritable, coming home two or three times a week with a sick headache induced, as I then supposed, by dyspepsia and catarrh. I grew serene and gentle, and the physical troubles entirely disappeared. I had been in the habit of approaching every business interview with an almost morbid dread. I now meet every one with confidence and inner calm.

"I may say that the growth has all been toward the elimination of selfishness. I do not mean simply the grosser, more sensual forms, but those subtler and generally unrecognized kinds, such as express themselves in sorrow, grief, regret, envy, etc. It has been in the direction of a practical, working realization of the immanence of God and the Divinity of man's true, inner self."

[pg 127]

Lectures VI And VII. The Sick Soul.

At our last meeting, we considered the healthy-minded temperament, the temperament which has a constitutional incapacity for prolonged suffering, and in which the tendency to see things optimistically is like a water of crystallization in which the individual's character is set. We saw how this temperament may become the basis for a peculiar type of religion, a religion in which good, even the good of this world's life, is regarded as the essential thing for a rational being to attend to. This religion directs him to settle his scores with the more evil aspects of the universe by systematically declining to lay them to heart or make much of them, by ignoring them in his reflective calculations, or even, on occasion, by denying outright that they exist. Evil is a disease; and worry over disease is itself an additional form of disease, which only adds to the original complaint. Even repentance and remorse, affections which come in the character of ministers of good, may be but sickly and relaxing impulses. The best repentance is to up and act for righteousness, and forget that you ever had relations with sin.

Spinoza's philosophy has this sort of healthy-mindedness woven into the heart of it, and this has been one secret of its fascination. He whom Reason leads, according to Spinoza, is led altogether by the influence over his mind of good. Knowledge of evil is an "inadequate" knowledge, fit only for slavish minds. So Spinoza [pg 128] categorically condemns repentance. When men make mistakes, he says,—

> "One might perhaps expect gnawings of conscience and repentance to help to bring them on the right path, and might thereupon conclude (as every one does conclude) that these affections are good things. Yet when we look at the matter closely, we shall find that not only are they not good, but on the contrary deleterious and evil passions. For it is manifest that we can always get along better by reason and love of truth than by worry of conscience and remorse. Harmful are these and evil, inasmuch as they form a particular kind of sadness; and the disadvantages of sadness," he continues, "I have already proved, and shown that we should strive to keep it from our life. Just so we should endeavor, since uneasiness of conscience and remorse are of this kind of complexion, to flee and shun these states of mind."[66]

Within the Christian body, for which repentance of sins has from the beginning been the critical religious act, healthy-mindedness has always come forward with its milder interpretation. Repentance according to such healthy-minded Christians means *getting away from* the sin, not groaning and writhing over its commission. The Catholic practice of confession and absolution is in one of its aspects little more than a systematic method of keeping healthy-mindedness on top. By it a man's accounts with evil are periodically squared and audited, so that he may start the clean page with no old debts inscribed. Any Catholic will tell us how clean and fresh and free he feels after the purging operation. Martin Luther by no means belonged to the healthy-minded type in the radical sense in which we have discussed it, and he repudiated priestly absolution for sin. Yet in this matter of repentance he had some very healthy-minded [pg 129] ideas, due in the main to the largeness of his conception of God.

> "When I was a monk," he says, "I thought that I was utterly cast away, if at any time I felt the lust of the flesh: that is to say, if I felt any evil motion, fleshly lust, wrath, hatred, or envy against any brother. I assayed many ways to help to quiet my conscience, but it would not be; for the concupiscence and lust of my flesh did always return, so that I could not rest, but was continually vexed with these thoughts: This or that sin thou hast committed: thou art infected with envy, with impatiency, and such other sins: therefore thou art entered into this holy order in vain, and all thy good works are

unprofitable. But if then I had rightly understood these sentences of Paul: 'The flesh lusteth contrary to the Spirit, and the Spirit contrary to the flesh; and these two are one against another, so that ye cannot do the things that ye would do,' I should not have so miserably tormented myself, but should have thought and said to myself, as now commonly I do, 'Martin, thou shalt not utterly be without sin, for thou hast flesh; thou shalt therefore feel the battle thereof.' I remember that Staupitz was wont to say, 'I have vowed unto God above a thousand times that I would become a better man: but I never performed that which I vowed. Hereafter I will make no such vow: for I have now learned by experience that I am not able to perform it. Unless, therefore, God be favorable and merciful unto me for Christ's sake, I shall not be able, with all my vows and all my good deeds, to stand before him.' This (of Staupitz's) was not only a true, but also a godly and a holy desperation; and this must they all confess, both with mouth and heart, who will be saved. For the godly trust not to their own righteousness. They look unto Christ their reconciler, who gave his life for their sins. Moreover, they know that the remnant of sin which is in their flesh is not laid to their charge, but freely pardoned. Notwithstanding, in the mean while they fight in spirit against the flesh, lest they should *fulfill* the lusts thereof; and although they feel the flesh to rage and rebel, and themselves also do fall sometimes into sin through infirmity, yet are they not discouraged, nor think therefore [pg 130]that their state and kind of life, and the works which are done according to their calling, displease God; but they raise up themselves by faith."[67]

One of the heresies for which the Jesuits got that spiritual genius, Molinos, the founder of Quietism, so abominably condemned was his healthy-minded opinion of repentance:—

"When thou fallest into a fault, in what matter soever it be, do not trouble nor afflict thyself for it. For they are effects of our frail Nature, stained by Original Sin. The common enemy will make thee believe, as soon as thou fallest into any fault, that thou walkest in error, and therefore art out of God and his favor, and herewith would he make thee distrust of the divine Grace, telling thee of thy misery, and making a giant of it; and putting it into thy head that every day thy soul grows worse instead of better, whilst it so often repeats these failings. O blessed Soul, open thine eyes; and shut the gate against these diabolical suggestions, knowing thy misery, and trusting in the mercy divine. Would not he be a mere fool who, running at tournament with others, and falling in the best of the career, should lie weeping on the ground and afflicting himself with discourses upon his fall? Man (they would tell him), lose no time, get up and take the course again, for he that rises again quickly and continues his race is as if he had never fallen. If thou seest thyself fallen once and a thousand times, thou oughtest to make use of the remedy which I have given thee, that is, a loving confidence in the divine mercy. These are the weapons with which thou must fight and conquer cowardice and vain thoughts. This is the means thou oughtest to use—not to lose time, not to disturb thyself, and reap no good."[68]

Now in contrast with such healthy-minded views as these, if we treat them as a way of deliberately minimizing evil, stands a radically opposite view, a way of maximizing [pg 131] evil, if you please so to call it, based on the persuasion that the evil aspects of our life are of its very essence, and that the world's meaning most comes home to us when we lay them most to heart. We have now to address ourselves to this more morbid way of looking at the situation. But as I closed our last hour with a general philosophical reflection on the healthy-minded way of taking life, I should like at this point to make another philosophical reflection upon it before turning to that heavier task. You will excuse the brief delay.

If we admit that evil is an essential part of our being and the key to the interpretation of our life, we load ourselves down with a difficulty that has always proved burdensome in philosophies of religion. Theism, whenever it has erected itself into a systematic philosophy of the universe, has shown a reluctance to let God be anything less than All-in-All. In other words, philosophic theism has always shown a tendency to become pantheistic and monistic, and to consider the world as one unit of absolute fact; and this has been at variance with popular or practical theism, which latter has ever been more or less frankly pluralistic, not to say polytheistic, and shown itself perfectly well satisfied with a universe composed of many original principles, provided we be only allowed to believe that the divine principle remains supreme, and that the others are subordinate. In this latter case God is not necessarily responsible for the existence of evil; he would only be responsible if it were not finally overcome. But on the monistic or pantheistic view, evil, like everything else, must have its foundation in God; and the difficulty is to see how this can possibly be the case if God be absolutely good. This difficulty faces us in every form of philosophy in which the world appears as one flawless unit of fact. Such a unit is an *Individual,* [pg 132] and in it the worst parts must be as essential as the best, must be as necessary to make the individual what he is; since if any part whatever in an individual were to vanish or alter, it would no longer be *that* individual at all. The philosophy of absolute idealism, so vigorously represented both in Scotland and America to-day, has to struggle with this difficulty quite as much as scholastic theism struggled in its time; and although it would be premature to say that there is no speculative issue whatever from the puzzle, it is perfectly fair to say that there is no clear or easy issue, and that the only *obvious* escape from paradox here is to cut loose from the monistic assumption altogether, and to allow the world to have existed from its origin in pluralistic form, as an aggregate or collection of higher and lower things and principles, rather than an absolutely unitary fact. For then evil would not need to be essential; it might be, and may always have been, an independent portion that had no rational or absolute right to live with the rest, and which we might conceivably hope to see got rid of at last.

Now the gospel of healthy-mindedness, as we have described it, casts its vote distinctly for this pluralistic view. Whereas the monistic philosopher finds himself more or less bound to say, as Hegel said, that everything actual is rational, and that evil, as an element dialectically required, must be pinned in and kept and consecrated and have a function awarded to it in the final system of truth, healthy-mindedness refuses to say anything of the sort.[69] Evil, it says, is emphatically irrational, [pg 133] and *not* to be pinned in, or preserved, or consecrated in any final system of truth. It is a pure abomination to the Lord, an alien unreality, a waste element, to be sloughed off and negated, and the very memory of it, if possible, wiped out and forgotten. The ideal, so far from being co-extensive with the whole actual, is a mere *extract* from the actual, marked by its deliverance from all contact with this diseased, inferior, and excrementitious stuff.

Here we have the interesting notion fairly and squarely presented to us, of there being elements of the universe which may make no rational whole in conjunction with the other elements, and which, from the point of view of any system which those other elements make up, can only be considered so much irrelevance and accident—so much "dirt," as it were, and matter out of place. I ask you now not to forget this notion; for although most philosophers seem either to forget it or to disdain it too much ever to mention it, I believe that we shall have to admit it ourselves in the end as containing an element of truth. The mind-cure gospel thus once more appears to us as having dignity and importance. We have seen it to be a genuine religion, and no mere silly appeal to imagination to cure disease;

we have seen its method of experimental verification to be not unlike the method of all science; and now here we find mind-cure as the champion of a perfectly definite conception of the metaphysical structure of the world. I hope that, in view of all this, you will not regret my having pressed it upon your attention at such length.

Let us now say good-by for a while to all this way of thinking, and turn towards those persons who cannot so swiftly throw off the burden of the consciousness of evil, [pg 134] but are congenitally fated to suffer from its presence. Just as we saw that in healthy-mindedness there are shallower and profounder levels, happiness like that of the mere animal, and more regenerate sorts of happiness, so also are there different levels of the morbid mind, and the one is much more formidable than the other. There are people for whom evil means only a mal-adjustment with *things*, a wrong correspondence of one's life with the environment. Such evil as this is curable, in principle at least, upon the natural plane, for merely by modifying either the self or the things, or both at once, the two terms may be made to fit, and all go merry as a marriage bell again. But there are others for whom evil is no mere relation of the subject to particular outer things, but something more radical and general, a wrongness or vice in his essential nature, which no alteration of the environment, or any superficial rearrangement of the inner self, can cure, and which requires a supernatural remedy. On the whole, the Latin races have leaned more towards the former way of looking upon evil, as made up of ills and sins in the plural, removable in detail; while the Germanic races have tended rather to think of Sin in the singular, and with a capital S, as of something ineradicably ingrained in our natural subjectivity, and never to be removed by any superficial piecemeal operations.[70] These comparisons of races are always open to exception, but undoubtedly the northern tone in religion has inclined to the more intimately pessimistic persuasion, and this way of feeling, being the more extreme, we shall find by far the more instructive for our study.

Recent psychology has found great use for the word "threshold" as a symbolic designation for the point at which one state of mind passes into another. Thus we [pg 135] speak of the threshold of a man's consciousness in general, to indicate the amount of noise, pressure, or other outer stimulus which it takes to arouse his attention at all. One with a high threshold will doze through an amount of racket by which one with a low threshold would be immediately waked. Similarly, when one is sensitive to small differences in any order of sensation, we say he has a low "difference-threshold"—his mind easily steps over it into the consciousness of the differences in question. And just so we might speak of a "pain-threshold," a "fear-threshold," a "misery-threshold," and find it quickly overpassed by the consciousness of some individuals, but lying too high in others to be often reached by their consciousness. The sanguine and healthy-minded live habitually on the sunny side of their misery-line, the depressed and melancholy live beyond it, in darkness and apprehension. There are men who seem to have started in life with a bottle or two of champagne inscribed to their credit; whilst others seem to have been born close to the pain-threshold, which the slightest irritants fatally send them over.

Does it not appear as if one who lived more habitually on one side of the pain-threshold might need a different sort of religion from one who habitually lived on the other? This question, of the relativity of different types of religion to different types of need, arises naturally at this point, and will become a serious problem ere we have done. But before we confront it in general terms, we must address ourselves to the unpleasant task of hearing what the sick souls, as we may call them in contrast to the healthy-minded, have to say of the secrets of their prison-house, their own peculiar form of consciousness. Let us then resolutely turn our backs on the once-born and their sky-blue optimistic gospel; let us not simply cry [pg 136] out, in spite of all appearances, "Hurrah for the Universe!—God's in his Heaven, all's right with the world." Let us see rather whether pity, pain, and fear, and the sentiment of human helplessness may not open a profounder view and put into our hands a more complicated key to the meaning of the situation.

To begin with, how *can* things so insecure as the successful experiences of this world afford a stable anchorage? A chain is no stronger than its weakest link, and life is after all a chain. In the healthiest and most prosperous existence, how many links of illness, danger, and disaster are always interposed? Unsuspectedly from the bottom of every fountain of pleasure, as the old poet said, something bitter rises up: a touch of nausea, a falling dead of the delight, a whiff of melancholy, things that sound a knell, for fugitive as they may be, they bring a feeling of coming from a deeper region and often have an appalling convincingness. The buzz of life ceases at their touch as a piano-string stops sounding when the damper falls upon it.

Of course the music can commence again;—and again and again,—at intervals. But with this the healthy-minded consciousness is left with an irremediable sense of precariousness. It is a bell with a crack; it draws its breath on sufferance and by an accident.

Even if we suppose a man so packed with healthy-mindedness as never to have experienced in his own person any of these sobering intervals, still, if he is a reflecting being, he must generalize and class his own lot with that of others; and, doing so, he must see that his escape is just a lucky chance and no essential difference. He might just as well have been born to an entirely different fortune. And then indeed the hollow security! What [pg 137] kind of a frame of things is it of which the best you can say is, "Thank God, it has let me off clear this time!" Is not its blessedness a fragile fiction? Is not your joy in it a very vulgar glee, not much unlike the snicker of any rogue at his success? If indeed it were all success, even on such terms as that! But take the happiest man, the one most envied by the world, and in nine cases out of ten his inmost consciousness is one of failure. Either his ideals in the line of his achievements are pitched far higher than the achievements themselves, or else he has secret ideals of which the world knows nothing, and in regard to which he inwardly knows himself to be found wanting.

When such a conquering optimist as Goethe can express himself in this wise, how must it be with less successful men?

> "I will say nothing," writes Goethe in 1824, "against the course of my existence. But at bottom it has been nothing but pain and burden, and I can

> affirm that during the whole of my 75 years, I have not had four weeks of genuine well-being. It is but the perpetual rolling of a rock that must be raised up again forever."

What single-handed man was ever on the whole as successful as Luther? yet when he had grown old, he looked back on his life as if it were an absolute failure.

> "I am utterly weary of life. I pray the Lord will come forthwith and carry me hence. Let him come, above all, with his last Judgment: I will stretch out my neck, the thunder will burst forth, and I shall be at rest."—And having a necklace of white agates in his hand at the time he added: "O God, grant that it may come without delay. I would readily eat up this necklace to-day, for the Judgment to come to-morrow."—The Electress Dowager, one day when Luther was dining with her, said to him: "Doctor, I wish you may live forty years to [pg 138]come." "Madam," replied he, "rather than live forty years more, I would give up my chance of Paradise."

Failure, then, failure! so the world stamps us at every turn. We strew it with our blunders, our misdeeds, our lost opportunities, with all the memorials of our inadequacy to our vocation. And with what a damning emphasis does it then blot us out! No easy fine, no mere apology or formal expiation, will satisfy the world's demands, but every pound of flesh exacted is soaked with all its blood. The subtlest forms of suffering known to man are connected with the poisonous humiliations incidental to these results.

And they are pivotal human experiences. A process so ubiquitous and everlasting is evidently an integral part of life. "There is indeed one element in human destiny," Robert Louis Stevenson writes, "that not blindness itself can controvert. Whatever else we are intended to do, we are not intended to succeed; failure is the fate allotted."[71] And our nature being thus rooted in failure, is it any wonder that theologians should have held it to be essential, and thought that only through the personal experience of humiliation which it engenders the deeper sense of life's significance is reached?[72]

[pg 139]
But this is only the first stage of the world-sickness. Make the human being's sensitiveness a little greater, carry him a little farther over the

misery-threshold, and the good quality of the successful moments themselves when they occur is spoiled and vitiated. All natural goods perish. Riches take wings; fame is a breath; love is a cheat; youth and health and pleasure vanish. Can things whose end is always dust and disappointment be the real goods which our souls require? Back of everything is the great spectre of universal death, the all-encompassing blackness:—

> "What profit hath a man of all his labour which he taketh under the Sun? I looked on all the works that my hands had wrought, and behold, all was vanity and vexation of spirit. For that which befalleth the sons of men befalleth beasts; as the one dieth, so dieth the other; all are of the dust, and all turn to dust again.... The dead know not anything, neither have they any more a reward; for the memory of them is forgotten. Also their love and their hatred and their envy is now perished; neither have they any more a portion for ever in anything that is done under the Sun.... Truly the light is sweet, and a pleasant thing it is for the eyes to behold the Sun: but if a man live many years and rejoice in them all, yet let him remember the days of darkness; for they shall be many."

In short, life and its negation are beaten up inextricably together. But if the life be good, the negation of it must be bad. Yet the two are equally essential facts of existence; and all natural happiness thus seems infected with a contradiction. The breath of the sepulchre surrounds it.

To a mind attentive to this state of things and rightly subject to the joy-destroying chill which such a contemplation engenders, the only relief that healthy-mindedness can give is by saying: "Stuff and nonsense, get out into the open air!" or "Cheer up, old fellow, you'll [pg 140] be all right erelong, if you will only drop your morbidness!" But in all seriousness, can such bald animal talk as that be treated as a rational answer? To ascribe religious value to mere happy-go-lucky contentment with one's brief chance at natural good is but the very consecration of forgetfulness and superficiality. Our troubles lie indeed too deep for *that* cure. The fact that we *can* die, that we *can* be ill at all, is what perplexes us; the fact that we now for a moment live and are well is irrelevant to that perplexity. We need a life not correlated with death, a health not liable to illness, a kind of good that will not perish, a good in fact that flies beyond the Goods of nature.

It all depends on how sensitive the soul may become to discords. "The trouble with me is that I believe too much in common happiness and goodness," said a friend of mine whose consciousness was of this sort, "and nothing can console me for their transiency. I am appalled and disconcerted at its being possible." And so with most of us: a little cooling down of animal excitability and instinct, a little loss of animal toughness, a little irritable weakness and descent of the pain-threshold, will bring the worm at the core of all our usual springs of delight into full view, and turn us into melancholy metaphysicians. The pride of life and glory of the world will shrivel. It is after all but the standing quarrel of hot youth and hoary eld. Old age has the last word: the purely naturalistic look at life, however enthusiastically it may begin, is sure to end in sadness.

This sadness lies at the heart of every merely positivistic, agnostic, or naturalistic scheme of philosophy. Let sanguine healthy-mindedness do its best with its strange power of living in the moment and ignoring and forgetting, still the evil background is really there to be [pg 141] thought of, and the skull will grin in at the banquet. In the practical life of the individual, we know how his whole gloom or glee about any present fact depends on the remoter schemes and hopes with which it stands related. Its significance and framing give it the chief part of its value. Let it be known to lead nowhere, and however agreeable it may be in its immediacy, its glow and gilding vanish. The old man, sick with an insidious internal disease, may laugh and quaff his wine at first as well as ever, but he knows his fate now, for the doctors have revealed it; and the knowledge knocks the satisfaction out of all these functions. They are partners of death and the worm is their brother, and they turn to a mere flatness.

The lustre of the present hour is always borrowed from the background of possibilities it goes with. Let our common experiences be enveloped in an eternal moral order; let our suffering have an immortal significance; let Heaven smile upon the earth, and deities pay their visits; let faith and hope be the atmosphere which man breathes in;—and his days pass by with zest; they stir with prospects, they thrill with remoter values. Place round them on the contrary the curdling cold and gloom and absence of all permanent meaning which for pure naturalism and the popular science evolutionism of our time are all that is visible ultimately, and the thrill stops short, or turns rather to an anxious trembling.

For naturalism, fed on recent cosmological speculations, mankind is in a position similar to that of a set of people living on a frozen lake, surrounded by cliffs over which there is no escape, yet knowing that little by little the ice is melting, and the inevitable day drawing near when the last film of it will disappear, and to be drowned ignominiously will be the human creature's portion. The [pg 142] merrier the skating, the warmer and more sparkling the sun by day, and the ruddier the bonfires at night, the more poignant the sadness with which one must take in the meaning of the total situation.

The early Greeks are continually held up to us in literary works as models of the healthy-minded joyousness which the religion of nature may engender. There was indeed much joyousness among the Greeks—Homer's flow of enthusiasm for most things that the sun shines upon is steady. But even in Homer the reflective passages are cheerless,[73] and the moment the Greeks grew systematically pensive and thought of ultimates, they became unmitigated pessimists.[74] The jealousy of the gods, the nemesis that follows too much happiness, the all-encompassing death, fate's dark opacity, the ultimate and unintelligible cruelty, were the fixed background of [pg 143] their imagination. The beautiful joyousness of their polytheism is only a poetic modern fiction. They knew no joys comparable in quality of preciousness to those which we shall erelong see that Brahmans, Buddhists, Christians, Mohammedans, twice-born people whose religion is non-naturalistic, get from their several creeds of mysticism and renunciation.

Stoic insensibility and Epicurean resignation were the farthest advance which the Greek mind made in that direction. The Epicurean said: "Seek not to be happy, but rather to escape unhappiness; strong happiness is always linked with pain; therefore hug the safe shore, and do not tempt the deeper raptures. Avoid disappointment by expecting little, and by aiming low; and above all do not fret." The Stoic said: "The only genuine good that life can yield a man is the free possession of his own soul; all other goods are lies." Each of these philosophies is in its degree a philosophy of despair in nature's boons. Trustful self-abandonment to the joys that freely offer has entirely departed from both Epicurean and Stoic; and what each proposes is a way of rescue from the resultant dust-and-ashes state of mind. The Epicurean still awaits results from economy of indulgence and damping of desire. The Stoic hopes for no results, and gives up natural good altogether. There is dignity in both these forms of resignation. They represent distinct stages in the sobering process which man's primitive intoxication with sense-happiness is sure to undergo. In the one the hot blood has grown cool, in the other it has become quite cold; and although I have spoken of them in the past tense, as if they were merely historic, yet Stoicism and Epicureanism will probably be to all time typical attitudes, marking a certain definite stage accomplished in the evolution of the world-sick [pg 144] soul.[75] They mark the conclusion of what we call the once-born period, and represent the highest flights of what twice-born religion would call the purely natural man—Epicureanism, which can only by great courtesy be called a religion, showing his refinement, and Stoicism exhibiting his moral will. They leave the world in the shape of an unreconciled contradiction, and seek no higher unity. Compared with the complex ecstasies which the supernaturally regenerated Christian may enjoy, or the oriental pantheist indulge in, their receipts for equanimity are expedients which seem almost crude in their simplicity.

Please observe, however, that I am not yet pretending finally to *judge* any of these attitudes. I am only describing their variety.

The securest way to the rapturous sorts of happiness of which the twice-born make report has as an historic matter of fact been through a more radical pessimism than anything that we have yet considered. We have seen how the lustre and enchantment may be rubbed off from the goods of nature. But there is a pitch of unhappiness so great that the goods of nature may be entirely forgotten, and all sentiment of their existence vanish from the mental field. For this extremity of pessimism to be reached, something more is needed than observation of [pg 145] life and reflection upon death. The individual must in his own person become the prey of a pathological melancholy. As the healthy-minded enthusiast succeeds in ignoring evil's very existence, so the subject of melancholy is forced in spite of himself to ignore that of all good whatever: for him it may no longer have the least reality. Such sensitiveness and susceptibility to mental pain is a rare occurrence where the nervous constitution is entirely normal; one seldom finds it in a healthy subject even where he is the victim of the most atrocious cruelties of outward fortune. So we note here the neurotic constitution, of which I said so much in my first lecture, making its active entrance on our scene, and destined to play a part in much that follows. Since these experiences of melancholy are in the first instance absolutely private and individual, I can now help myself out with personal documents. Painful indeed they will be to listen to, and there is almost an indecency in handling them in public. Yet they lie right in the middle of our path; and if we are to touch the psychology of religion at all seriously, we must be willing to forget conventionalities, and dive below the smooth and lying official conversational surface.

One can distinguish many kinds of pathological depression. Sometimes it is mere passive joylessness and dreariness, discouragement, dejection, lack of taste and zest and spring. Professor Ribot has proposed the name *anhedonia* to designate this condition.

> "The state of *anhedonia*, if I may coin a new word to pair off with *analgesia*," he writes, "has been very little studied, but it exists. A young girl was smitten with a liver disease which for some time altered her constitution. She felt no longer any affection for her father and mother. She would have played with her doll, but it was impossible to find the least pleasure in [pg 146]the act. The same things which formerly convulsed her with laughter entirely failed to interest her now. Esquirol observed the case of a very intelligent magistrate who was also a prey to hepatic disease. Every emotion appeared dead within him. He manifested neither perversion nor violence, but complete absence of emotional reaction. If he went to the theatre, which he did out of habit, he could find no pleasure there. The thought of his house, of his home, of his wife, and of his absent children moved him as little, he said, as a theorem of Euclid."[76]

Prolonged seasickness will in most persons produce a temporary condition of anhedonia. Every good, terrestrial or celestial, is imagined only to be turned from with disgust. A temporary condition of this sort, connected with the religious evolution of a singularly lofty character, both intellectual and moral, is well described by the Catholic philosopher, Father Gratry, in his autobiographical recollections. In consequence of mental isolation and excessive study at the Polytechnic school, young Gratry fell into a state of nervous exhaustion with symptoms which he thus describes:—

> "I had such a universal terror that I woke at night with a start, thinking that the Pantheon was tumbling on the Polytechnic school, or that the school was in flames, or that the Seine was pouring into the Catacombs, and that Paris was being swallowed up. And when these impressions were past, all day long without respite I suffered an incurable and intolerable desolation, verging on despair. I thought myself, in fact, rejected by God, lost, damned! I felt something like the suffering of hell. Before that I had never even thought of hell. My mind had never turned in that direction. Neither discourses nor reflections had impressed me in that way. I took no account of hell. Now, and all at once, I suffered in a measure what is suffered there.
>
> "But what was perhaps still more dreadful is that every idea of heaven was taken away from me: I could no longer conceive [pg 147]of anything of the sort. Heaven did not seem to me worth going to. It was like a vacuum; a mythological elysium, an abode of shadows less real than the earth. I could conceive no joy, no pleasure in inhabiting it. Happiness, joy, light, affection, love—all these words were now devoid of sense. Without doubt I could still have talked of all these things, but I had become incapable of feeling anything in them, of understanding anything about them, of hoping anything from them, or of believing them to exist. There was my great and inconsolable grief! I neither perceived nor conceived any longer the existence of happiness or perfection. An abstract heaven over a naked rock. Such was my present abode for eternity."[77]

So much for melancholy in the sense of incapacity for joyous feeling. A much worse form of it is positive and active anguish, a sort of psychical neuralgia wholly unknown to healthy life. Such anguish may partake of various characters, having sometimes more the quality of loathing; sometimes that of irritation and exasperation; or again of self-mistrust and self-despair; or of suspicion, anxiety, trepidation, fear. The patient may rebel or submit; [pg 148] may accuse himself, or accuse outside powers; and he may or he may not be tormented by the theoretical mystery of why he should so have to suffer. Most cases are mixed cases, and we should not treat our classifications with too much respect. Moreover, it is only a relatively small proportion of cases that connect themselves with the religious sphere of experience at all. Exasperated cases, for instance, as a rule do not. I quote now literally from the first case of melancholy on which I lay my hand. It is a letter from a patient in a French asylum.

"I suffer too much in this hospital, both physically and morally. Besides the burnings and the sleeplessness (for I no longer sleep since I am shut up here, and the little rest I get is broken by bad dreams, and I am waked with a jump by nightmares, dreadful visions, lightning, thunder, and the rest), fear, atrocious fear, presses me down, holds me without respite, never lets me go. Where is the justice in it all! What have I done to deserve this excess of severity? Under what form will this fear crush me? What would I not owe to any one who would rid me of my life! Eat, drink, lie awake all night, suffer without interruption—such is the fine legacy I have received from my mother! What I fail to understand is this abuse of power. There are limits to everything, there is a middle way. But God knows neither middle way nor limits. I say God, but why? All I have known so far has been the devil. After all, I am afraid of God as much as of the devil, so I drift along, thinking of nothing but suicide, but with neither courage nor means here to execute the act. As you read this, it will easily prove to you my insanity. The style and the ideas are incoherent enough—I can see that myself. But I cannot keep myself from being either crazy or an idiot; and, as things are, from whom should I ask pity? I am defenseless against the invisible enemy who is tightening his coils around me. I should be no better armed against him even if I saw him, or had seen him. Oh, if he would but kill me, devil take him! Death, [pg 149]death, once for all! But I stop. I have raved to you long enough. I say raved, for I can write no otherwise, having neither brain nor thoughts left. O God! what a misfortune to be born! Born like a mushroom, doubtless between an evening and a morning; and how true and right I was when in our philosophy-year in college I chewed the cud of bitterness with the pessimists. Yes, indeed, there is more pain in life than gladness—it is one long agony until the grave. Think how gay it makes me to remember that this horrible misery of mine, coupled with this unspeakable fear, may last fifty, one hundred, who knows how many more years!"[78]

This letter shows two things. First, you see how the entire consciousness of the poor man is so choked with the feeling of evil that the sense of there being any good in the world is lost for him altogether. His attention excludes it, cannot admit it: the sun has left his heaven. And secondly you see how the querulous temper of his misery keeps his mind from taking a religious direction. Querulousness of mind tends in fact rather towards irreligion; and it has played, so far as I know, no part whatever in the construction of religious systems.

Religious melancholy must be cast in a more melting mood. Tolstoy has left us, in his book called My Confession, a wonderful account of the attack of melancholy which led him to his own religious conclusions. The latter in some respects are peculiar; but the melancholy presents two characters which make it a typical document for our present purpose. First it is a well-marked case of anhedonia, of passive loss of appetite for all life's values; and second, it shows how the altered and estranged aspect which the world assumed in consequence of this stimulated Tolstoy's intellect to a gnawing, carking questioning and effort for philosophic relief. I mean [pg 150] to quote Tolstoy at some length; but before doing so, I will make a general remark on each of these two points.

First on our spiritual judgments and the sense of value in general.

It is notorious that facts are compatible with opposite emotional comments, since the same fact will inspire entirely different feelings in different persons, and at different times in the same person; and there is no rationally deducible connection between any outer fact and the sentiments it may happen to provoke. These have their source in another sphere of existence altogether, in the animal and spiritual region of the subject's being. Conceive yourself, if possible, suddenly stripped of all the emotion with which your world now inspires you, and try to imagine it *as it exists*, purely by itself, without your favorable or unfavorable, hopeful or apprehensive comment. It will be almost impossible for you to realize such a condition of negativity and deadness. No one portion of the universe would then have importance beyond another; and the whole collection of its things and series of its events would be without significance, character, expression, or perspective. Whatever of value, interest, or meaning our respective worlds may appear endued with are thus pure gifts of the spectator's mind. The passion of love is the most familiar and extreme example of this fact. If it comes, it comes; if it does not come, no process of reasoning can force it. Yet it transforms the value of the creature loved as utterly as the sunrise transforms Mont Blanc from a corpse-like gray to a rosy enchantment; and it sets the whole world to a new tune for the lover and gives a new issue to his life. So with fear, with indignation, jealousy, ambition, worship. If they are there, life changes. And whether they shall be there or not depends almost always upon [pg 151] non-logical, often on organic conditions. And as the excited interest which these passions put into the world is our gift to the world, just so are the passions themselves *gifts*,—gifts to us, from sources sometimes low and sometimes high; but almost always non-logical and beyond our control. How can the moribund old man reason back to himself the romance, the mystery, the imminence of great things with which our old earth tingled for him in the days when he was young and well? Gifts, either of the flesh or of the spirit; and the spirit bloweth where it listeth; and the world's materials lend their surface passively to all the gifts alike, as the stage-setting receives indifferently whatever alternating colored lights may be shed upon it from the optical apparatus in the gallery.

Meanwhile the practically real world for each one of us, the effective world of the individual, is the compound world, the physical facts and emotional values in indistinguishable combination. Withdraw or pervert either factor of this complex resultant, and the kind of experience we call pathological ensues.

In Tolstoy's case the sense that life had any meaning whatever was for a time wholly withdrawn. The result was a transformation in the whole expression of reality. When we come to study the phenomenon of conversion or religious regeneration, we shall see that a not infrequent consequence of the change operated in the subject is a transfiguration of the face of nature in his eyes. A new heaven seems to shine upon a new earth. In melancholiacs there is usually a similar change, only it is in the reverse direction. The world now looks remote, strange, sinister, uncanny. Its color is gone, its breath is cold, there is no speculation in the eyes it glares with. "It is as if I lived in another century," says one asylum patient.—"I [pg 152] see everything through a cloud," says another, "things are not as they were, and I am changed."—"I see," says a third, "I touch, but the things do not come near me, a thick veil alters the hue and look of everything."—"Persons move like shadows, and sounds seem to come from a distant world."—"There is no longer any past for me; people appear so strange; it is as if I could not see any reality, as if I were in a theatre; as if people were actors, and everything were scenery; I can no longer find myself; I walk, but why? Everything floats before my eyes, but leaves no impression."—"I weep false tears, I have unreal hands: the things I see are not real things."—Such are expressions that naturally rise to the lips of melancholy subjects describing their changed state.[79]

Now there are some subjects whom all this leaves a prey to the profoundest astonishment. The strangeness is wrong. The unreality cannot be. A mystery is concealed, and a metaphysical solution must exist. If the natural world is so double-faced and unhomelike, what world, what thing is real? An urgent wondering and questioning is set up, a poring theoretic activity, and in the desperate effort to get into right relations with the matter, the sufferer is often led to what becomes for him a satisfying religious solution.

At about the age of fifty, Tolstoy relates that he began to have moments of perplexity, of what he calls arrest, as if he knew not "how to live," or what to do. It is obvious that these were moments in which the excitement and interest which our functions naturally bring had ceased. Life had been enchanting, it was now flat sober, more than sober, dead. Things were meaningless whose [pg 153] meaning had always been self-evident. The questions "Why?" and "What next?" began to beset him more and more frequently. At first it seemed as if such questions must be answerable, and as if he could easily find the answers if he would take the time; but as they ever became more urgent, he perceived that it was like those first discomforts of a sick man, to which he pays but little attention till they run into one continuous suffering, and then he realizes that what he took for a passing disorder means the most momentous thing in the world for him, means his death.

These questions "Why?" "Wherefore?" "What for?" found no response.

> "I felt," says Tolstoy, "that something had broken within me on which my life had always rested, that I had nothing left to hold on to, and that morally my life had stopped. An invincible force impelled me to get rid of my existence, in one way or another. It cannot be said exactly that I *wished* to kill myself, for the force which drew me away from life was fuller, more powerful, more general than any mere desire. It was a force like my old aspiration to live, only it impelled me in the opposite direction. It was an aspiration of my whole being to get out of life.
>
> "Behold me then, a man happy and in good health, hiding the rope in order not to hang myself to the rafters of the room where every night I went to sleep alone; behold me no longer going shooting, lest I should yield to the too easy temptation of putting an end to myself with my gun.

"I did not know what I wanted. I was afraid of life; I was driven to leave it; and in spite of that I still hoped something from it.

"All this took place at a time when so far as all my outer circumstances went, I ought to have been completely happy. I had a good wife who loved me and whom I loved; good children and a large property which was increasing with no pains taken on my part. I was more respected by my kinsfolk and [pg 154]acquaintance than I had ever been; I was loaded with praise by strangers; and without exaggeration I could believe my name already famous. Moreover I was neither insane nor ill. On the contrary, I possessed a physical and mental strength which I have rarely met in persons of my age. I could mow as well as the peasants, I could work with my brain eight hours uninterruptedly and feel no bad effects.

"And yet I could give no reasonable meaning to any actions of my life. And I was surprised that I had not understood this from the very beginning. My state of mind was as if some wicked and stupid jest was being played upon me by some one. One can live only so long as one is intoxicated, drunk with life; but when one grows sober one cannot fail to see that it is all a stupid cheat. What is truest about it is that there is nothing even funny or silly in it; it is cruel and stupid, purely and simply.

"The oriental fable of the traveler surprised in the desert by a wild beast is very old.

"Seeking to save himself from the fierce animal, the traveler jumps into a well with no water in it; but at the bottom of this well he sees a dragon waiting with open mouth to devour him. And the unhappy man, not daring to go out lest he should be the prey of the beast, not daring to jump to the bottom lest he should be devoured by the dragon, clings to the branches of a wild bush which grows out of one of the cracks of the well. His hands weaken, and he feels that he must soon give way to certain fate; but still he clings, and sees two mice, one white, the other black, evenly moving round the bush to which he hangs, and gnawing off its roots.

"The traveler sees this and knows that he must inevitably perish; but while thus hanging he looks about him and finds on the leaves of the bush some drops of honey. These he reaches with his tongue and licks them off with rapture.

"Thus I hang upon the boughs of life, knowing that the inevitable dragon of death is waiting ready to tear me, and I cannot comprehend why I am thus made a martyr. I try to suck the honey which formerly consoled me; but the honey pleases me no longer, and day and night the white mouse and [pg 155]the black mouse gnaw the branch to which I cling. I can see but one thing: the inevitable dragon and the mice—I cannot turn my gaze away from them.

> "This is no fable, but the literal incontestable truth which every one may understand. What will be the outcome of what I do to-day? Of what I shall do to-morrow? What will be the outcome of all my life? Why should I live? Why should I do anything? Is there in life any purpose which the inevitable death which awaits me does not undo and destroy?
>
> "These questions are the simplest in the world. From the stupid child to the wisest old man, they are in the soul of every human being. Without an answer to them, it is impossible, as I experienced, for life to go on.
>
> " 'But perhaps,' I often said to myself, 'there may be something I have failed to notice or to comprehend. It is not possible that this condition of despair should be natural to mankind.' And I sought for an explanation in all the branches of knowledge acquired by men. I questioned painfully and protractedly and with no idle curiosity. I sought, not with indolence, but laboriously and obstinately for days and nights together. I sought like a man who is lost and seeks to save himself,—and I found nothing. I became convinced, moreover, that all those who before me had sought for an answer in the sciences have also found nothing. And not only this, but that they have recognized that the very thing which was leading me to despair—the meaningless absurdity of life—is the only incontestable knowledge accessible to man."

To prove this point, Tolstoy quotes the Buddha, Solomon, and Schopenhauer. And he finds only four ways in which men of his own class and society are accustomed to meet the situation. Either mere animal blindness, sucking the honey without seeing the dragon or the mice,—"and from such a way," he says, "I can learn nothing, after what I now know;" or reflective epicureanism, snatching what it can while the day lasts,—which is only a more deliberate sort of stupefaction than the first; [pg 156] or manly suicide; or seeing the mice and dragon and yet weakly and plaintively clinging to the bush of life.

Suicide was naturally the consistent course dictated by the logical intellect.

> "Yet," says Tolstoy, "whilst my intellect was working, something else in me was working too, and kept me from the deed—a consciousness of life, as I may call it, which was like a force that obliged my mind to fix itself in another direction and draw me out of my situation of despair.... During the whole course of this year, when I almost unceasingly kept asking myself how to end the business, whether by the rope or by the bullet, during all that time, alongside of all those movements of my ideas and observations, my heart kept languishing with another pining emotion. I can call this by no other

> name than that of a thirst for God. This craving for God had nothing to do with the movement of my ideas,—in fact, it was the direct contrary of that movement,—but it came from my heart. It was like a feeling of dread that made me seem like an orphan and isolated in the midst of all these things that were so foreign. And this feeling of dread was mitigated by the hope of finding the assistance of some one."[80]

Of the process, intellectual as well as emotional, which, starting from this idea of God, led to Tolstoy's recovery, I will say nothing in this lecture, reserving it for a later hour. The only thing that need interest us now is the phenomenon of his absolute disenchantment with ordinary life, and the fact that the whole range of habitual values may, to a man as powerful and full of faculty as he was, come to appear so ghastly a mockery.

When disillusionment has gone as far as this, there is seldom a *restitutio ad integrum*. One has tasted of the fruit of the tree, and the happiness of Eden never comes again. The happiness that comes, when any does come,—and [pg 157] often enough it fails to return in an acute form, though its form is sometimes very acute,—is not the simple ignorance of ill, but something vastly more complex, including natural evil as one of its elements, but finding natural evil no such stumbling-block and terror because it now sees it swallowed up in supernatural good. The process is one of redemption, not of mere reversion to natural health, and the sufferer, when saved, is saved by what seems to him a second birth, a deeper kind of conscious being than he could enjoy before.

We find a somewhat different type of religious melancholy enshrined in literature in John Bunyan's autobiography. Tolstoy's preoccupations were largely objective, for the purpose and meaning of life in general was what so troubled him; but poor Bunyan's troubles were over the condition of his own personal self. He was a typical case of the psychopathic temperament, sensitive of conscience to a diseased degree, beset by doubts, fears, and insistent ideas, and a victim of verbal automatisms, both motor and sensory. These were usually texts of Scripture which, sometimes damnatory and sometimes favorable, would come in a half-hallucinatory form as if they were voices, and fasten on his mind and buffet it between them like a shuttlecock. Added to this were a fearful melancholy self-contempt and despair.

> "Nay, thought I, now I grow worse and worse; now I am farther from conversion than ever I was before. If now I should have burned at the stake, I could not believe that Christ had love for me; alas, I could neither hear him, nor see him, nor feel him, nor savor any of his things. Sometimes I would tell my condition to the people of God, which, when they heard, they would pity me, and would tell of the Promises. But they had as good have told me that I must reach the Sun with my finger as have bidden me receive or rely upon the Promise. [pg 158][Yet] all this while as to the act of sinning, I never was more tender than now; I durst not take a pin or stick, though but so big as a straw, for my conscience now was sore, and would smart at every touch; I could not tell how to speak my words, for fear I should misplace them. Oh, how gingerly did I then go, in all I did or said! I found myself as on a miry bog that shook if I did but stir; and was as there left both by God and Christ, and the spirit, and all good things.
>
> "But my original and inward pollution, that was my plague and my affliction. By reason of that, I was more loathsome in my own eyes than was a toad; and I thought I was so in God's eyes too. Sin and corruption, I said, would as naturally bubble out of my heart as water would bubble out of a fountain. I could have changed heart with anybody. I thought none but the Devil himself could equal me for inward wickedness and pollution of mind. Sure, thought I, I am forsaken of God; and thus I continued a long while, even for some years together.
>
> "And now I was sorry that God had made me a man. The beasts, birds, fishes, etc., I blessed their condition, for they had not a sinful nature; they were not obnoxious to the wrath of God; they were not to go to hell-fire after death. I could therefore have rejoiced, had my condition been as any of theirs. Now I blessed the condition of the dog and toad, yea, gladly would I have been in the condition of the dog or horse, for I knew they had no soul to perish under the everlasting weight of Hell or Sin, as mine was like to do. Nay, and though I saw this, felt this, and was broken to pieces with it, yet that which added to my sorrow was, that I could not find with all my soul that I did desire deliverance. My heart was at times exceedingly hard. If I would have given a thousand pounds for a tear, I could not shed one; no, nor sometimes scarce desire to shed one.
>
> "I was both a burthen and a terror to myself; nor did I ever so know, as now, what it was to be weary of my life, and yet afraid to die. How gladly would I have been anything but myself! Anything but a man! and in any condition but my own."[81]

Poor patient Bunyan, like Tolstoy, saw the light again, but we must also postpone that part of his story to another hour. In a later lecture I will also give the end of the experience of Henry Alline, a devoted evangelist who worked in Nova Scotia a hundred years ago, and who thus vividly describes the high-water mark of the religious melancholy which formed its beginning. The type was not unlike Bunyan's.

> "Everything I saw seemed to be a burden to me; the earth seemed accursed for my sake: all trees, plants, rocks, hills, and vales seemed to be dressed in mourning and groaning, under the weight of the curse, and everything around me seemed to be conspiring my ruin. My sins seemed to be laid open; so that I thought that every one I saw knew them, and sometimes I was almost ready to acknowledge many things, which I thought they knew: yea sometimes it seemed to me as if every one was pointing me out as the most guilty wretch upon earth. I had now so great a sense of the vanity and emptiness of all things here below, that I knew the whole world could not possibly make me happy, no, nor the whole system of creation. When I waked in the morning, the first thought would be, Oh, my wretched soul, what shall I do, where shall I go? And when I laid down, would say, I shall be perhaps in hell before morning. I would many times look on the beasts with envy, wishing with all my heart I was in their place, that I might have no soul to lose; and when I have seen birds flying over my head, have often thought within myself, Oh, that I could fly away from my danger and distress! Oh, how happy should I be, if I were in their place!"[82]

Envy of the placid beasts seems to be a very widespread affection in this type of sadness.

The worst kind of melancholy is that which takes the form of panic fear. Here is an excellent example, for permission to print which I have to thank the sufferer. The original is in French, and though the subject was evidently in a bad nervous condition at the time of which he writes, his case has otherwise the merit of extreme simplicity. I translate freely.

> "Whilst in this state of philosophic pessimism and general depression of spirits about my prospects, I went one evening into a dressing-room in the twilight to procure some article that was there; when suddenly there fell upon

me without any warning, just as if it came out of the darkness, a horrible fear of my own existence. Simultaneously there arose in my mind the image of an epileptic patient whom I had seen in the asylum, a black-haired youth with greenish skin, entirely idiotic, who used to sit all day on one of the benches, or rather shelves against the wall, with his knees drawn up against his chin, and the coarse gray undershirt, which was his only garment, drawn over them inclosing his entire figure. He sat there like a sort of sculptured Egyptian cat or Peruvian mummy, moving nothing but his black eyes and looking absolutely non-human. This image and my fear entered into a species of combination with each other. *That shape am I*, I felt, potentially. Nothing that I possess can defend me against that fate, if the hour for it should strike for me as it struck for him. There was such a horror of him, and such a perception of my own merely momentary discrepancy from him, that it was as if something hitherto solid within my breast gave way entirely, and I became a mass of quivering fear. After this the universe was changed for me altogether. I awoke morning after morning with a horrible dread at the pit of my stomach, and with a sense of the insecurity of life that I never knew before, and that I have never felt since.[83] It was like a revelation; and although the immediate [pg 161] feelings passed away, the experience has made me sympathetic with the morbid feelings of others ever since. It gradually faded, but for months I was unable to go out into the dark alone.

"In general I dreaded to be left alone. I remember wondering how other people could live, how I myself had ever lived, so unconscious of that pit of insecurity beneath the surface of life. My mother in particular, a very cheerful person, seemed to me a perfect paradox in her unconsciousness of danger, which you may well believe I was very careful not to disturb by revelations of my own state of mind. I have always thought that this experience of melancholia of mine had a religious bearing."

On asking this correspondent to explain more fully what he meant by these last words, the answer he wrote was this:—

"I mean that the fear was so invasive and powerful that if I had not clung to scripture-texts like 'The eternal God is my refuge,' etc., 'Come unto me, all ye that labor and are heavy-laden,' etc., 'I am the resurrection and the life,' etc., I think I should have grown really insane."[84]

There is no need of more examples. The cases we have looked at are enough. One of them gives us the vanity of mortal things; another the sense of sin; and the remaining one describes the fear of the universe;—and in one or other of these three ways it always is that man's original optimism and self-satisfaction get leveled with the dust.

In none of these cases was there any intellectual insanity [pg 162] or delusion about matters of fact; but were we disposed to open the chapter of really insane melancholia, with its hallucinations and delusions, it would be a worse story still—desperation absolute and complete, the whole universe coagulating about the sufferer into a material of overwhelming horror, surrounding him without opening or end. Not the conception or intellectual perception of evil, but the grisly blood-freezing heart-palsying sensation of it close upon one, and no other conception or sensation able to live for a moment in its presence. How irrelevantly remote seem all our usual refined optimisms and intellectual and moral consolations in presence of a need of help like this! Here is the real core of the religious problem: Help! help! No prophet can claim to bring a final message unless he says things that will have a sound of reality in the ears of victims such as these. But the deliverance must come in as strong a form as the complaint, if it is to take effect; and that seems a reason why the coarser religions, revivalistic, orgiastic, with blood and miracles and supernatural operations, may possibly never be displaced. Some constitutions need them too much.

Arrived at this point, we can see how great an antagonism may naturally arise between the healthy-minded way of viewing life and the way that takes all this experience of evil as something essential. To this latter way, the morbid-minded way, as we might call it, healthy-mindedness pure and simple seems unspeakably blind and shallow. To the healthy-minded way, on the other hand, the way of the sick soul seems unmanly and diseased. With their grubbing in rat-holes instead of living in the light; with their manufacture of fears, and preoccupation with every unwholesome kind of misery, there is something [pg 163] almost obscene about these children of wrath and cravers of a second birth. If religious intolerance and hanging and burning could again become the order of the day, there is little doubt that, however it may have been in the past, the healthy-minded would at present show themselves the less indulgent party of the two.

In our own attitude, not yet abandoned, of impartial onlookers, what are we to say of this quarrel? It seems to me that we are bound to say that morbid-mindedness ranges over the wider scale of experience, and that its survey is the one that overlaps. The method of averting one's attention from evil, and living simply in the light of good is splendid as long as it will work. It will work with many persons; it will work far more generally than most of us are ready to suppose; and within the sphere of its successful operation there is nothing to be said against it as a religious solution. But it breaks down impotently as soon as melancholy comes; and even though one be quite free from melancholy one's self, there is no doubt that healthy-mindedness is inadequate as a philosophical doctrine, because the evil facts which it refuses positively to account for are a genuine portion of reality; and they may after all be the best key to life's significance, and possibly the only openers of our eyes to the deepest levels of truth.

The normal process of life contains moments as bad as any of those which insane melancholy is filled with, moments in which radical evil gets its innings and takes its solid turn. The lunatic's visions of horror are all drawn from the material of daily fact. Our civilization is founded on the shambles, and every individual existence goes out in a lonely spasm of helpless agony. If you protest, my friend, wait till you arrive there yourself! To believe in the carnivorous reptiles of geologic [pg 164] times is hard for our imagination—they seem too much like mere museum specimens. Yet there is no tooth in any one of those museum-skulls that did not daily through long years of the foretime hold fast to the body struggling in despair of some fated living victim. Forms of horror just as dreadful to their victims, if on a smaller spatial scale, fill the world about us to-day. Here on our very hearths and in our gardens the infernal cat plays with the panting mouse, or holds the hot bird fluttering in her jaws. Crocodiles and rattlesnakes and pythons are at this moment vessels of life as real as we are; their loathsome existence fills every minute of every day that drags its length along; and whenever they or other wild beasts clutch their living prey, the deadly horror which an agitated melancholiac feels is the literally right reaction on the situation.[85]

It may indeed be that no religious reconciliation with the absolute totality of things is possible. Some evils, indeed, are ministerial to higher forms of good; but it [pg 165] may be that there are forms of evil so extreme as to enter into no good system whatsoever, and that, in respect of such evil, dumb submission or neglect to notice is the only practical resource. This question must confront us on a later day. But provisionally, and as a mere matter of program and method, since the evil facts are as genuine parts of nature as the good ones, the philosophic presumption should be that they have some rational significance, and that systematic healthy-mindedness, failing as it does to accord to sorrow, pain, and death any positive and active attention whatever, is formally less complete than systems that try at least to include these elements in their scope.

The completest religions would therefore seem to be those in which the pessimistic elements are best developed. Buddhism, of course, and Christianity are the best known to us of these. They are essentially religions of deliverance: the man must die to an unreal life before he can be born into the real life. In my next lecture, I will try to discuss some of the psychological conditions of this second birth. Fortunately from now onward we shall have to deal with more cheerful subjects than those which we have recently been dwelling on.

Lecture VIII. The Divided Self, And The Process Of Its Unification.

The last lecture was a painful one, dealing as it did with evil as a pervasive element of the world we live in. At the close of it we were brought into full view of the contrast between the two ways of looking at life which are characteristic respectively of what we called the healthy-minded, who need to be born only once, and of the sick souls, who must be twice-born in order to be happy. The result is two different conceptions of the universe of our experience. In the religion of the once-born the world is a sort of rectilinear or one-storied affair, whose accounts are kept in one denomination, whose parts have just the values which naturally they appear to have, and of which a simple algebraic sum of pluses and minuses will give the total worth. Happiness and religious peace consist in living on the plus side of the account. In the religion of the twice-born, on the other hand, the world is a double-storied mystery. Peace cannot be reached by the simple addition of pluses and elimination of minuses from life. Natural good is not simply insufficient in amount and transient, there lurks a falsity in its very being. Cancelled as it all is by death if not by earlier enemies, it gives no final balance, and can never be the thing intended for our lasting worship. It keeps us from our real good, rather; and renunciation and despair of it are our first step in the direction of the truth. There are two lives, the natural [pg 167] and the spiritual, and we must lose the one before we can participate in the other.

In their extreme forms, of pure naturalism and pure salvationism, the two types are violently contrasted; though here as in most other current classifications, the radical extremes are somewhat ideal abstractions, and the concrete human beings whom we oftenest meet are intermediate varieties and mixtures. Practically, however, you all recognize the difference: you understand, for example, the disdain of the methodist convert for the mere sky-blue healthy-minded moralist; and you likewise enter into the aversion of the latter to what seems to him the diseased subjectivism of the Methodist, dying to live, as he calls it, and making of paradox and the inversion of natural appearances the essence of God's truth.[86]

The psychological basis of the twice-born character seems to be a certain discordancy or heterogeneity in the native temperament of the subject, an incompletely unified moral and intellectual constitution.

> "Homo duplex, homo duplex!" writes Alphonse Daudet. "The first time that I perceived that I was two was at the death of my brother Henri, when my father cried out so dramatically, 'He is dead, he is dead!' While my first self wept, my second self thought, 'How truly given was that cry, how fine it would be at the theatre.' I was then fourteen years old.
>
> "This horrible duality has often given me matter for reflection. Oh, this terrible second me, always seated whilst the other is on foot, acting, living, suffering, bestirring itself. This [pg 168]second me that I have never been able to intoxicate, to make shed tears, or put to sleep. And how it sees into things, and how it mocks!"[87]

Recent works on the psychology of character have had much to say upon this point.[88] Some persons are born with an inner constitution which is harmonious and well balanced from the outset. Their impulses are consistent with one another, their will follows without trouble the guidance of their intellect, their passions are not excessive, and their lives are little haunted by regrets. Others are oppositely constituted; and are so in degrees which may vary from something so slight as to result in a merely odd or whimsical inconsistency, to a discordancy of which the consequences may be inconvenient in the extreme. Of the more innocent kinds of heterogeneity I find a good example in Mrs. Annie Besant's autobiography.

> "I have ever been the queerest mixture of weakness and strength, and have paid heavily for the weakness. As a child I used to suffer tortures of shyness, and if my shoe-lace was untied would feel shamefacedly that every eye was fixed on the unlucky string; as a girl I would shrink away from strangers and think myself unwanted and unliked, so that I was full of eager gratitude to any one who noticed me kindly; as the young mistress of a house I was afraid of my servants, and would let careless work pass rather than bear the pain of reproving the ill-doer; when I have been lecturing and debating with no lack of spirit on the platform, I have preferred to go without what I wanted at the hotel rather than to ring and make the waiter fetch it. Combative on the platform in defense of any cause I cared for, I shrink from quarrel or disapproval in the house, and am a coward at heart in private while a good [pg 169]fighter in public. How often have I passed unhappy quarters of an hour screwing up my courage to find fault with some subordinate whom my duty compelled me to reprove, and how often have I jeered at myself for a fraud as the doughty platform combatant, when shrinking from blaming some lad or lass for doing their work badly. An unkind look or word has availed to make me shrink into myself as a snail into its shell, while, on the platform, opposition makes me speak my best."[89]

This amount of inconsistency will only count as amiable weakness; but a stronger degree of heterogeneity may make havoc of the subject's life. There are persons whose existence is little more than a series of zigzags, as now one tendency and now another gets the upper hand. Their spirit wars with their flesh, they wish for incompatibles, wayward impulses interrupt their most deliberate plans, and their lives are one long drama of repentance and of effort to repair misdemeanors and mistakes.

Heterogeneous personality has been explained as the result of inheritance— the traits of character of incompatible and antagonistic ancestors are supposed to be preserved alongside of each other.[90] This explanation may pass for what it is worth—it certainly needs corroboration. But whatever the cause of heterogeneous personality may be, we find the extreme examples of it in the psychopathic temperament, of which I spoke in my first lecture. All writers about that temperament make the inner heterogeneity prominent in their descriptions. Frequently, indeed, it is only this trait that leads us to ascribe that temperament to a man at all. A "dégénéré supérieur" is simply a man of sensibility in many directions, who finds more difficulty than is common in [pg 170] keeping his spiritual house in order and running his furrow straight, because his feelings and impulses are too keen and too discrepant mutually. In the haunting and insistent ideas, in the irrational impulses, the morbid scruples, dreads, and inhibitions which beset the psychopathic temperament when it is thoroughly pronounced, we have exquisite examples of heterogeneous personality. Bunyan had an obsession of the words, "Sell Christ for this, sell him for that, sell him, sell him!" which would run through his mind a hundred times together, until one day out of breath with retorting, "I will not, I will not," he impulsively said, "Let him go if he will," and this loss of the battle kept him in despair for over a year. The lives of the saints are full of such blasphemous obsessions, ascribed invariably to the direct agency of Satan. The phenomenon connects itself with the life of the subconscious self, so-called, of which we must ere-long speak more directly.

Now in all of us, however constituted, but to a degree the greater in proportion as we are intense and sensitive and subject to diversified temptations, and to the greatest possible degree if we are decidedly psychopathic, does the normal evolution of character chiefly consist in the straightening out and unifying of the inner self. The higher and the lower feelings, the useful and the erring impulses, begin by being a comparative chaos within us—they must end by forming a stable system of functions in right subordination. Unhappiness is apt to characterize the period of order-making and struggle. If the individual be of tender conscience and religiously quickened, the unhappiness will take the form of moral remorse and compunction, of feeling inwardly vile and wrong, and of standing in false relations to the author of one's being and appointer of one's spiritual fate. This is the religious [pg 171] melancholy and "conviction of sin" that have played so large a part in the history of Protestant Christianity. The man's interior is a battle-ground for what he feels to be two deadly hostile selves, one actual, the other ideal. As Victor Hugo makes his Mahomet say: —

> "Je suis le champ vil des sublimes combats:
> Tantôt l'homme d'en haut, et tantôt l'homme d'en bas;
> Et le mal dans ma bouche avec le bien alterne,
> Comme dans le désert le sable et la citerne."

Wrong living, impotent aspirations; "What I would, that do I not; but what I hate, that do I," as Saint Paul says; self-loathing, self-despair; an unintelligible and intolerable burden to which one is mysteriously the heir.

Let me quote from some typical cases of discordant personality, with melancholy in the form of self-condemnation and sense of sin. Saint Augustine's case is a classic example. You all remember his half-pagan, half-Christian bringing up at Carthage, his emigration to Rome and Milan, his adoption of Manicheism and subsequent skepticism, and his restless search for truth and purity of life; and finally how, distracted by the struggle between the two souls in his breast, and ashamed of his own weakness of will, when so many others whom he knew and knew of had thrown off the shackles of sensuality and dedicated themselves to chastity and the higher life, he heard a voice in the garden say, *"Sume, lege"* (take and read), and opening the Bible at random, saw the text, "not in chambering and wantonness," etc., which seemed directly sent to his address, and laid the inner storm to rest forever.[91] Augustine's psychological genius has [pg 172] given an account of the trouble of having a divided self which has never been surpassed.

> "The new will which I began to have was not yet strong enough to overcome that other will, strengthened by long indulgence. So these two wills, one old, one new, one carnal, the other spiritual, contended with each other and disturbed my soul. I understood by my own experience what I had read,
>
> 'flesh lusteth against spirit, and spirit against flesh.' It was myself indeed in both the wills, yet more myself in that which I approved in myself than in that which I disapproved in myself. Yet it was through myself that habit had attained so fierce a mastery over me, because I had willingly come whither I willed not. Still bound to earth, I refused, O God, to fight on thy side, as much afraid to be freed from all bonds, as I ought to have feared being trammeled by them.
>
> "Thus the thoughts by which I meditated upon thee were like the efforts of one who would awake, but being overpowered with sleepiness is soon asleep again. Often does a man when heavy sleepiness is on his limbs defer to shake it off, and though not approving it, encourage it; even so I was sure it was better to surrender to thy love than to yield to my own lusts, yet, though the former course convinced me, the latter pleased and held me bound. There was naught in me to answer thy call, 'Awake, thou sleeper,' but only drawling, drowsy words, 'Presently; yes, presently; wait a little while.' But the 'presently' had no 'present,' and the 'little while' grew long…. For I was afraid thou wouldst hear me too soon, and heal me at once of my disease of lust, which I wished to satiate rather than to see extinguished. With what lashes of words did I not scourge my own soul. Yet it shrank back; it refused,

> though it had no excuse to offer.... I said within myself: 'Come, let it be done now,' and as I said it, I was on the point of the resolve. I all but did it, yet I did not do it. And I made another effort, and almost succeeded, yet I did not reach it, and did not grasp it, hesitating to die to death, and live to life; and the evil to which [pg 173] I was so wonted held me more than the better life I had not tried."[92]

There could be no more perfect description of the divided will, when the higher wishes lack just that last acuteness, that touch of explosive intensity, of dynamogenic quality (to use the slang of the psychologists), that enables them to burst their shell, and make irruption efficaciously into life and quell the lower tendencies forever. In a later lecture we shall have much to say about this higher excitability.

I find another good description of the divided will in the autobiography of Henry Alline, the Nova Scotian evangelist, of whose melancholy I read a brief account in my last lecture. The poor youth's sins were, as you will see, of the most harmless order, yet they interfered with what proved to be his truest vocation, so they gave him great distress.

> "I was now very moral in my life, but found no rest of conscience. I now began to be esteemed in young company, who knew nothing of my mind all this while, and their esteem began to be a snare to my soul, for I soon began to be fond of carnal mirth, though I still flattered myself that if I did not get drunk, nor curse, nor swear, there would be no sin in frolicking and carnal mirth, and I thought God would indulge young people with some (what I called simple or civil) recreation. I still kept a round of duties, and would not suffer myself to run into any open vices, and so got along very well in time of health and prosperity, but when I was distressed or threatened by sickness, death, or heavy storms of thunder, my religion would not do, and I found there was something wanting, and would begin to repent my going so much to frolics, but when the distress was over, the devil and my own wicked heart, with the solicitations of my associates, and my fondness for young company, [pg 174] were such strong allurements, I would again give way, and thus I got to be very wild and rude, at the same time kept up my rounds of secret prayer and reading; but God, not willing I should destroy myself, still followed me with his calls, and moved with such power upon my conscience, that I could not satisfy myself with my diversions, and in the midst of my mirth sometimes would have such a sense of my lost and undone condition,

that I would wish myself from the company, and after it was over, when I went home, would make many promises that I would attend no more on these frolics, and would beg forgiveness for hours and hours; but when I came to have the temptation again, I would give way: no sooner would I hear the music and drink a glass of wine, but I would find my mind elevated and soon proceed to any sort of merriment or diversion, that I thought was not debauched or openly vicious; but when I returned from my carnal mirth I felt as guilty as ever, and could sometimes not close my eyes for some hours after I had gone to my bed. I was one of the most unhappy creatures on earth.

"Sometimes I would leave the company (often speaking to the fiddler to cease from playing, as if I was tired), and go out and walk about crying and praying, as if my very heart would break, and beseeching God that he would not cut me off, nor give me up to hardness of heart. Oh, what unhappy hours and nights I thus wore away! When I met sometimes with merry companions, and my heart was ready to sink, I would labor to put on as cheerful a countenance as possible, that they might not distrust anything, and sometimes would begin some discourse with young men or young women on purpose, or propose a merry song, lest the distress of my soul would be discovered, or mistrusted, when at the same time I would then rather have been in a wilderness in exile, than with them or any of their pleasures or enjoyments. Thus for many months when I was in company, I would act the hypocrite and feign a merry heart, but at the same time would endeavor as much as I could to shun their company, oh wretched and unhappy mortal that I was! Everything I did, and wherever I went, I was still in a storm, and yet I continued to be the chief contriver and ringleader [pg 175]of the frolics for many months after; though it was a toil and torment to attend them; but the devil and my own wicked heart drove me about like a slave, telling me that I must do this and do that, and bear this and bear that, and turn here and turn there, to keep my credit up, and retain the esteem of my associates: and all this while I continued as strict as possible in my duties, and left no stone unturned to pacify my conscience, watching even against my thoughts, and praying continually wherever I went: for I did not think there was any sin in my conduct, when I was among carnal company, because I did not take any satisfaction there, but only followed it, I thought, for sufficient reasons.

"But still, all that I did or could do, conscience would roar night and day."

Saint Augustine and Alline both emerged into the smooth waters of inner unity and peace, and I shall next ask you to consider more closely some of the peculiarities of the process of unification, when it occurs. It may come gradually, or it may occur abruptly; it may come through altered feelings, or through altered powers of action; or it may come through new intellectual insights, or through experiences which we shall later have to designate as "mystical." However it come, it brings a characteristic sort of relief; and never such extreme relief as when it is cast into the religious mould.

Happiness! happiness! religion is only one of the ways in which men gain that gift. Easily, permanently, and successfully, it often transforms the most intolerable misery into the profoundest and most enduring happiness.

But to find religion is only one out of many ways of reaching unity; and the process of remedying inner incompleteness and reducing inner discord is a general psychological process, which may take place with any sort of mental material, and need not necessarily assume the religious form. In judging of the religious types of [pg 176] regeneration which we are about to study, it is important to recognize that they are only one species of a genus that contains other types as well. For example, the new birth may be away from religion into incredulity; or it may be from moral scrupulosity into freedom and license; or it may be produced by the irruption into the individual's life of some new stimulus or passion, such as love, ambition, cupidity, revenge, or patriotic devotion. In all these instances we have precisely the same psychological form of event,—a firmness, stability, and equilibrium succeeding a period of storm and stress and inconsistency. In these non-religious cases the new man may also be born either gradually or suddenly.

The French philosopher Jouffroy has left an eloquent memorial of his own "counter-conversion," as the transition from orthodoxy to infidelity has been well styled by Mr. Starbuck. Jouffroy's doubts had long harassed him; but he dates his final crisis from a certain night when his disbelief grew fixed and stable, and where the immediate result was sadness at the illusions he had lost.

> "I shall never forget that night of December," writes Jouffroy, "in which the veil that concealed from me my own incredulity was torn. I hear again my steps in that narrow naked chamber where long after the hour of sleep had come I had the habit of walking up and down. I see again that moon, half-veiled by clouds, which now and again illuminated the frigid window-panes. The hours of the night flowed on and I did not note their passage. Anxiously I followed my thoughts, as from layer to layer they descended towards the foundation of my consciousness, and, scattering one by one all the illusions which until then had screened its windings from my view, made them every moment more clearly visible.
>
> "Vainly I clung to these last beliefs as a shipwrecked sailor clings to the fragments of his vessel; vainly, frightened at the unknown void in which I

was about to float, I turned with them [pg 177]towards my childhood, my family, my country, all that was dear and sacred to me: the inflexible current of my thought was too strong,—parents, family, memory, beliefs, it forced me to let go of everything. The investigation went on more obstinate and more severe as it drew near its term, and did not stop until the end was reached. I knew then that in the depth of my mind nothing was left that stood erect.

"This moment was a frightful one; and when towards morning I threw myself exhausted on my bed, I seemed to feel my earlier life, so smiling and so full, go out like a fire, and before me another life opened, sombre and unpeopled, where in future I must live alone, alone with my fatal thought which had exiled me thither, and which I was tempted to curse. The days which followed this discovery were the saddest of my life."[93]

[pg 178]
In John Foster's Essay on Decision of Character, there is an account of a case of sudden conversion to avarice, which is illustrative enough to quote:—

A young man, it appears, "wasted, in two or three years, a large patrimony in profligate revels with a number of worthless associates who called themselves his friends, and who, when his last means were exhausted, treated him of course with neglect or contempt. Reduced to absolute want, he one day went out of the house with an intention to put an end to his life; but wandering awhile almost unconsciously, he came to the brow of an eminence which overlooked what were lately his estates. Here he sat down, and remained fixed in thought a number of hours, at the end of which he sprang from the ground with a vehement, exulting emotion. He had formed his resolution, which was, that all these estates should be his again; he had formed his plan, too, which he instantly began to execute. He walked hastily forward, determined to seize the first opportunity, of however humble a kind, to gain any money, though it were ever so despicable a trifle, and resolved absolutely not to [pg 179]spend, if he could help it, a farthing of whatever he might obtain. The first thing that drew his attention was a heap of coals shot out of carts on the pavement before a house. He offered himself to shovel or wheel them into the place where they were to be laid, and was employed. He received a few pence for the labor; and then, in pursuance of the saving part of his plan, requested some small gratuity of meat and drink, which was given him. He then looked out for the next thing that might chance; and went, with indefatigable industry, through a succession of servile employments in different places, of longer and shorter duration, still scrupulous in avoiding, as far as possible, the expense of a penny. He promptly seized every opportunity which could advance his design, without regarding the meanness of occupation or appearance. By this method he had gained, after a considerable time, money enough to purchase in order to sell again a few cattle, of which he had taken pains to understand the value. He speedily but cautiously turned his first gains into second advantages; retained without a single deviation his extreme parsimony; and thus advanced by degrees into larger transactions and incipient wealth. I did not hear, or have forgotten, the continued course of his life, but the final result was, that he more than recovered his lost possessions, and died an inveterate miser, worth £60,000."[94]

[pg 180]
Let me turn now to the kind of case, the religious case, namely, that immediately concerns us. Here is one of [pg 181] the simplest possible type, an account of the conversion to the systematic religion of healthy-mindedness of a man who must already have been naturally of the healthy-minded type. It shows how, when the fruit is ripe, a touch will make it fall.

Mr. Horace Fletcher, in his little book called Menticulture, relates that a friend with whom he was talking of the self-control attained by the Japanese through their practice of the Buddhist discipline said:—

> " 'You must first get rid of anger and worry.' 'But,' said I, 'is that possible?' 'Yes,' replied he; 'it is possible to the Japanese, and ought to be possible to us.'
>
> "On my way back I could think of nothing else but the words 'get rid, get rid'; and the idea must have continued to possess me during my sleeping hours, for the first consciousness in the morning brought back the same thought, with the revelation of a discovery, which framed itself into the reasoning, 'If it is possible to get rid of anger and worry, why is it necessary to have them at all?' I felt the strength of the argument, and at once accepted the reasoning. The baby had discovered that it could walk. It would scorn to creep any longer.
>
> "From the instant I realized that these cancer spots of worry and anger were removable, they left me. With the discovery of their weakness they were exorcised. From that time life has had an entirely different aspect.
>
> "Although from that moment the possibility and desirability of freedom from the depressing passions has been a reality to me, it took me some months to feel absolute security in my new position; but, as the usual occasions for worry and anger have presented themselves over and over again, and I have been unable to feel them in the slightest degree, I no longer dread or guard against them, and I am amazed at my increased energy and vigor of mind; at

my strength to meet situations of all kinds, and at my disposition to love and appreciate everything.

"I have had occasion to travel more than ten thousand miles by rail since that morning. The same Pullman porter, conductor, hotel-waiter, peddler, book-agent, cabman, and others [pg 182]who were formerly a source of annoyance and irritation have been met, but I am not conscious of a single incivility. All at once the whole world has turned good to me. I have become, as it were, sensitive only to the rays of good.

"I could recount many experiences which prove a brand-new condition of mind, but one will be sufficient. Without the slightest feeling of annoyance or impatience, I have seen a train that I had planned to take with a good deal of interested and pleasurable anticipation move out of the station without me, because my baggage did not arrive. The porter from the hotel came running and panting into the station just as the train pulled out of sight. When he saw me, he looked as if he feared a scolding, and began to tell of being blocked in a crowded street and unable to get out. When he had finished, I said to him: 'It doesn't matter at all, you couldn't help it, so we will try again to-morrow. Here is your fee, I am sorry you had all this trouble in earning it.' The look of surprise that came over his face was so filled with pleasure that I was repaid on the spot for the delay in my departure. Next day he would not accept a cent for the service, and he and I are friends for life.

"During the first weeks of my experience I was on guard only against worry and anger; but, in the mean time, having noticed the absence of the other depressing and dwarfing passions, I began to trace a relationship, until I was convinced that they are all growths from the two roots I have specified. I have felt the freedom now for so long a time that I am sure of my relation toward it; and I could no more harbor any of the thieving and depressing influences that once I nursed as a heritage of humanity than a fop would voluntarily wallow in a filthy gutter.

"There is no doubt in my mind that pure Christianity and pure Buddhism, and the Mental Sciences and all Religions, fundamentally teach what has been a discovery to me; but none of them have presented it in the light of a simple and easy process of elimination. At one time I wondered if the elimination would not yield to indifference and sloth. In my experience, the contrary is the result. I feel such an increased [pg 183]desire to do something useful that it seems as if I were a boy again and the energy for play had returned. I could fight as readily as (and better than) ever, if there were occasion for it. It does not make one a coward. It can't, since fear is one of the things eliminated. I notice the absence of timidity in the presence of any audience. When a boy, I was standing under a tree which was struck by lightning, and received a shock from the effects of which I never knew exemption until I had dissolved partnership with worry. Since then, lightning and thunder have been encountered under conditions which would formerly have caused great depression and discomfort, without [my] experiencing a trace of either.

> Surprise is also greatly modified, and one is less liable to become startled by unexpected sights or noises.
>
> "As far as I am individually concerned, I am not bothering myself at present as to what the results of this emancipated condition may be. I have no doubt that the perfect health aimed at by Christian Science may be one of the possibilities, for I note a marked improvement in the way my stomach does its duty in assimilating the food I give it to handle, and I am sure it works better to the sound of a song than under the friction of a frown. Neither am I wasting any of this precious time formulating an idea of a future existence or a future Heaven. The Heaven that I have within myself is as attractive as any that has been promised or that I can imagine; and I am willing to let the growth lead where it will, as long as the anger and their brood have no part in misguiding it."[95]

The older medicine used to speak of two ways, *lysis* and *crisis,* one gradual, the other abrupt, in which one might recover from a bodily disease. In the spiritual realm there are also two ways, one gradual, the other sudden, in which inner unification may occur. Tolstoy and Bunyan may again serve us as examples, examples, as it happens, of the gradual way, though it must be confessed at the outset that it is hard to follow these windings [pg 184] of the hearts of others, and one feels that their words do not reveal their total secret.

Howe'er this be, Tolstoy, pursuing his unending questioning, seemed to come to one insight after another. First he perceived that his conviction that life was meaningless took only this finite life into account. He was looking for the value of one finite term in that of another, and the whole result could only be one of those indeterminate equations in mathematics which end with $0=0$. Yet this is as far as the reasoning intellect by itself can go, unless irrational sentiment or faith brings in the infinite. Believe in the infinite as common people do, and life grows possible again.

> "Since mankind has existed, wherever life has been, there also has been the faith that gave the possibility of living. Faith is the sense of life, that sense by virtue of which man does not destroy himself, but continues to live on. It is the force whereby we live. If Man did not believe that he must live for something, he would not live at all. The idea of an infinite God, of the divinity of the soul, of the union of men's actions with God—these are ideas elaborated in the infinite secret depths of human thought. They are ideas
>
> without which there would be no life, without which I myself," said Tolstoy, "would not exist. I began to see that I had no right to rely on my individual

> reasoning and neglect these answers given by faith, for they are the only answers to the question."

Yet how believe as the common people believe, steeped as they are in grossest superstition? It is impossible,—but yet their life! their life! It is normal. It is happy! It is an answer to the question!

Little by little, Tolstoy came to the settled conviction—he says it took him two years to arrive there—that his trouble had not been with life in general, not with the common life of common men, but with the life of the upper, intellectual, artistic classes, the life which he had [pg 185] personally always led, the cerebral life, the life of conventionality, artificiality, and personal ambition. He had been living wrongly and must change. To work for animal needs, to abjure lies and vanities, to relieve common wants, to be simple, to believe in God, therein lay happiness again.

> "I remember," he says, "one day in early spring, I was alone in the forest, lending my ear to its mysterious noises. I listened, and my thought went back to what for these three years it always was busy with—the quest of God. But the idea of him, I said, how did I ever come by the idea?
>
> "And again there arose in me, with this thought, glad aspirations towards life. Everything in me awoke and received a meaning.... Why do I look farther? a voice within me asked. He is there: he, without whom one cannot live. To acknowledge God and to live are one and the same thing. God is what life is. Well, then! live, seek God, and there will be no life without him....
>
> "After this, things cleared up within me and about me better than ever, and the light has never wholly died away. I was saved from suicide. Just how or when the change took place I cannot tell. But as insensibly and gradually as the force of life had been annulled within me, and I had reached my moral death-bed, just as gradually and imperceptibly did the energy of life come back. And what was strange was that this energy that came back was nothing new. It was my ancient juvenile force of faith, the belief that the sole purpose of my life was to be *better*. I gave up the life of the conventional world, recognizing it to be no life, but a parody on life, which its superfluities simply keep us from comprehending,"—and Tolstoy thereupon embraced the life of the peasants, and has felt right and happy, or at least relatively so, ever since.[96]

As I interpret his melancholy, then, it was not merely an accidental vitiation of his humors, though it was doubtless also that. It was logically called for by the clash [pg 186] between his inner character and his outer activities and aims. Although a literary artist, Tolstoy was one of those primitive oaks of men to whom the superfluities and insincerities, the cupidities, complications, and cruelties of our polite civilization are profoundly unsatisfying, and for whom the eternal veracities lie with more natural and animal things. His crisis was the getting of his soul in order, the discovery of its genuine habitat and vocation, the escape from falsehoods into what for him were ways of truth. It was a case of heterogeneous personality tardily and slowly finding its unity and level. And though not many of us can imitate Tolstoy, not having enough, perhaps, of the aboriginal human marrow in our bones, most of us may at least feel as if it might be better for us if we could.

Bunyan's recovery seems to have been even slower. For years together he was alternately haunted with texts of Scripture, now up and now down, but at last with an ever growing relief in his salvation through the blood of Christ.

> "My peace would be in and out twenty times a day; comfort now and trouble presently; peace now and before I could go a furlong as full of guilt and fear as ever heart could hold." When a good text comes home to him, "This," he writes, "gave me good encouragement for the space of two or three hours"; or "This was a good day to me, I hope I shall not forget it"; or "The glory of these words was then so weighty on me that I was ready to swoon as I sat; yet not with grief and trouble, but with solid joy and peace"; or "This made a strange seizure on my spirit; it brought light with it, and commanded a silence in my heart of all those tumultuous thoughts that before did use, like masterless hell-hounds, to roar and bellow and make a hideous noise within me. It showed me that Jesus Christ had not quite forsaken and cast off my Soul."

> Such periods accumulate until he can write: "And now [pg 187] remained only the hinder part of the tempest, for the thunder was gone beyond me, only some drops would still remain, that now and then would fall upon me";
> —and at last: "Now did my chains fall off my legs indeed; I was loosed from my afflictions and irons; my temptations also fled away; so that from that time, those dreadful Scriptures of God left off to trouble me; now went I also home rejoicing, for the grace and love of God.... Now could I see myself in Heaven and Earth at once; in Heaven by my Christ, by my Head, by my

> Righteousness and Life, though on Earth by my body or person.... Christ was a precious Christ to my soul that night; I could scarce lie in my bed for joy and peace and triumph through Christ."

Bunyan became a minister of the gospel, and in spite of his neurotic constitution, and of the twelve years he lay in prison for his non-conformity, his life was turned to active use. He was a peacemaker and doer of good, and the immortal Allegory which he wrote has brought the very spirit of religious patience home to English hearts.

But neither Bunyan nor Tolstoy could become what we have called healthy-minded. They had drunk too deeply of the cup of bitterness ever to forget its taste, and their redemption is into a universe two stories deep. Each of them realized a good which broke the effective edge of his sadness; yet the sadness was preserved as a minor ingredient in the heart of the faith by which it was overcome. The fact of interest for us is that as a matter of fact they could and did find *something* welling up in the inner reaches of their consciousness, by which such extreme sadness could be overcome. Tolstoy does well to talk of it as *that by which men live*; for that is exactly what it is, a stimulus, an excitement, a faith, a force that re-infuses the positive willingness to live, even in full presence of the evil perceptions that erewhile made life seem unbearable. For Tolstoy's perceptions of evil [pg 188] appear within their sphere to have remained unmodified. His later works show him implacable to the whole system of official values: the ignobility of fashionable life; the infamies of empire; the spuriousness of the church, the vain conceit of the professions; the meannesses and cruelties that go with great success; and every other pompous crime and lying institution of this world. To all patience with such things his experience has been for him a permanent ministry of death.

Bunyan also leaves this world to the enemy.

> "I must first pass a sentence of death," he says, "upon everything that can properly be called a thing of this life, even to reckon myself, my wife, my children, my health, my enjoyments, and all, as dead to me, and myself as dead to them; to trust in God through Christ, as touching the world to come; and as touching this world, to count the grave my house, to make my bed in darkness, and to say to corruption, Thou art my father, and to the worm, Thou art my mother and sister.... The parting with my wife and my poor

children hath often been to me as the pulling of my flesh from my bones, especially my poor blind child who lay nearer my heart than all I had besides. Poor child, thought I, what sorrow art thou like to have for thy portion in this world! Thou must be beaten, must beg, suffer hunger, cold, nakedness, and a thousand calamities, though I cannot now endure that the wind should blow upon thee. But yet I must venture you all with God, though it goeth to the quick to leave you."[97]

The "hue of resolution" is there, but the full flood of ecstatic liberation seems never to have poured over poor John Bunyan's soul.

These examples may suffice to acquaint us in a general way with the phenomenon technically called "Conversion." In the next lecture I shall invite you to study its peculiarities and concomitants in some detail.

Lecture IX. Conversion.

To be converted, to be regenerated, to receive grace, to experience religion, to gain an assurance, are so many phrases which denote the process, gradual or sudden, by which a self hitherto divided, and consciously wrong inferior and unhappy, becomes unified and consciously right superior and happy, in consequence of its firmer hold upon religious realities. This at least is what conversion signifies in general terms, whether or not we believe that a direct divine operation is needed to bring such a moral change about.

Before entering upon a minuter study of the process, let me enliven our understanding of the definition by a concrete example. I choose the quaint case of an unlettered man, Stephen H. Bradley, whose experience is related in a scarce American pamphlet.[98]

I select this case because it shows how in these inner alterations one may find one unsuspected depth below another, as if the possibilities of character lay disposed in a series of layers or shells, of whose existence we have no premonitory knowledge.

Bradley thought that he had been already fully converted at the age of fourteen.

> "I thought I saw the Saviour, by faith, in human shape, for about one second in the room, with arms extended, appearing [pg 190] to say to me, Come. The next day I rejoiced with trembling; soon after, my happiness was so great that I said that I wanted to die; this world had no place in my affections, as I knew of, and every day appeared as solemn to me as the Sabbath. I had an ardent desire that all mankind might feel as I did; I wanted to have them all love God supremely. Previous to this time I was very selfish and self-righteous; but now I desired the welfare of all mankind, and could with a

feeling heart forgive my worst enemies, and I felt as if I should be willing to bear the scoffs and sneers of any person, and suffer anything for His sake, if I could be the means in the hands of God, of the conversion of one soul."

Nine years later, in 1829, Mr. Bradley heard of a revival of religion that had begun in his neighborhood. "Many of the young converts," he says, "would come to me when in meeting and ask me if I had religion, and my reply generally was, I hope I have. This did not appear to satisfy them; they said they *knew they* had it. I requested them to pray for me, thinking with myself, that if I had not got religion now, after so long a time professing to be a Christian, that it was time I had, and hoped their prayers would be answered in my behalf.

"One Sabbath, I went to hear the Methodist at the Academy. He spoke of the ushering in of the day of general judgment; and he set it forth in such a solemn and terrible manner as I never heard before. The scene of that day appeared to be taking place, and so awakened were all the powers of my mind that, like Felix, I trembled involuntarily on the bench where I was sitting, though I felt nothing at heart. The next day evening I went to hear him again. He took his text from Revelation: 'And I saw the dead, small and great, stand before God.' And he represented the terrors of that day in such a manner that it appeared as if it would melt the heart of stone. When he finished his discourse, an old gentleman turned to me and said, 'This is what I call preaching.' I thought the same; but my feelings were still unmoved by what he said, and I did not enjoy religion, but I believe he did.

"I will now relate my experience of the power of the Holy Spirit which took place on the same night. Had any person told me previous to this that I could have experienced the power of the Holy Spirit in the manner which I did, I could not have believed it, and should have thought the person deluded that told me so. I went directly home after the meeting, and when I got home I wondered what made me feel so stupid. I retired to rest soon after I got home, and felt indifferent to the things of religion until I began to be exercised by the Holy Spirit, which began in about five minutes after, in the following manner:—

"At first, I began to feel my heart beat very quick all on a sudden, which made me at first think that perhaps something is going to ail me, though I was not alarmed, for I felt no pain. My heart increased in its beating, which soon convinced me that it was the Holy Spirit from the effect it had on me. I began to feel exceedingly happy and humble, and such a sense of unworthiness as I never felt before. I could not very well help speaking out, which I did, and said, Lord, I do not deserve this happiness, or words to that effect, while there was a stream (resembling air in feeling) came into my mouth and heart in a more sensible manner than that of drinking anything, which continued, as near as I could judge, five minutes or more, which appeared to be the cause of such a palpitation of my heart. It took complete possession of my soul, and I am certain that I desired the Lord, while in the midst of it, not to give me any more happiness, for it seemed as if I could not contain what I had got. My heart seemed as if it would burst, but it did not stop until I felt as if I was unutterably full of the love and grace of God. In the mean time while thus exercised, a thought arose in my mind, what can it mean? and all at once, as if to answer it, my memory became exceedingly clear, and it appeared to me just as if the New Testament was placed open before me, eighth chapter of Romans, and as light as if some candle lighted was held for me to read the 26th and 27th verses of that chapter, and I read these words: 'The Spirit helpeth our infirmities with groanings which cannot be uttered.' And all the time that my heart was a-beating, it made me groan like a person in distress, which was not very easy to stop, though I was in no pain at all, and my brother being in bed in [pg 192]another room came and opened the door, and asked me if I had got the toothache. I told him no, and that he might get to sleep. I tried to stop. I felt unwilling to go to sleep myself, I was so happy, fearing I should lose it—thinking within myself

'My willing soul would stay
    In such a frame as this.'

And while I lay reflecting, after my heart stopped beating, feeling as if my soul was full of the Holy Spirit, I thought that perhaps there might be angels hovering round my bed. I felt just as if I wanted to converse with them, and finally I spoke, saying, 'O ye affectionate angels! how is it that ye can take so much interest in our welfare, and we take so little interest in our own.' After this, with difficulty I got to sleep; and when I awoke in the morning my first thoughts were: What has become of my happiness? and, feeling a degree of it in my heart, I asked for more, which was given to me as quick as thought. I then got up to dress myself, and found to my surprise that I could but just stand. It appeared to me as if it was a little heaven upon earth. My soul felt as completely raised above the fears of death as of going to sleep; and like a bird in a cage, I had a desire, if it was the will of God, to get released from my body and to dwell with Christ, though willing to live to do good to others, and to warn sinners to repent. I went downstairs feeling as solemn as if I had lost all my friends, and thinking with myself, that I would not let my parents know it until I had first looked into the Testament. I went directly to the shelf and looked into it, at the eighth chapter of Romans, and every verse seemed to almost speak and to confirm it to be truly the Word of God, and as if my feelings corresponded with the meaning of the word. I then told my parents of it, and told them that I thought that they must see that when I spoke, that it was not my own voice, for it appeared so to me. My speech seemed entirely under the control of the Spirit within me; I do not mean that the words which I spoke were not my own, for they were. I thought that I was influenced similar to the Apostles on the day of Pentecost (with the exception of having power to give it to others, and doing [pg 193]what they did). After breakfast I went round to converse with my neighbors on religion, which I could not have been hired to have done before this, and at their request I prayed with them, though I had never prayed in public before.

> "I now feel as if I had discharged my duty by telling the truth, and hope by the blessing of God, it may do some good to all who shall read it. He has fulfilled his promise in sending the Holy Spirit down into our hearts, or mine at least, and I now defy all the Deists and Atheists in the world to shake my faith in Christ."

So much for Mr. Bradley and his conversion, of the effect of which upon his later life we gain no information. Now for a minuter survey of the constituent elements of the conversion process.

If you open the chapter on Association, of any treatise on Psychology, you will read that a man's ideas, aims, and objects form diverse internal groups and systems, relatively independent of one another. Each "aim" which he follows awakens a certain specific kind of interested excitement, and gathers a certain group of ideas together in subordination to it as its associates; and if the aims and excitements are distinct in kind, their groups of ideas may have little in common. When one group is present and engrosses the interest, all the ideas connected with other groups may be excluded from the mental field. The President of the United States when, with paddle, gun, and fishing-rod, he goes camping in the wilderness for a vacation, changes his system of ideas from top to bottom. The presidential anxieties have lapsed into the background entirely; the official habits are replaced by the habits of a son of nature, and those who knew the man only as the strenuous magistrate would not "know him for the same person" if they saw him as the camper.

If now he should never go back, and never again [pg 194] suffer political interests to gain dominion over him, he would be for practical intents and purposes a permanently transformed being. Our ordinary alterations of character, as we pass from one of our aims to another, are not commonly called transformations, because each of them is so rapidly succeeded by another in the reverse direction; but whenever one aim grows so stable as to expel definitively its previous rivals from the individual's life, we tend to speak of the phenomenon, and perhaps to wonder at it, as a "transformation."

These alternations are the completest of the ways in which a self may be divided. A less complete way is the simultaneous coexistence of two or more different groups of aims, of which one practically holds the right of way and instigates activity, whilst the others are only pious wishes, and never practically come to anything. Saint Augustine's aspirations to a purer life, in our last lecture, were for a while an example. Another would be the President in his full pride of office, wondering whether it were not all vanity, and whether the life of a wood-chopper were not the wholesomer destiny. Such fleeting aspirations are mere *velleitates*, whimsies. They exist on the remoter outskirts of the mind, and the real self of the man, the centre of his energies, is occupied with an entirely different system. As life goes on, there is a constant change of our interests, and a consequent change of place in our systems of ideas, from more central to more peripheral, and from more peripheral to more central parts of consciousness. I remember, for instance, that one evening when I was a youth, my father read aloud from a Boston newspaper that part of Lord Gifford's will which founded these four lectureships. At that time I did not think of being a teacher of philosophy: and what I listened to was as remote from my own life [pg 195] as if it related to the planet Mars. Yet here I am, with the Gifford system part and parcel of my very self, and all my energies, for the time being, devoted to successfully identifying myself with it. My soul stands now planted in what once was for it a practically unreal object, and speaks from it as from its proper habitat and centre.

When I say "Soul," you need not take me in the ontological sense unless you prefer to; for although ontological language is instinctive in such matters, yet Buddhists or Humians can perfectly well describe the facts in the phenomenal terms which are their favorites. For them the soul is only a succession of fields of consciousness: yet there is found in each field a part, or sub-field, which figures as focal and contains the excitement, and from which, as from a centre, the aim seems to be taken. Talking of this part, we involuntarily apply words of perspective to distinguish it from the rest, words like "here," "this," "now," "mine," or "me"; and we ascribe to the other parts the positions "there," "then," "that," "his" or "thine," "it," "not me." But a "here" can change to a "there," and a "there" become a "here," and what was "mine" and what was "not mine" change their places.

What brings such changes about is the way in which emotional excitement alters. Things hot and vital to us to-day are cold to-morrow. It is as if seen from the hot parts of the field that the other parts appear to us, and from these hot parts personal desire and volition make their sallies. They are in short the centres of our dynamic energy, whereas the cold parts leave us indifferent and passive in proportion to their coldness.

Whether such language be rigorously exact is for the present of no importance. It is exact enough, if you [pg 196] recognize from your own experience the facts which I seek to designate by it.

Now there may be great oscillation in the emotional interest, and the hot places may shift before one almost as rapidly as the sparks that run through burnt-up paper. Then we have the wavering and divided self we heard so much of in the previous lecture. Or the focus of excitement and heat, the point of view from which the aim is taken, may come to lie permanently within a certain system; and then, if the change be a religious one, we call it a *conversion*, especially if it be by crisis, or sudden.

Let us hereafter, in speaking of the hot place in a man's consciousness, the group of ideas to which he devotes himself, and from which he works, call it *the habitual centre of his personal energy*. It makes a great difference to a man whether one set of his ideas, or another, be the centre of his energy; and it makes a great difference, as regards any set of ideas which he may possess, whether they become central or remain peripheral in him. To say that a man is "converted" means, in these terms, that religious ideas, previously peripheral in his consciousness, now take a central place, and that religious aims form the habitual centre of his energy.

Now if you ask of psychology just *how* the excitement shifts in a man's mental system, and *why* aims that were peripheral become at a certain moment central, psychology has to reply that although she can give a general description of what happens, she is unable in a given case to account accurately for all the single forces at work. Neither an outside observer nor the Subject who undergoes the process can explain fully how particular experiences are able to change one's centre of energy so decisively, or why they so often have to bide their hour to do so. We have a thought, or we perform an act, [pg 197] repeatedly, but on a certain day the real meaning of the thought peals through us for the first time, or the act has suddenly turned into a moral impossibility. All we know is that there are dead feelings, dead ideas, and cold beliefs, and there are hot and live ones; and when one grows hot and alive within us, everything has to re-crystallize about it. We may say that the heat and liveliness mean only the "motor efficacy," long deferred but now operative, of the idea; but such talk itself is only circumlocution, for whence the sudden motor efficacy? And our explanations then get so vague and general that one realizes all the more the intense individuality of the whole phenomenon.

In the end we fall back on the hackneyed symbolism of a mechanical equilibrium. A mind is a system of ideas, each with the excitement it arouses, and with tendencies impulsive and inhibitive, which mutually check or reinforce one another. The collection of ideas alters by subtraction or by addition in the course of experience, and the tendencies alter as the organism gets more aged. A mental system may be undermined or weakened by this interstitial alteration just as a building is, and yet for a time keep upright by dead habit. But a new perception, a sudden emotional shock, or an occasion which lays bare the organic alteration, will make the whole fabric fall together; and then the centre of gravity sinks into an attitude more stable, for the new ideas that reach the centre in the rearrangement seem now to be locked there, and the new structure remains permanent.

Formed associations of ideas and habits are usually factors of retardation in such changes of equilibrium. New information, however acquired, plays an accelerating part in the changes; and the slow mutation of our instincts and propensities, under the "unimaginable touch [pg 198] of time" has an enormous influence. Moreover, all these influences may work subconsciously or half unconsciously.[99] And when you get a Subject in whom the subconscious life—of which I must speak more fully soon—is largely developed, and in whom motives habitually ripen in silence, you get a case of which you can never give a full account, and in which, both to the Subject and the onlookers, there may appear an element of marvel. Emotional occasions, especially violent ones, are extremely potent in precipitating mental rearrangements. The sudden and explosive ways in which love, jealousy, guilt, fear, remorse, or anger can seize upon one are known to everybody.[100] Hope, happiness, security, resolve, emotions characteristic of conversion, can be equally explosive. And emotions that come in this explosive way seldom leave things as they found them.

In his recent work on the Psychology of Religion, Professor Starbuck of California has shown by a statistical [pg 199] inquiry how closely parallel in its manifestations the ordinary "conversion" which occurs in young people brought up in evangelical circles is to that growth into a larger spiritual life which is a normal phase of adolescence in every class of human beings. The age is the same, falling usually between fourteen and seventeen. The symptoms are the same,—sense of incompleteness and imperfection; brooding, depression, morbid introspection, and sense of sin; anxiety about the hereafter; distress over doubts, and the like. And the result is the same,—a happy relief and objectivity, as the confidence in self gets greater through the adjustment of the faculties to the wider outlook. In spontaneous religious awakening, apart from revivalistic examples, and in the ordinary storm and stress and moulting-time of adolescence, we also may meet with mystical experiences, astonishing the subjects by their suddenness, just as in revivalistic conversion. The analogy, in fact, is complete; and Starbuck's conclusion as to these ordinary youthful conversions would seem to be the only sound one: Conversion is in its essence a normal adolescent phenomenon, incidental to the passage from the child's small universe to the wider intellectual and spiritual life of maturity.

"Theology," says Dr. Starbuck, "takes the adolescent tendencies and builds upon them; it sees that the essential thing in adolescent growth is bringing the person out of childhood into the new life of maturity and personal insight. It accordingly brings those means to bear which will intensify the normal tendencies. It shortens up the period of duration of storm and stress." The conversion phenomena of "conviction of sin" last, by this investigator's statistics, about one fifth as long as the periods of adolescent storm and stress phenomena of which he also got statistics, but they are very much more intense. [pg 200] Bodily accompaniments, loss of sleep and appetite, for example, are much more frequent in them. "The essential distinction appears to be that conversion intensifies but shortens the period by bringing the person to a definite crisis."[101]

The conversions which Dr. Starbuck here has in mind are of course mainly those of very commonplace persons, kept true to a pre-appointed type by instruction, appeal, and example. The particular form which they affect is the result of suggestion and imitation.[102] If they went through their growth-crisis in other faiths and other countries, although the essence of the change would be the same (since it is one in the main so inevitable), its accidents would be different. In Catholic lands, for example, and in our own Episcopalian sects, no such anxiety and conviction of sin is usual as in sects that encourage revivals. The sacraments being more relied on in these more strictly ecclesiastical bodies, the individual's personal acceptance of salvation needs less to be accentuated and led up to.

[pg 201]
But every imitative phenomenon must once have had its original, and I propose that for the future we keep as close as may be to the more first-hand and original forms of experience. These are more likely to be found in sporadic adult cases.

Professor Leuba, in a valuable article on the psychology of conversion,[103] subordinates the theological aspect of the religious life almost entirely to its moral aspect. The religious sense he defines as "the feeling of unwholeness, of moral imperfection, of sin, to use the technical word, accompanied by the yearning after the peace of unity." "The word 'religion,'" he says, "is getting more and more to signify the conglomerate of desires and emotions springing from the sense of sin and its release"; and he gives a large number of examples, in which the sin ranges from drunkenness to spiritual pride, to show that the sense of it may beset one and crave relief as urgently as does the anguish of the sickened flesh or any form of physical misery.

Undoubtedly this conception covers an immense number of cases. A good one to use as an example is that of Mr. S. H. Hadley, who after his conversion became an active and useful rescuer of drunkards in New York. His experience runs as follows:—

> "One Tuesday evening I sat in a saloon in Harlem, a homeless, friendless, dying drunkard. I had pawned or sold everything that would bring a drink. I could not sleep unless I was dead drunk. I had not eaten for days, and for four

nights preceding I had suffered with delirium tremens, or the horrors, from midnight till morning. I had often said, 'I will never be a tramp. I will never be cornered, for when that time comes, if ever it comes, I will find a home in the bottom of the river.' But the Lord so ordered it that when that time did come I was [pg 202]not able to walk one quarter of the way to the river. As I sat there thinking, I seemed to feel some great and mighty presence. I did not know then what it was. I did learn afterwards that it was Jesus, the sinner's friend. I walked up to the bar and pounded it with my fist till I made the glasses rattle. Those who stood by drinking looked on with scornful curiosity. I said I would never take another drink, if I died on the street, and really I felt as though that would happen before morning. Something said, 'If you want to keep this promise, go and have yourself locked up.' I went to the nearest station-house and had myself locked up.

"I was placed in a narrow cell, and it seemed as though all the demons that could find room came in that place with me. This was not all the company I had, either. No, praise the Lord; that dear Spirit that came to me in the saloon was present, and said, Pray. I did pray, and though I did not feel any great help, I kept on praying. As soon as I was able to leave my cell I was taken to the police court and remanded back to the cell. I was finally released, and found my way to my brother's house, where every care was given me. While lying in bed the admonishing Spirit never left me, and when I arose the following Sabbath morning I felt that day would decide my fate, and toward evening it came into my head to go to Jerry M'Auley's Mission. I went. The house was packed, and with great difficulty I made my way to the space near the platform. There I saw the apostle to the drunkard and the outcast—that man of God, Jerry M'Auley. He rose, and amid deep silence told his experience. There was a sincerity about this man that carried conviction with it, and I found myself saying, 'I wonder if God can save *me*?' I listened to the testimony of twenty-five or thirty persons, every one of whom had been saved from rum, and I made up my mind that I would be saved or die right there. When the invitation was given, I knelt down with a crowd of drunkards. Jerry made the first prayer. Then Mrs. M'Auley prayed fervently for us. Oh, what a conflict was going on for my poor soul! A blessed whisper said, 'Come'; the devil said, 'Be careful.' I halted but a moment, and then, with a breaking heart, I said, 'Dear [pg 203]Jesus, can you help me?' Never with mortal tongue can I describe that moment. Although up to that moment my soul had been filled with indescribable gloom, I felt the glorious brightness of the noonday sun shine into my heart. I felt I was a free man. Oh, the precious feeling of safety, of freedom, of resting on Jesus! I felt that Christ with all his brightness and power had come into my life; that, indeed, old things had passed away and all things had become new.

"From that moment till now I have never wanted a drink of whiskey, and I have never seen money enough to make me take one. I promised God that night that if he would take away the appetite for strong drink, I would work for him all my life. He has done his part, and I have been trying to do mine."[104]

Dr. Leuba rightly remarks that there is little doctrinal theology in such an experience, which starts with the absolute need of a higher helper, and ends with the sense that he has helped us. He gives other cases of drunkards' conversions which are purely ethical, containing, as recorded, no theological beliefs whatever. John B. Gough's case, for instance, is practically, says Dr. Leuba, the conversion of an atheist—neither God nor Jesus being mentioned.[105] But in spite of the importance of this type of regeneration, with little or no intellectual readjustment, this writer surely makes it too exclusive. It corresponds to the subjectively centred form of morbid melancholy, of which Bunyan and Alline were examples. But we saw in our seventh lecture that there are objective forms of melancholy also, in which the lack of rational [pg 204] meaning of the universe, and of life anyhow, is the burden that weighs upon one—you remember Tolstoy's case.[106] So there are distinct elements in conversion, and their relations to individual lives deserve to be discriminated.[107]

Some persons, for instance, never are, and possibly never under any circumstances could be, converted. Religious ideas cannot become the centre of their spiritual energy. They may be excellent persons, servants of God in practical ways, but they are not children of his kingdom. They are either incapable of imagining the invisible; or else, in the language of devotion, they are life-long subjects of "barrenness" and "dryness." Such inaptitude for religious faith may in some cases be intellectual in its origin. Their religious faculties may be checked in their natural tendency to expand, by beliefs about the world that are inhibitive, the pessimistic and materialistic beliefs, for example, within which so many good souls, who in former times would have freely indulged their religious propensities, find themselves nowadays, as it were, frozen; or the agnostic vetoes upon faith as something weak and shameful, under which so many of us to-day lie cowering, afraid to use our instincts. In many persons such inhibitions are never overcome. To the end of their days they refuse to believe, their personal energy never gets to its religious centre, and the latter remains inactive in perpetuity.

In other persons the trouble is profounder. There are men anæsthetic on the religious side, deficient in that [pg 205] category of sensibility. Just as a bloodless organism can never, in spite of all its goodwill, attain to the reckless "animal spirits" enjoyed by those of sanguine temperament; so the nature which is spiritually barren may admire and envy faith in others, but can never compass the enthusiasm and peace which those who are temperamentally qualified for faith enjoy. All this may, however, turn out eventually to have been a matter of temporary inhibition. Even late in life some thaw, some release may take place, some bolt be shot back in the barrenest breast, and the man's hard heart may soften and break into religious feeling. Such cases more than any others suggest the idea that sudden conversion is by miracle. So long as they exist, we must not imagine ourselves to deal with irretrievably fixed classes.

Now there are two forms of mental occurrence in human beings, which lead to a striking difference in the conversion process, a difference to which Professor Starbuck has called attention. You know how it is when you try to recollect a forgotten name. Usually you help the recall by working for it, by mentally running over the places, persons, and things with which the word was connected. But sometimes this effort fails: you feel then as if the harder you tried the less hope there would be, as though the name were *jammed*, and pressure in its direction only kept it all the more from rising. And then the opposite expedient often succeeds. Give up the effort entirely; think of something altogether different, and in half an hour the lost name comes sauntering into your mind, as Emerson says, as carelessly as if it had never been invited. Some hidden process was started in you by the effort, which went on after the effort ceased, and made the result come as if it came spontaneously. [pg 206] A certain music teacher, says Dr. Starbuck, says to her pupils after the thing to be done has been clearly pointed out, and unsuccessfully attempted: "Stop trying and it will do itself!"[108]

There is thus a conscious and voluntary way and an involuntary and unconscious way in which mental results may get accomplished; and we find both ways exemplified in the history of conversion, giving us two types, which Starbuck calls the *volitional type* and the *type by self-surrender* respectively.

In the volitional type the regenerative change is usually gradual, and consists in the building up, piece by piece, of a new set of moral and spiritual habits. But there are always critical points here at which the movement forward seems much more rapid. This psychological fact is abundantly illustrated by Dr. Starbuck. Our education in any practical accomplishment proceeds apparently by jerks and starts, just as the growth of our physical bodies does.

> "An athlete ... sometimes awakens suddenly to an understanding of the fine points of the game and to a real enjoyment of it, just as the convert awakens to an appreciation of religion. If he keeps on engaging in the sport, there may come a day when all at once the game plays itself through him—when he loses himself in some great contest. In the same way, a musician may suddenly reach a point at which pleasure in the technique of the art entirely falls away, and in some moment of inspiration he becomes the instrument through which music flows. The writer has chanced to hear two different married persons, both of whose wedded lives had been beautiful from the beginning, relate that not until a year or more after marriage did they awake to the full blessedness of married life. So it is with the religious experience of these persons we are studying."[109]

[pg 207]
We shall erelong hear still more remarkable illustrations of subconsciously maturing processes eventuating in results of which we suddenly grow conscious. Sir William Hamilton and Professor Laycock of Edinburgh were among the first to call attention to this class of effects; but Dr. Carpenter first, unless I am mistaken, introduced the term "unconscious cerebration," which has since then been a popular phrase of explanation. The facts are now known to us far more extensively than he could know them, and the adjective "unconscious," being for many of them almost certainly a misnomer, is better replaced by the vaguer term "subconscious" or "subliminal."

Of the volitional type of conversion it would be easy to give examples,[110] but they are as a rule less interesting [pg 208] than those of the self-surrender type, in which the subconscious effects are more abundant and often startling. I will therefore hurry to the latter, the more so because the difference between the two types is after all not radical. Even in the most voluntarily built-up sort of regeneration there are passages of partial self-surrender interposed; and in the great majority of all cases, when the will has done its uttermost towards bringing one close to the complete unification aspired after, it seems that the very last step must be left to other forces and performed without the help of its activity. In other words, self-surrender becomes then indispensable. "The personal will," says Dr. Starbuck, "must be given up. In many cases relief persistently refuses to come until the person ceases to resist, or to make an effort in the direction he desires to go."

> "I had said I would not give up; but when my will was broken, it was all over," writes one of Starbuck's correspondents.—Another says: "I simply said: 'Lord, I have done all I can; I leave the whole matter with Thee;' and immediately there came to me a great peace."—Another: "All at once it occurred to me that I might be saved, too, if I would stop trying to do it all myself, and follow Jesus: somehow I lost my load."—Another: "I finally ceased to resist, and gave myself up, though it was a hard struggle. Gradually the feeling came over me that I had done my part, and God was willing to do his."[111]—"Lord, Thy will be done; damn or save!" cries John Nelson,[112] exhausted with the anxious struggle to escape damnation; and at that moment his soul was filled with peace.

[pg 209]
Dr. Starbuck gives an interesting, and it seems to me a true, account—so far as conceptions so schematic can claim truth at all—of the reasons why self-surrender at the last moment should be so indispensable. To begin with, there are two things in the mind of the candidate for conversion: first, the present incompleteness or wrongness, the "sin" which he is eager to escape from; and, second, the positive ideal which he longs to compass. Now with most of us the sense of our present wrongness is a far more distinct piece of our consciousness than is the imagination of any positive ideal we can aim at. In a majority of cases, indeed, the "sin" almost exclusively engrosses the attention, so that conversion is *"a process of struggling away from sin rather than of striving towards righteousness."*[113] A man's conscious wit and will, so far as they strain towards the ideal, are aiming at something only dimly and inaccurately imagined. Yet all the while the forces of mere organic ripening within him are going on towards their own prefigured result, and his conscious strainings are letting loose subconscious allies behind the scenes, which in their way work towards rearrangement; and the

rearrangement towards which all these deeper forces tend is pretty surely definite, and definitely different from what he consciously conceives and determines. It may consequently be actually interfered with (*jammed*, as it were, like the lost word when we seek too energetically to recall it), by his voluntary efforts slanting from the true direction.

Starbuck seems to put his finger on the root of the matter when he says that to exercise the personal will is still to live in the region where the imperfect self is the thing most emphasized. Where, on the contrary, the subconscious forces take the lead, it is more probably [pg 210] the better self *in posse* which directs the operation. Instead of being clumsily and vaguely aimed at from without, it is then itself the organizing centre. What then must the person do? "He must relax," says Dr. Starbuck,—"that is, he must fall back on the larger Power that makes for righteousness, which has been welling up in his own being, and let it finish in its own way the work it has begun.... The act of yielding, in this point of view, is giving one's self over to the new life, making it the centre of a new personality, and living, from within, the truth of it which had before been viewed objectively."[114]

"Man's extremity is God's opportunity" is the theological way of putting this fact of the need of self-surrender; whilst the physiological way of stating it would be, "Let one do all in one's power, and one's nervous system will do the rest." Both statements acknowledge the same fact.[115]

To state it in terms of our own symbolism: When the new centre of personal energy has been subconsciously incubated so long as to be just ready to open into flower, "hands off" is the only word for us, it must burst forth unaided!

We have used the vague and abstract language of psychology. But since, in any terms, the crisis described is the throwing of our conscious selves upon the mercy of powers which, whatever they may be, are more ideal than we are actually, and make for our redemption, you see why self-surrender has been and always must be regarded as the vital turning-point of the religious life, so far as the religious life is spiritual and no affair of outer works and ritual and sacraments. One may say that the whole development of Christianity in inwardness [pg 211] has consisted in little more than the greater and greater emphasis attached to this crisis of self-surrender. From

Catholicism to Lutheranism, and then to Calvinism; from that to Wesleyanism; and from this, outside of technical Christianity altogether, to pure "liberalism" or transcendental idealism, whether or not of the mind-cure type, taking in the mediæval mystics, the quietists, the pietists, and quakers by the way, we can trace the stages of progress towards the idea of an immediate spiritual help, experienced by the individual in his forlornness and standing in no essential need of doctrinal apparatus or propitiatory machinery.

Psychology and religion are thus in perfect harmony up to this point, since both admit that there are forces seemingly outside of the conscious individual that bring redemption to his life. Nevertheless psychology, defining these forces as "subconscious," and speaking of their effects as due to "incubation," or "cerebration," implies that they do not transcend the individual's personality; and herein she diverges from Christian theology, which insists that they are direct supernatural operations of the Deity. I propose to you that we do not yet consider this divergence final, but leave the question for a while in abeyance—continued inquiry may enable us to get rid of some of the apparent discord.

Revert, then, for a moment more to the psychology of self-surrender.

When you find a man living on the ragged edge of his consciousness, pent in to his sin and want and incompleteness, and consequently inconsolable, and then simply tell him that all is well with him, that he must stop his worry, break with his discontent, and give up his anxiety, you seem to him to come with pure absurdities. The [pg 212] only positive consciousness he has tells him that all is *not* well, and the better way you offer sounds simply as if you proposed to him to assert cold-blooded falsehoods. "The will to believe" cannot be stretched as far as that. We can make ourselves more faithful to a belief of which we have the rudiments, but we cannot create a belief out of whole cloth when our perception actively assures us of its opposite. The better mind proposed to us comes in that case in the form of a pure negation of the only mind we have, and we cannot actively will a pure negation.

There are only two ways in which it is possible to get rid of anger, worry, fear, despair, or other undesirable affections. One is that an opposite affection should overpoweringly break over us, and the other is by getting so exhausted with the struggle that we have to stop,—so we drop down, give up, and *don't care* any longer. Our emotional brain-centres strike work, and we lapse into a temporary apathy. Now there is documentary proof that this state of temporary exhaustion not infrequently forms part of the conversion crisis. So long as the egoistic worry of the sick soul guards the door, the expansive confidence of the soul of faith gains no presence. But let the former faint away, even but for a moment, and the latter can profit by the opportunity, and, having once acquired possession, may retain it. Carlyle's Teufelsdröckh passes from the everlasting No to the everlasting Yes through a "Centre of Indifference."

Let me give you a good illustration of this feature in the conversion process. That genuine saint, David Brainerd, describes his own crisis in the following words:—

> "One morning, while I was walking in a solitary place as usual, I at once saw that all my contrivances and projects to effect or procure deliverance and salvation for myself were utterly in [pg 213]vain; I was brought quite to a stand, as finding myself totally lost. I saw that it was forever impossible for me to do anything towards helping or delivering myself, that I had made all the pleas I ever could have made to all eternity; and that all my pleas were vain, for I saw that self-interest had led me to pray, and that I had never once prayed from any respect to the glory of God. I saw that there was no necessary connection between my prayers and the bestowment of divine mercy; that they laid not the least obligation upon God to bestow his grace upon me; and that there was no more virtue or goodness in them than there would be in my paddling with my hand in the water. I saw that I had been heaping up my devotions before God, fasting, praying, etc., pretending, and indeed really thinking sometimes that I was aiming at the glory of God; whereas I never once truly intended it, but only my own happiness. I saw that as I had never done anything for God, I had no claim on anything from him but perdition, on account of my hypocrisy and mockery. When I saw evidently that I had regard to nothing but self-interest, then my duties appeared a vile mockery and a continual course of lies, for the whole was nothing but self-worship, and an horrid abuse of God.
>
> "I continued, as I remember, in this state of mind, from Friday morning till the Sabbath evening following (July 12, 1739), when I was walking again in the same solitary place. Here, in a mournful melancholy state *I was attempting to pray; but found no heart to engage in that or any other duty;*

my former concern, exercise, and religious affections were now gone. I thought that the Spirit of God had quite left me; but still was not distressed; yet disconsolate, as if there was nothing in heaven or earth could make me happy. Having been thus endeavoring to pray—though, as I thought, very stupid and senseless—for near half an hour; then, as I was walking in a thick grove, unspeakable glory seemed to open to the apprehension of my soul. I do not mean any external brightness, nor any imagination of a body of light, but it was a new inward apprehension or view that I had of God, such as I never had before, nor anything which had the least resemblance to it. I had no particular apprehension of any one person in [pg 214]the Trinity, either the Father, the Son, or the Holy Ghost; but it appeared to be Divine glory. My soul rejoiced with joy unspeakable, to see such a God, such a glorious Divine Being; and I was inwardly pleased and satisfied that he should be God over all for ever and ever. My soul was so captivated and delighted with the excellency of God that I was even swallowed up in him; at least to that degree that I had no thought about my own salvation, and scarce reflected that there was such a creature as myself. I continued in this state of inward joy, peace, and astonishing, till near dark without any sensible abatement; and then began to think and examine what I had seen; and felt sweetly composed in my mind all the evening following. I felt myself in a new world, and everything about me appeared with a different aspect from what it was wont to do. At this time, the way of salvation opened to me with such infinite wisdom, suitableness, and excellency, that I wondered I should ever think of any other way of salvation; was amazed that I had not dropped my own contrivances, and complied with this lovely, blessed, and excellent way before. If I could have been saved by my own duties or any other way that I had formerly contrived, my whole soul would now have refused it. I wondered that all the world did not see and comply with this way of salvation, entirely by the righteousness of Christ."[116]

I have italicized the passage which records the exhaustion of the anxious emotion hitherto habitual. In a large proportion, perhaps the majority, of reports, the writers speak as if the exhaustion of the lower and the entrance of the higher emotion were simultaneous,[117] yet [pg 215] often again they speak as if the higher actively drove the lower out. This is undoubtedly true in a great many instances, as we shall presently see. But often there seems little doubt that both conditions—subconscious ripening of the one affection and exhaustion of the other—must simultaneously have conspired, in order to produce the result.

> T. W. B., a convert of Nettleton's, being brought to an acute paroxysm of conviction of sin, ate nothing all day, locked himself in his room in the evening in complete despair, crying aloud, "How long, O Lord, how long?"
> "After repeating this and similar language," he says, "several times, *I*

seemed to sink away into a state of insensibility. When I came to myself again I was on my knees, praying not for myself but for others. I felt submission to the will of God, willing that he should do with me as should seem good in his sight. My concern seemed all lost in concern for others."[118]

Our great American revivalist Finney writes: "I said to myself: 'What is this? I must have grieved the Holy Ghost entirely away. I have lost all my conviction. I have not a particle of concern about my soul; and it must be that the Spirit has left me.' 'Why!' thought I, 'I never was so far from being concerned about my own salvation in my life.'... I tried to recall my convictions, to get back again the load of sin under which I had been laboring. I tried in vain to make myself anxious. I was so quiet and peaceful that I tried to feel concerned about that, lest it should be the result of my having grieved the Spirit away."[119]

But beyond all question there are persons in whom, quite independently of any exhaustion in the Subject's capacity for feeling, or even in the absence of any acute [pg 216] previous feeling, the higher condition, having reached the due degree of energy, bursts through all barriers and sweeps in like a sudden flood. These are the most striking and memorable cases, the cases of instantaneous conversion to which the conception of divine grace has been most peculiarly attached. I have given one of them at length—the case of Mr. Bradley. But I had better reserve the other cases and my comments on the rest of the subject for the following lecture.

[pg 217]

Lecture X. Conversion—Concluded.

In this lecture we have to finish the subject of Conversion, considering at first those striking instantaneous instances of which Saint Paul's is the most eminent, and in which, often amid tremendous emotional excitement or perturbation of the senses, a complete division is established in the twinkling of an eye between the old life and the new. Conversion of this type is an important phase of religious experience, owing to the part which it has played in Protestant theology, and it behooves us to study it conscientiously on that account.

I think I had better cite two or three of these cases before proceeding to a more generalized account. One must know concrete instances first; for, as Professor Agassiz used to say, one can see no farther into a generalization than just so far as one's previous acquaintance with particulars enables one to take it in. I will go back, then, to the case of our friend Henry Alline, and quote his report of the 26th of March, 1775, on which his poor divided mind became unified for good.

> "As I was about sunset wandering in the fields lamenting my miserable lost and undone condition, and almost ready to sink under my burden, I thought I was in such a miserable case as never any man was before. I returned to the house, and when I got to the door, just as I was stepping off the threshold, the following impressions came into my mind like a powerful but small still voice. You have been seeking, praying, [pg 218]reforming, laboring, reading, hearing, and meditating, and what have you done by it towards your salvation? Are you any nearer to conversion now than when you first began? Are you any more prepared for heaven, or fitter to appear before the impartial bar of God, than when you first began to seek?
>
> "It brought such conviction on me that I was obliged to say that I did not think I was one step nearer than at first, but as much condemned, as much

exposed, and as miserable as before. I cried out within myself, O Lord God, I am lost, and if thou, O Lord, dost not find out some new way, I know nothing of, I shall never be saved, for the ways and methods I have prescribed to myself have all failed me, and I am willing they should fail. O Lord, have mercy! O Lord, have mercy!

"These discoveries continued until I went into the house and sat down. After I sat down, being all in confusion, like a drowning man that was just giving up to sink, and almost in an agony, I turned very suddenly round in my chair, and seeing part of an old Bible lying in one of the chairs, I caught hold of it in great haste; and opening it without any premeditation, cast my eyes on the 38th Psalm, which was the first time I ever saw the word of God: it took hold of me with such power that it seemed to go through my whole soul, so that it seemed as if God was praying in, with, and for me. About this time my father called the family to attend prayers; I attended, but paid no regard to what he said in his prayer, but continued praying in those words of the Psalm. Oh, help me, help me! cried I, thou Redeemer of souls, and save me, or I am gone forever; thou canst this night, if thou pleasest, with one drop of thy blood atone for my sins, and appease the wrath of an angry God. At that instant of time when I gave all up to him to do with me as he pleased, and was willing that God should rule over me at his pleasure, redeeming love broke into my soul with repeated scriptures, with such power that my whole soul seemed to be melted down with love; the burden of guilt and condemnation was gone, darkness was expelled, my heart humbled and filled with gratitude, and my whole soul, that was a few minutes ago groaning under mountains of death, and crying to an unknown God for help, was now filled with [pg 219]immortal love, soaring on the wings of faith, freed from the chains of death and darkness, and crying out, My Lord and my God; thou art my rock and my fortress, my shield and my high tower, my life, my joy, my present and my everlasting portion. Looking up, I thought I saw that same light [he had on more than one previous occasion seen subjectively a bright blaze of light], though it appeared different; and as soon as I saw it, the design was opened to me, according to his promise, and I was obliged to cry out: Enough, enough, O blessed God! The work of conversion, the change, and the manifestations of it are no more disputable than that light which I see, or anything that ever I saw.

"In the midst of all my joys, in less than half an hour after my soul was set at liberty, the Lord discovered to me my labor in the ministry and call to preach the gospel. I cried out, Amen, Lord, I'll go; send me, send me. I spent the greatest part of the night in ecstasies of joy, praising and adoring the Ancient of Days for his free and unbounded grace. After I had been so long in this transport and heavenly frame that my nature seemed to require sleep, I thought to close my eyes for a few moments; then the devil stepped in, and told me that if I went to sleep, I should lose it all, and when I should awake in the morning I would find it to be nothing but a fancy and delusion. I immediately cried out, O Lord God, if I am deceived, undeceive me.

> "I then closed my eyes for a few minutes, and seemed to be refreshed with sleep; and when I awoke, the first inquiry was, Where is my God? And in an instant of time, my soul seemed awake in and with God, and surrounded by the arms of everlasting love. About sunrise I arose with joy to relate to my parents what God had done for my soul, and declared to them the miracle of God's unbounded grace. I took a Bible to show them the words that were impressed by God on my soul the evening before; but when I came to open the Bible, it appeared all new to me.
>
> "I so longed to be useful in the cause of Christ, in preaching the gospel, that it seemed as if I could not rest any longer, but go I must and tell the wonders of redeeming love. I lost all taste for carnal pleasures, and carnal company, and was enabled to forsake them."[120]

Young Mr. Alline, after the briefest of delays, and with no book-learning but his Bible, and no teaching save that of his own experience, became a Christian minister, and thenceforward his life was fit to rank, for its austerity and single-mindedness, with that of the most devoted saints. But happy as he became in his strenuous way, he never got his taste for even the most innocent carnal pleasures back. We must class him, like Bunyan and Tolstoy, amongst those upon whose soul the iron of melancholy left a permanent imprint. His redemption was into another universe than this mere natural world, and life remained for him a sad and patient trial. Years later we can find him making such an entry as this in his diary: "On Wednesday the 12th I preached at a wedding, and had the happiness thereby to be the means of excluding carnal mirth."

The next case I will give is that of a correspondent of Professor Leuba, printed in the latter's article, already cited, in vol. vi. of the American Journal of Psychology. This subject was an Oxford graduate, the son of a clergyman, and the story resembles in many points the classic case of Colonel Gardiner, which everybody may be supposed to know. Here it is, somewhat abridged:—

> "Between the period of leaving Oxford and my conversion I never darkened the door of my father's church, although I lived with him for eight years, making what money I wanted by journalism, and spending it in high carousal with any one who would sit with me and drink it away. So I lived, sometimes drunk for a week together, and then a terrible repentance, and would not touch a drop for a whole month.

[pg 221]

"In all this period, that is, up to thirty-three years of age, I never had a desire to reform on religious grounds. But all my pangs were due to some terrible remorse I used to feel after a heavy carousal, the remorse taking the shape of regret after my folly in wasting my life in such a way—a man of superior talents and education. This terrible remorse turned me gray in one night, and whenever it came upon me I was perceptibly grayer the next morning. What I suffered in this way is beyond the expression of words. It was hell-fire in all its most dreadful tortures. Often did I vow that if I got over 'this time' I would reform. Alas, in about three days I fully recovered, and was as happy as ever. So it went on for years, but, with a physique like a rhinoceros, I always recovered, and as long as I let drink alone, no man was as capable of enjoying life as I was.

"I was converted in my own bedroom in my father's rectory house at precisely three o'clock in the afternoon of a hot July day (July 13, 1886). I was in perfect health, having been off from the drink for nearly a month. I was in no way troubled about my soul. In fact, God was not in my thoughts that day. A young lady friend sent me a copy of Professor Drummond's Natural Law in the Spiritual World, asking me my opinion of it as a literary work only. Being proud of my critical talents and wishing to enhance myself in my new friend's esteem, I took the book to my bedroom for quiet, intending to give it a thorough study, and then write her what I thought of it. It was here that God met me face to face, and I shall never forget the meeting. 'He that hath the Son hath life eternal, he that hath not the Son hath not life.' I had read this scores of times before, but this made all the difference. I was now in God's presence and my attention was absolutely 'soldered' on to this verse, and I was not allowed to proceed with the book till I had fairly considered what these words really involved. Only then was I allowed to proceed, feeling all the while that there was another being in my bedroom, though not seen by me. The stillness was very marvelous, and I felt supremely happy. It was most unquestionably shown me, in one second of time, that I had never touched the Eternal: and [pg 222] that if I died then, I must inevitably be lost. I was undone. I knew it as well as I now know I am saved. The Spirit of God showed it me in ineffable love; there was no terror in it; I felt God's love so powerfully upon me that only a mighty sorrow crept over me that I had lost all through my own folly; and what was I to do? What could I do? I did not repent even; God never asked me to repent. All I felt was 'I am undone,' and God cannot help it, although he loves me. No fault on the part of the Almighty. All the time I was supremely happy: I felt like a little child before his father. I had done wrong, but my Father did not scold me, but loved me most wondrously. Still my doom was sealed. I was lost to a certainty, and being naturally of a brave disposition I did not quail under it, but deep sorrow for the past, mixed with regret for what I had lost, took hold upon me, and my soul thrilled within me to think it was all over. Then there crept in upon me so gently, so lovingly, so unmistakably, a way of escape, and what was it after all? The old, old story over again, told in the simplest way: 'There is no name under heaven whereby ye can be saved except that of the Lord Jesus Christ.' No words were spoken to me; my soul seemed to see my Saviour in the spirit, and from that hour to this, nearly nine years now, there has never been in my life one doubt that the Lord Jesus Christ and God the Father both worked upon me that afternoon in July, both differently, and both in the most perfect love conceivable, and I rejoiced there and then in a conversion so astounding that the whole village heard of it in less than twenty-four hours.

"But a time of trouble was yet to come. The day after my conversion I went into the hay-field to lend a hand with the harvest, and not having made any promise to God to abstain or drink in moderation only, I took too much and came home drunk. My poor sister was heart-broken; and I felt ashamed of myself and got to my bedroom at once, where she followed me, weeping copiously. She said I had been converted and fallen away instantly. But although I was quite full of drink (not muddled, however), I knew that God's work begun in me was not going to be wasted. About midday I [pg 223]made on my knees the first prayer before God for twenty years. I did not ask to be forgiven; I felt that was no good, for I would be sure to fall again. Well, what did I do? I committed myself to him in the profoundest belief that my individuality was going to be destroyed, that he would take all from me, and I was willing. In such a surrender lies the secret of a holy life. From that hour drink has had no terrors for me: I never touch it, never want it. The same thing occurred with my pipe: after being a regular smoker from my twelfth year the desire for it went at once, and has never returned. So with every known sin, the deliverance in each case being permanent and complete. I have had no temptation since conversion, God seemingly having shut out Satan from that course with me. He gets a free hand in other ways, but never on sins of the flesh. Since I gave up to God all ownership in my own life, he has guided me in a thousand ways, and has opened my path in a way almost incredible to those who do not enjoy the blessing of a truly surrendered life."

So much for our graduate of Oxford, in whom you notice the complete abolition of an ancient appetite as one of the conversion's fruits.

The most curious record of sudden conversion with which I am acquainted is that of M. Alphonse Ratisbonne, a freethinking French Jew, to Catholicism, at Rome in 1842. In a letter to a clerical friend, written a few months later, the convert gives a palpitating account of the circumstances.[121] The predisposing conditions appear to have been slight. He had an elder brother who had been converted and was a Catholic priest. He was himself irreligious, and nourished an antipathy to the apostate brother and generally to his "cloth." Finding himself at Rome in his twenty-ninth year, he fell in with a [pg 224] French gentleman who tried to make a proselyte of him, but who succeeded no farther after two or three conversations than to get him to hang (half jocosely) a religious medal round his neck, and to accept and read a copy of a short prayer to the Virgin. M. Ratisbonne represents his own part in the conversations as having been of a light and chaffing order; but he notes the fact that for some days he was unable to banish the words of the prayer from his mind, and that the night before the crisis he had a sort of nightmare, in the imagery of which a black cross with no Christ upon it figured. Nevertheless, until noon of the next day he was free in mind and spent the time in trivial conversations. I now give his own words.

> "If at this time any one had accosted me, saying: 'Alphonse, in a quarter of an hour you shall be adoring Jesus Christ as your God and Saviour; you shall lie prostrate with your face upon the ground in a humble church; you shall be smiting your breast at the foot of a priest; you shall pass the carnival in a college of Jesuits to prepare yourself to receive baptism, ready to give your life for the Catholic faith; you shall renounce the world and its pomps and pleasures; renounce your fortune, your hopes, and if need be, your betrothed; the affections of your family, the esteem of your friends, and your attachment to the Jewish people; you shall have no other aspiration than to follow Christ and bear his cross till death;'—if, I say, a prophet had come to me with such a prediction, I should have judged that only one person could be more mad than he,—whosoever, namely, might believe in the possibility of such senseless folly becoming true. And yet that folly is at present my only wisdom, my sole happiness.
>
> "Coming out of the café I met the carriage of Monsieur B. [the proselyting friend]. He stopped and invited me in for a drive, but first asked me to wait for a few minutes whilst he attended to some duty at the church of San Andrea delle Fratte. Instead of waiting in the carriage, I entered the church myself to look at it. The church of San Andrea was poor, small, and [pg 225]empty; I believe that I found myself there almost alone. No work of art attracted my attention; and I passed my eyes mechanically over its interior without being arrested by any particular thought. I can only remember an entirely black dog which went trotting and turning before me as I mused. In an instant the dog had disappeared, the whole church had vanished, I no longer saw anything, ... or more truly I saw, O my God, one thing alone.
>
> "Heavens, how can I speak of it? Oh no! human words cannot attain to expressing the inexpressible. Any description, however sublime it might be, could be but a profanation of the unspeakable truth.
>
> "I was there prostrate on the ground, bathed in my tears, with my heart beside itself, when M. B. called me back to life. I could not reply to the questions which followed from him one upon the other. But finally I took the medal which I had on my breast, and with all the effusion of my soul I kissed the

image of the Virgin, radiant with grace, which it bore. Oh, indeed, it was She! It was indeed She! [What he had seen had been a vision of the Virgin.]

"I did not know where I was: I did not know whether I was Alphonse or another. I only felt myself changed and believed myself another me; I looked for myself in myself and did not find myself. In the bottom of my soul I felt an explosion of the most ardent joy; I could not speak; I had no wish to reveal what had happened. But I felt something solemn and sacred within me which made me ask for a priest. I was led to one; and there, alone, after he had given me the positive order, I spoke as best I could, kneeling, and with my heart still trembling. I could give no account to myself of the truth of which I had acquired a knowledge and a faith. All that I can say is that in an instant the bandage had fallen from my eyes; and not one bandage only, but the whole manifold of bandages in which I had been brought up. One after another they rapidly disappeared, even as the mud and ice disappear under the rays of the burning sun.

"I came out as from a sepulchre, from an abyss of darkness; and I was living, perfectly living. But I wept, for at the bottom [pg 226] of that gulf I saw the extreme of misery from which I had been saved by an infinite mercy; and I shuddered at the sight of my iniquities, stupefied, melted, overwhelmed with wonder and with gratitude. You may ask me how I came to this new insight, for truly I had never opened a book of religion nor even read a single page of the Bible, and the dogma of original sin is either entirely denied or forgotten by the Hebrews of to-day, so that I had thought so little about it that I doubt whether I ever knew its name. But how came I, then, to this perception of it? I can answer nothing save this, that on entering that church I was in darkness altogether, and on coming out of it I saw the fullness of the light. I can explain the change no better than by the simile of a profound sleep or the analogy of one born blind who should suddenly open his eyes to the day. He sees, but cannot define the light which bathes him and by means of which he sees the objects which excite his wonder. If we cannot explain physical light, how can we explain the light which is the truth itself? And I think I remain within the limits of veracity when I say that without having any knowledge of the letter of religious doctrine, I now intuitively perceived its sense and spirit. Better than if I saw them, I *felt* those hidden things; I felt them by the inexplicable effects they produced in me. It all happened in my interior mind; and those impressions, more rapid than thought, shook my soul, revolved and turned it, as it were, in another direction, towards other aims, by other paths. I express myself badly. But do you wish, Lord, that I should inclose in poor and barren words sentiments which the heart alone can understand?"

I might multiply cases almost indefinitely, but these will suffice to show you how real, definite, and memorable an event a sudden conversion may be to him who has the experience. Throughout the height of it he undoubtedly seems to himself a passive spectator or undergoer of an astounding process performed upon him from above. There is too much evidence of this for any doubt of it to be possible. Theology, combining this fact with the doctrines of election and grace, has concluded that [pg 227] the spirit of God is with us at these dramatic moments in a peculiarly miraculous way, unlike what happens at any other juncture of our lives. At that moment, it believes, an absolutely new nature is breathed into us, and we become partakers of the very substance of the Deity.

That the conversion should be instantaneous seems called for on this view, and the Moravian Protestants appear to have been the first to see this logical consequence. The Methodists soon followed suit, practically if not dogmatically, and a short time ere his death, John Wesley wrote:—

> "In London alone I found 652 members of our Society who were exceeding clear in their experience, and whose testimony I could see no reason to doubt. And every one of these (without a single exception) has declared that his deliverance from sin was instantaneous; that the change was wrought in a moment. Had half of these, or one third, or one in twenty, declared it was *gradually* wrought in *them*, I should have believed this, with regard to *them*, and thought that *some* were gradually sanctified and some instantaneously. But as I have not found, in so long a space of time, a single person speaking thus, I cannot but believe that sanctification is commonly, if not always, an instantaneous work." Tyerman's Life of Wesley, i. 463.

All this while the more usual sects of Protestantism have set no such store by instantaneous conversion. For them as for the Catholic Church, Christ's blood, the sacraments, and the individual's ordinary religious duties are practically supposed to suffice to his salvation, even though no acute crisis of self-despair and surrender followed by relief should be experienced. For Methodism, on the contrary, unless there have been a crisis of this sort, salvation is only offered, not effectively received, and Christ's sacrifice in so far forth is incomplete. Methodism surely here follows, if not the healthier-minded, yet on [pg 228] the whole the profounder spiritual instinct. The individual models which it has set up as typical and worthy of imitation are not only the more interesting dramatically, but psychologically they have been the more complete.

In the fully evolved Revivalism of Great Britain and America we have, so to speak, the codified and stereotyped procedure to which this way of thinking has led. In spite of the unquestionable fact that saints of the once-born type exist, that there may be a gradual growth in holiness without a cataclysm; in spite of the obvious leakage (as one may say) of much mere natural goodness into the scheme of salvation; revivalism has always assumed that only its own type of religious experience can be perfect; you must first be nailed on the cross of natural despair and agony, and then in the twinkling of an eye be miraculously released.

It is natural that those who personally have traversed such an experience should carry away a feeling of its being a miracle rather than a natural process. Voices are often heard, lights seen, or visions witnessed; automatic motor phenomena occur; and it always seems, after the surrender of the personal will, as if an extraneous higher power had flooded in and taken possession. Moreover the sense of renovation, safety, cleanness, rightness, can be so marvelous and jubilant as well to warrant one's belief in a radically new substantial nature.

> "Conversion," writes the New England Puritan, Joseph Alleine, "is not the putting in a patch of holiness; but with the true convert holiness is woven into all his powers, principles, and practice. The sincere Christian is quite a new fabric, from the foundation to the top-stone. He is a new man, a new creature."

> And Jonathan Edwards says in the same strain: "Those gracious influences which are the effects of the Spirit of God [pg 229]are altogether supernatural—are quite different from anything that unregenerate men experience. They are what no improvement, or composition of natural qualifications or principles will ever produce; because they not only differ from what is natural, and from everything that natural men experience in degree and circumstances, but also in kind, and are of a nature far more excellent. From hence it follows that in gracious affections there are [also] new perceptions and sensations entirely different in their nature and kind from anything experienced by the [same] saints before they were sanctified.... The conceptions which the saints have of the loveliness of God, and that kind of delight which they experience in it, are quite peculiar, and entirely different from anything which a natural man can possess, or of which he can form any proper notion."

And that such a glorious transformation as this ought of necessity to be preceded by despair is shown by Edwards in another passage.

> "Surely it cannot be unreasonable," he says, "that before God delivers us from a state of sin and liability to everlasting woe, he should give us some considerable sense of the evil from which he delivers us, in order that we may know and feel the importance of salvation, and be enabled to appreciate the value of what God is pleased to do for us. As those who are saved are successively in two extremely different states—first in a state of condemnation and then in a state of justification and blessedness—and as God, in the salvation of men, deals with them as rational and intelligent creatures, it appears agreeable to this wisdom, that those who are saved should be made sensible of their Being, in those two different states. In the first place, that they should be made sensible of their state of condemnation; and afterwards, of their state of deliverance and happiness."

Such quotations express sufficiently well for our purpose the doctrinal interpretation of these changes. Whatever part suggestion and imitation may have played in producing them in men and women in excited assemblies, [pg 230] they have at any rate been in countless individual instances an original and unborrowed experience. Were we writing the story of the mind from the purely natural-history point of view, with no religious interest whatever, we should still have to write down man's liability to sudden and complete conversion as one of his most curious peculiarities.

What, now, must we ourselves think of this question? Is an instantaneous conversion a miracle in which God is present as he is present in no change of heart less strikingly abrupt? Are there two classes of human beings, even among the apparently regenerate, of which the one class really partakes of Christ's nature while the other merely seems to do so? Or, on the contrary, may the whole phenomenon of regeneration, even in these startling instantaneous examples, possibly be a strictly natural process, divine in its fruits, of course, but in one case more and in another less so, and neither more nor less divine in its mere causation and mechanism than any other process, high or low, of man's interior life?

Before proceeding to answer this question, I must ask you to listen to some more psychological remarks. At our last lecture, I explained the shifting of men's centres of personal energy within them and the lighting up of new crises of emotion. I explained the phenomena as partly due to explicitly conscious processes of thought and will, but as due largely also to the subconscious incubation and maturing of motives deposited by the experiences of life. When ripe, the results hatch out, or burst into flower. I have now to speak of the subconscious region, in which such processes of flowering may occur, in a somewhat less vague way. I only regret that my limits of time here force me to be so short.

[pg 231]
The expression "field of consciousness" has but recently come into vogue in the psychology books. Until quite lately the unit of mental life which figured most was the single "idea" supposed to be a definitely outlined thing. But at present psychologists are tending, first, to admit that the actual unit is more probably the total mental state, the entire wave of consciousness or field of objects present to the thought at any time; and, second, to see that it is impossible to outline this wave, this field, with any definiteness.

As our mental fields succeed one another, each has its centre of interest, around which the objects of which we are less and less attentively conscious fade to a margin so faint that its limits are unassignable. Some fields are narrow fields and some are wide fields. Usually when we have a wide field we rejoice, for we then see masses of truth together, and often get glimpses of relations which we divine rather than see, for they shoot beyond the field into still remoter regions of objectivity, regions which we seem rather to be about to perceive than to perceive actually. At other times, of drowsiness, illness, or fatigue, our fields may narrow almost to a point, and we find ourselves correspondingly oppressed and contracted.

Different individuals present constitutional differences in this matter of width of field. Your great organizing geniuses are men with habitually vast fields of mental vision, in which a whole programme of future operations will appear dotted out at once, the rays shooting far ahead into definite directions of advance. In common people there is never this magnificent inclusive view of a topic. They stumble along, feeling their way, as it were, from point to point, and often stop entirely. In certain diseased conditions consciousness is a mere spark, without memory of the past or thought of the future, and with the [pg 232] present narrowed down to some one simple emotion or sensation of the body.

The important fact which this "field" formula commemorates is the indetermination of the margin. Inattentively realized as is the matter which the margin contains, it is nevertheless there, and helps both to guide our behavior and to determine the next movement of our attention. It lies around us like a "magnetic field," inside of which our centre of energy turns like a compass-needle, as the present phase of consciousness alters into its successor. Our whole past store of memories floats beyond this margin, ready at a touch to come in; and the entire mass of residual powers, impulses, and knowledges that constitute our empirical self stretches continuously beyond it. So vaguely drawn are the outlines between what is actual and what is only potential at any moment of our conscious life, that it is always hard to say of certain mental elements whether we are conscious of them or not.

The ordinary psychology, admitting fully the difficulty of tracing the marginal outline, has nevertheless taken for granted, first, that all the consciousness the person now has, be the same focal or marginal, inattentive or attentive, is there in the "field" of the moment, all dim and impossible to assign as the latter's outline may be; and, second, that what is absolutely extra-marginal is absolutely non-existent, and cannot be a fact of consciousness at all.

And having reached this point, I must now ask you to recall what I said in my last lecture about the subconscious life. I said, as you may recollect, that those who first laid stress upon these phenomena could not know the facts as we now know them. My first duty now is to tell you what I meant by such a statement.

[pg 233]
I cannot but think that the most important step forward that has occurred in psychology since I have been a student of that science is the discovery, first made in 1886, that, in certain subjects at least, there is not only the

consciousness of the ordinary field, with its usual centre and margin, but an addition thereto in the shape of a set of memories, thoughts, and feelings which are extra-marginal and outside of the primary consciousness altogether, but yet must be classed as conscious facts of some sort, able to reveal their presence by unmistakable signs. I call this the most important step forward because, unlike the other advances which psychology has made, this discovery has revealed to us an entirely unsuspected peculiarity in the constitution of human nature. No other step forward which psychology has made can proffer any such claim as this.

In particular this discovery of a consciousness existing beyond the field, or subliminally as Mr. Myers terms it, casts light on many phenomena of religious biography. That is why I have to advert to it now, although it is naturally impossible for me in this place to give you any account of the evidence on which the admission of such a consciousness is based. You will find it set forth in many recent books, Binet's Alterations of Personality[122] being perhaps as good a one as any to recommend.

The human material on which the demonstration has been made has so far been rather limited and, in part at least, eccentric, consisting of unusually suggestible hypnotic subjects, and of hysteric patients. Yet the elementary mechanisms of our life are presumably so uniform that what is shown to be true in a marked degree of some persons is probably true in some degree of all, and may in a few be true in an extraordinarily high degree.

[pg 234]
The most important consequence of having a strongly developed ultra-marginal life of this sort is that one's ordinary fields of consciousness are liable to incursions from it of which the subject does not guess the source, and which, therefore, take for him the form of unaccountable impulses to act, or inhibitions of action, of obsessive ideas, or even of hallucinations of sight or hearing. The impulses may take the direction of automatic speech or writing, the meaning of which the subject himself may not understand even while he utters it; and generalizing this phenomenon, Mr. Myers has given the name of *automatism*, sensory or motor, emotional or intellectual, to this whole sphere of effects, due to "uprushes" into the ordinary consciousness of energies originating in the subliminal parts of the mind.

The simplest instance of an automatism is the phenomenon of post-hypnotic suggestion, so-called. You give to a hypnotized subject, adequately susceptible, an order to perform some designated act—usual or eccentric, it makes no difference—after he wakes from his hypnotic sleep. Punctually, when the signal comes or the time elapses upon which you have told him that the act must ensue, he performs it;—but in so doing he has no recollection of your suggestion, and he always trumps up an improvised pretext for his behavior if the act be of an eccentric kind. It may even be suggested to a subject to have a vision or to hear a voice at a certain interval after waking, and when the time comes the vision is seen or the voice heard, with no inkling on the subject's part of its source. In the wonderful explorations by Binet, Janet, Breuer, Freud, Mason, Prince, and others, of the subliminal consciousness of patients with hysteria, we have revealed to us whole systems of underground life, in the shape of memories of a painful sort which lead a [pg 235] parasitic existence, buried outside of the primary fields of consciousness, and making irruptions thereinto with hallucinations, pains, convulsions, paralyses of feeling and of motion, and the whole procession of symptoms of hysteric disease of body and of mind. Alter or abolish by suggestion these subconscious memories, and the patient immediately gets well. His symptoms were automatisms, in Mr. Myers's sense of the word. These clinical records sound like fairy-tales when one first reads them, yet it is impossible to doubt their accuracy; and, the path having been once opened by these first observers, similar observations have been made elsewhere. They throw, as I said, a wholly new light upon our natural constitution.

And it seems to me that they make a farther step inevitable. Interpreting the unknown after the analogy of the known, it seems to me that hereafter, wherever we meet with a phenomenon of automatism, be it motor impulses, or obsessive idea, or unaccountable caprice, or delusion, or hallucination, we are bound first of all to make search whether it be not an explosion, into the fields of ordinary consciousness, of ideas elaborated outside of those fields in subliminal regions of the mind. We should look, therefore, for its source in the Subject's subconscious life. In the hypnotic cases, we ourselves create the source by our suggestion, so we know it directly. In the hysteric cases, the lost memories which are the source have to be extracted from the patient's Subliminal by a number of ingenious methods, for an account of which you must consult the books. In other pathological cases, insane delusions, for example, or psychopathic obsessions, the source is yet to seek, but by analogy it also should be in subliminal regions which improvements in our methods may yet conceivably put on tap. There lies the mechanism logically to be assumed,—but the assumption [pg 236] involves a vast program of work to be done in the way of verification, in which the religious experiences of man must play their part.[123]

And thus I return to our own specific subject of instantaneous conversions. You remember the cases of Alline, Bradley, Brainerd, and the graduate of Oxford converted at three in the afternoon. Similar occurrences abound, some with and some without luminous visions, all with a sense of astonished happiness, and of being wrought on by a higher control. If, abstracting altogether from the question of their value for the future spiritual life of the individual, we take them on their psychological [pg 237] side exclusively, so many peculiarities in them remind us of what we find outside of conversion that we are tempted to class them along with other automatisms, and to suspect that what makes the difference between a sudden and a gradual convert is not necessarily the presence of divine miracle in the case of one and of something less divine in that of the other, but rather a simple psychological peculiarity, the fact, namely, that in the recipient of the more instantaneous grace we have one of those Subjects who are in possession of a large region in which mental work can go on subliminally, and from which invasive experiences, abruptly upsetting the equilibrium of the primary consciousness, may come.

I do not see why Methodists need object to such a view. Pray go back and recollect one of the conclusions to which I sought to lead you in my very first lecture. You may remember how I there argued against the notion that the worth of a thing can be decided by its origin. Our spiritual judgment, I said, our opinion of the significance and value of a human event or condition, must be decided on empirical grounds exclusively. If the *fruits for life* of the state of conversion are good, we ought to idealize and venerate it, even though it be a piece of natural psychology; if not, we ought to make short work with it, no matter what supernatural being may have infused it.

Well, how is it with these fruits? If we except the class of preëminent saints of whom the names illumine history, and consider only the usual run of "saints," the shopkeeping church-members and ordinary youthful or middle-aged recipients of instantaneous conversion, whether at revivals or in the spontaneous course of methodistic growth, you will probably agree that no splendor worthy of a wholly supernatural creature fulgurates from [pg 238] them, or sets them apart from the mortals who have never experienced that favor. Were it true that a suddenly converted man as such is, as Edwards says,[124] of an entirely different kind from a natural man, partaking as he does directly of Christ's substance, there surely ought to be some exquisite class-mark, some distinctive radiance attaching even to the lowliest specimen of this genus, to which no one of us could remain insensible, and which, so far as it went, would prove him more excellent than ever the most highly gifted among mere natural men. But notoriously there is no such radiance. Converted men as a class are indistinguishable from natural men; some natural men even excel some converted men in their fruits; and no one ignorant of doctrinal theology could guess by mere every-day inspection of the "accidents" of the two groups of persons before him, that their substance differed as much as divine differs from human substance.

The believers in the non-natural character of sudden conversion have had practically to admit that there is no unmistakable class-mark distinctive of all true converts. The super-normal incidents, such as voices and visions and overpowering impressions of the meaning of suddenly presented scripture texts, the melting emotions and tumultuous affections connected with the crisis of change, may all come by way of nature, or worse still, be counterfeited by Satan. The real witness of the spirit to the second birth is to be found only in the disposition of the genuine child of God, the permanently patient heart, the love of self eradicated. And this, it has to be admitted, [pg 239] is also found in those who pass no crisis, and may even be found outside of Christianity altogether.

Throughout Jonathan Edwards's admirably rich and delicate description of the supernaturally infused condition, in his Treatise on Religious Affections, there is not one decisive trait, not one mark, that unmistakably parts it off from what may possibly be only an exceptionally high degree of natural goodness. In fact, one could hardly read a clearer argument than this book unwittingly offers in favor of the thesis that no chasm exists between the orders of human excellence, but that here as elsewhere, nature shows continuous differences, and generation and regeneration are matters of degree.

All which denial of two objective classes of human beings separated by a chasm must not leave us blind to the extraordinary momentousness of the fact of his conversion to the individual himself who gets converted. There are higher and lower limits of possibility set to each personal life. If a flood but goes above one's head, its absolute elevation becomes a matter of small importance; and when we touch our own upper limit and live in our own highest centre of energy, we may call ourselves saved, no matter how much higher some one else's centre may be. A small man's salvation will always be a great salvation and the greatest of all facts *for him*, and we should remember this when the fruits of our ordinary evangelicism look discouraging. Who knows how much less ideal still the lives of these spiritual grubs and earthworms, these Crumps and Stigginses, might have been, if such poor grace as they have received had never touched them at all?[125]

[pg 240]
If we roughly arrange human beings in classes, each class standing for a grade of spiritual excellence, I believe we shall find natural men and converts both sudden and gradual in all the classes. The forms which regenerative change effects have, then, no general spiritual significance, but only a psychological significance. We have seen how Starbuck's laborious statistical studies tend to assimilate conversion to ordinary spiritual growth. Another American psychologist, Prof. George A. Coe,[126] has analyzed the cases of seventy-seven converts or ex-candidates for conversion, known to him, and the results strikingly confirm the view that sudden conversion is connected with the possession of an active subliminal self. Examining his subjects with reference to their hypnotic sensibility and to such

automatisms as hypnagogic hallucinations, odd impulses, religious dreams about the time of their conversion, etc., he found these relatively much more frequent in the group of converts whose transformation had been "striking," "striking" transformation being defined as a change which, though not necessarily instantaneous, seems to the subject of it to be distinctly different from a process of growth, however rapid.[127] Candidates for conversion at revivals are, as you know, often disappointed: they experience nothing striking. Professor Coe had a number of persons of this class among his seventy-seven subjects, and they almost all, when tested by hypnotism, proved to belong to a subclass which he [pg 241] calls "spontaneous," that is, fertile in self-suggestions, as distinguished from a "passive" subclass, to which most of the subjects of striking transformation belonged. His inference is that self-suggestion of impossibility had prevented the influence upon these persons of an environment which, on the more "passive" subjects, had easily brought forth the effects they looked for. Sharp distinctions are difficult in these regions, and Professor Coe's numbers are small. But his methods were careful, and the results tally with what one might expect; and they seem, on the whole, to justify his practical conclusion, which is that if you should expose to a converting influence a subject in whom three factors unite: first, pronounced emotional sensibility; second, tendency to automatisms; and third, suggestibility of the passive type; you might then safely predict the result: there would be a sudden conversion, a transformation of the striking kind.

Does this temperamental origin diminish the significance of the sudden conversion when it has occurred? Not in the least, as Professor Coe well says; for "the ultimate test of religious values is nothing psychological, nothing definable in terms of *how it happens,* but something ethical, definable only in terms of *what is attained.*"[128]

As we proceed farther in our inquiry we shall see that what is attained is often an altogether new level of spiritual vitality, a relatively heroic level, in which impossible things have become possible, and new energies and endurances are shown. The personality is changed, the man *is* born anew, whether or not his psychological idiosyncrasies are what give the particular shape to his metamorphosis. "Sanctification" is the technical name of this result; and erelong examples of it shall be brought [pg 242] before you. In this lecture I have still only to add a few remarks on the assurance and peace which fill the hour of change itself.

One word more, though, before proceeding to that point, lest the final purpose of my explanation of suddenness by subliminal activity be misunderstood. I do indeed believe that if the Subject have no liability to such subconscious activity, or if his conscious fields have a hard rind of a margin that resists incursions from beyond it, his conversion must be gradual if it occur, and must resemble any simple growth into new habits. His possession of a developed subliminal self, and of a leaky or pervious margin, is thus a *conditio sine qua non* of the Subject's becoming converted in the instantaneous way. But if you, being orthodox Christians, ask me as a psychologist whether the reference of a phenomenon to a subliminal self does not exclude the notion of the direct presence of the Deity altogether, I have to say frankly that as a psychologist I do not see why it necessarily should. The lower manifestations of the Subliminal, indeed, fall within the resources of the personal subject: his ordinary sense-material, inattentively taken in and subconsciously remembered and combined, will account for all his usual automatisms. But just as our primary wide-awake consciousness throws open our senses to the touch of things material, so it is logically conceivable that *if there be* higher spiritual agencies that can directly touch us, the psychological condition of their doing so *might be* our possession of a subconscious region which alone should yield access to them. The hubbub of the waking life might close a door which in the dreamy Subliminal might remain ajar or open.

Thus that perception of external control which is so [pg 243] essential a feature in conversion might, in some cases at any rate, be interpreted as the orthodox interpret it: forces transcending the finite individual might impress him, on condition of his being what we may call a subliminal human specimen. But in any case the *value* of these forces would have to be determined by their effects, and the mere fact of their transcendency would of itself establish no presumption that they were more divine than diabolical.

I confess that this is the way in which I should rather see the topic left lying in your minds until I come to a much later lecture, when I hope once more to gather these dropped threads together into more definitive conclusions. The notion of a subconscious self certainly ought not at this point of our inquiry to be held to *exclude* all notion of a higher penetration. If there be higher powers able to impress us, they may get access to us only through the subliminal door. (See below, p. 515 ff.)

Let us turn now to the feelings which immediately fill the hour of the conversion experience. The first one to be noted is just this sense of higher control. It is not always, but it is very often present. We saw examples of it in Alline, Bradley, Brainerd, and elsewhere. The need of such a higher controlling agency is well expressed in the short reference which the eminent French Protestant Adolphe Monod makes to the crisis of his own conversion. It was at Naples in his early manhood, in the summer of 1827.

> "My sadness," he says, "was without limit, and having got entire possession of me, it filled my life from the most indifferent external acts to the most secret thoughts, and corrupted at their source my feelings, my judgment, and my happiness. It was then that I saw that to expect to put a stop to this disorder [pg 244]by my reason and my will, which were themselves diseased, would be to act like a blind man who should pretend to correct one of his eyes by the aid of the other equally blind one. I had then no resource save in *some influence from without*. I remembered the promise of the Holy Ghost; and what the positive declarations of the Gospel had never succeeded in bringing home to me, I learned at last from necessity, and believed, for the first time in my life, in this promise, in the only sense in which it answered the needs of my soul, in that, namely, of a real external supernatural action, capable of giving me thoughts, and taking them away from me, and exerted on me by a God as truly master of my heart as he is of the rest of nature. Renouncing then all merit, all strength, abandoning all my personal resources, and acknowledging no other title to his mercy than my own utter misery, I went home and threw myself on my knees, and prayed as I never yet prayed in my life. From this day onwards a new interior life began for me: not that my melancholy had disappeared, but it had lost its sting. Hope had entered into my heart, and once entered on the path, the God of Jesus Christ, to whom I then had learned to give myself up, little by little did the rest."[129]

It is needless to remind you once more of the admirable congruity of Protestant theology with the structure of the mind as shown in such experiences. In the extreme of melancholy the self that consciously *is* can do absolutely nothing. It is completely bankrupt and without resource, and no works it can accomplish will avail. Redemption from such subjective conditions must be a free gift or nothing, and grace through Christ's accomplished sacrifice is such a gift.

> "God," says Luther, "is the God of the humble, the miserable, the oppressed, and the desperate, and of those that are brought even to nothing; and his nature is to give sight to the [pg 245]blind, to comfort the broken-hearted, to justify sinners, to save the very desperate and damned. Now that pernicious and pestilent opinion of man's own righteousness, which will not be a sinner, unclean, miserable, and damnable, but righteous and holy, suffereth not God to come to his own natural and proper work. Therefore God must take this maul in hand (the law, I mean) to beat in pieces and bring to nothing this beast with her vain confidence, that she may so learn at length by her own misery that she is utterly forlorn and damned. But here lieth the difficulty, that when a man is terrified and cast down, he is so little able to raise himself up again and say, 'Now I am bruised and afflicted enough; now is the time of grace; now is the time to hear Christ.' The foolishness of man's heart is so great that then he rather seeketh to himself more laws to satisfy his conscience. 'If I live,' saith he, 'I will amend my life: I will do this, I will do that.' But here, except thou do the quite contrary, except thou send Moses away with his law, and in these terrors and this anguish lay hold upon Christ who died for thy sins, look for no salvation. Thy cowl, thy shaven crown, thy chastity, thy obedience, thy poverty, thy works, thy merits? what shall all these do? what shall the law of Moses avail? If I, wretched and damnable sinner, through works or merits could have loved the Son of God, and so come to him, what needed he to deliver himself for me? If I, being a wretch and damned sinner, could be redeemed by any other price, what needed the Son of God to be given? But because there was no other price, therefore he delivered neither sheep, ox, gold, nor silver, but even God himself, entirely and wholly 'for me,' even 'for me,' I say, a miserable, wretched sinner. Now, therefore, I take comfort and apply this to *myself*. And this manner of applying is the very true force and power of faith. For he died *not* to justify the righteous, but the *un*-righteous, and to make *them* the children of God."[130]

That is, the more literally lost you are, the more literally you are the very being whom Christ's sacrifice has already saved. Nothing in Catholic theology, I imagine, [pg 246] has ever spoken to sick souls as straight as this message from Luther's personal experience. As Protestants are not all sick souls, of course reliance on what Luther exults in calling the dung of one's merits, the filthy puddle of one's own righteousness, has come to the front again in their religion; but the adequacy of his view of Christianity to the deeper parts of our human mental structure is shown by its wildfire contagiousness when it was a new and quickening thing.

Faith that Christ has genuinely done his work was part of what Luther meant by faith, which so far is faith in a fact intellectually conceived of. But this is only one part of Luther's faith, the other part being far more vital. This other part is something not intellectual but immediate and intuitive, the assurance, namely, that I, this individual I, just as I stand, without one plea, etc., am saved now and forever.[131]

Professor Leuba is undoubtedly right in contending that the conceptual belief about Christ's work, although so often efficacious and antecedent, is really accessory and non-essential, and that the "joyous conviction" can also [pg 247] come by far other channels than this conception. It is to the joyous conviction itself, the assurance that all is well with one, that he would give the name of faith *par excellence*.

> "When the sense of estrangement," he writes, "fencing man about in a narrowly limited ego, breaks down, the individual finds himself 'at one with all creation.' He lives in the universal life; he and man, he and nature, he and God, are one. That state of confidence, trust, union with all things, following upon the achievement of moral unity, is the *Faith-state*. Various dogmatic beliefs suddenly, on the advent of the faith-state, acquire a character of certainty, assume a new reality, become an object of faith. As the ground of assurance here is not rational, argumentation is irrelevant. But such conviction being a mere casual offshoot of the faith-state, it is a gross error to imagine that the chief practical value of the faith-state is its power to stamp with the seal of reality certain particular theological conceptions.[132] On the contrary, its value lies solely in the fact that it is the psychic correlate of a biological growth reducing contending desires to one direction; a growth which expresses itself in new affective states and new reactions; in larger, nobler, more Christ-like activities. The ground of the specific assurance in religious dogmas is then an affective experience. The objects of faith may even be preposterous; the affective stream will float them along, and invest them with unshakable certitude. The more startling the affective experience,

the less explicable it seems, the easier it is to make it the carrier of unsubstantiated notions."[133]

The characteristics of the affective experience which, to avoid ambiguity, should, I think, be called the state of assurance rather than the faith-state, can be easily enumerated, though it is probably difficult to realize their [pg 248] intensity, unless one have been through the experience one's self.

The central one is the loss of all the worry, the sense that all is ultimately well with one, the peace, the harmony, the *willingness to be,* even though the outer conditions should remain the same. The certainty of God's "grace," of "justification," "salvation," is an objective belief that usually accompanies the change in Christians; but this may be entirely lacking and yet the affective peace remain the same—you will recollect the case of the Oxford graduate: and many might be given where the assurance of personal salvation was only a later result. A passion of willingness, of acquiescence, of admiration, is the glowing centre of this state of mind.

The second feature is the sense of perceiving truths not known before. The mysteries of life become lucid, as Professor Leuba says; and often, nay usually, the solution is more or less unutterable in words. But these more intellectual phenomena may be postponed until we treat of mysticism.

A third peculiarity of the assurance state is the objective change which the world often appears to undergo. "An appearance of newness beautifies every object," the precise opposite of that other sort of newness, that dreadful unreality and strangeness in the appearance of the world, which is experienced by melancholy patients, and of which you may recall my relating some examples.[134] This sense of clean and beautiful newness within and without is one of the commonest entries in conversion records. Jonathan Edwards thus describes it in himself:—

> "After this my sense of divine things gradually increased, and became more and more lively, and had more of that inward sweetness. The appearance of everything was altered; there [pg 249] seemed to be, as it were, a calm, sweet cast, or appearance of divine glory, in almost everything. God's excellency, his wisdom, his purity and love, seemed to appear in everything; in the sun, moon, and stars; in the clouds and blue sky; in the grass, flowers,

and trees; in the water and all nature; which used greatly to fix my mind. And scarce anything, among all the works of nature, was so sweet to me as thunder and lightning; formerly nothing had been so terrible to me. Before, I used to be uncommonly terrified with thunder, and to be struck with terror when I saw a thunderstorm rising; but now, on the contrary, it rejoices me."[135]

Billy Bray, an excellent little illiterate English evangelist, records his sense of newness thus:—

"I said to the Lord: 'Thou hast said, they that ask shall receive, they that seek shall find, and to them that knock the door shall be opened, and I have faith to believe it.' In an instant the Lord made me so happy that I cannot express what I felt. I shouted for joy. I praised God with my whole heart.... I think this was in November, 1823, but what day of the month I do not know. I remember this, that everything looked new to me, the people, the fields, the cattle, the trees. I was like a new man in a new world. I spent the greater part of my time in praising the Lord."[136]

Starbuck and Leuba both illustrate this sense of newness by quotations. I take the two following from Starbuck's manuscript collection. One, a woman, says:—

"I was taken to a camp-meeting, mother and religious friends seeking and praying for my conversion. My emotional nature was stirred to its depths; confessions of depravity and pleading with God for salvation from sin made me oblivious of all surroundings. I plead for mercy, and had a vivid realization of forgiveness and renewal of my nature. When rising from my knees I exclaimed, 'Old things have passed away, all things [pg 250]have become new.' It was like entering another world, a new state of existence. Natural objects were glorified, my spiritual vision was so clarified that I saw beauty in every material object in the universe, the woods were vocal with heavenly music; my soul exulted in the love of God, and I wanted everybody to share in my joy."

The next case is that of a man:—

"I know not how I got back into the encampment, but found myself staggering up to Rev. ——'s Holiness tent—and as it was full of seekers and a terrible noise inside, some groaning, some laughing, and some shouting, and by a large oak, ten feet from the tent, I fell on my face by a bench, and tried to pray, and every time I would call on God, something like a man's hand would strangle me by choking. I don't know whether there were any one around or near me or not. I thought I should surely die if I did not get help, but just as often as I would pray, that unseen hand was felt on my throat and my breath squeezed off. Finally something said: 'Venture on the atonement, for you will die anyway if you don't.' So I made one final struggle to call on God for mercy, with the same choking and strangling, determined to finish the sentence of prayer for Mercy, if I did strangle and die, and the last I remember that time was falling back on the ground with the same unseen hand on my throat. I don't know how long I lay there or what was going on. None of my folks were present. When I came to myself, there were a crowd around me praising God. The very heavens seemed to open and pour down rays of light and glory. Not for a moment only, but all day and night, floods of light and glory seemed to pour through my soul, and oh, how I was changed, and everything became new. My horses and hogs and even everybody seemed changed."

This man's case introduces the feature of automatisms, which in suggestible subjects have been so startling a feature at revivals since, in Edwards's, Wesley's, and Whitfield's time, these became a regular means of gospel propagation. They were at first supposed to be semi-miraculous [pg 251] proofs of "power" on the part of the Holy Ghost; but great divergence of opinion quickly arose concerning them. Edwards, in his Thoughts on the Revival of Religion in New England, has to defend them against their critics; and their value has long been matter of debate even within the revivalistic denominations.[137] They undoubtedly have no essential spiritual significance, and although their presence makes his conversion more memorable to the convert, it has never been proved that converts who show them are more persevering or fertile in good fruits than those whose change of heart has had less violent accompaniments. On the whole, unconsciousness, convulsions, visions, involuntary vocal utterances, and suffocation, must be simply ascribed to the subject's having a large subliminal region, involving nervous instability. This is often the subject's own view of the matter afterwards. One of Starbuck's correspondents writes, for instance:—

"I have been through the experience which is known as conversion. My explanation of it is this: the subject works his emotions up to the breaking point, at the same time resisting their physical manifestations, such as quickened pulse, etc., and then suddenly lets them have their full sway over his body. The relief is something wonderful, and the pleasurable effects of the emotions are experienced to the highest degree."

There is one form of sensory automatism which possibly deserves special notice on account of its frequency. I refer to hallucinatory or pseudo-hallucinatory luminous phenomena, *photisms*, to use the term of the psychologists. Saint Paul's blinding heavenly vision seems to have been a phenomenon of this sort; so does Constantine's [pg 252] cross in the sky. The last case but one which I quoted mentions floods of light and glory. Henry Alline mentions a light, about whose externality he seems uncertain. Colonel Gardiner sees a blazing light. President Finney writes:—

> "All at once the glory of God shone upon and round about me in a manner almost marvelous.... A light perfectly ineffable shone in my soul, that almost prostrated me on the ground.... This light seemed like the brightness of the sun in every direction. It was too intense for the eyes.... I think I knew something then, by actual experience, of that light that prostrated Paul on the way to Damascus. It was surely a light such as I could not have endured long."[138]

Such reports of photisms are indeed far from uncommon. Here is another from Starbuck's collection, where the light appeared evidently external:—

> "I had attended a series of revival services for about two weeks off and on. Had been invited to the altar several times, all the time becoming more deeply impressed, when finally I decided I must do this, or I should be lost. Realization of conversion was very vivid, like a ton's weight being lifted from my heart; a strange light which seemed to light up the whole room (for it was dark); a conscious supreme bliss which caused me to repeat 'Glory to God' for a long time. Decided to be God's child for life, and to give up my pet ambition, wealth and social position. My former habits of life hindered my growth somewhat, but I set about overcoming these systematically, and in one year my whole nature was changed, i.e., my ambitions were of a different order."

Here is another one of Starbuck's cases, involving a luminous element:—

> "I had been clearly converted twenty-three years before, or rather reclaimed. My experience in regeneration was then clear and spiritual, and I had not

backslidden. But I experienced [pg 253]entire sanctification on the 15th day of March, 1893, about eleven o'clock in the morning. The particular accompaniments of the experience were entirely unexpected. I was quietly sitting at home singing selections out of Pentecostal Hymns. Suddenly there seemed to be a something sweeping into me and inflating my entire being— such a sensation as I had never experienced before. When this experience came, I seemed to be conducted around a large, capacious, well-lighted room. As I walked with my invisible conductor and looked around, a clear thought was coined in my mind, 'They are not here, they are gone.' As soon as the thought was definitely formed in my mind, though no word was spoken, the Holy Spirit impressed me that I was surveying my own soul. Then, for the first time in all my life, did I know that I was cleansed from all sin, and filled with the fullness of God."

Leuba quotes the case of a Mr. Peek, where the luminous affection reminds one of the chromatic hallucinations produced by the intoxicant cactus buds called mescal by the Mexicans:—

"When I went in the morning into the fields to work, the glory of God appeared in all his visible creation. I well remember we reaped oats, and how every straw and head of the oats seemed, as it were, arrayed in a kind of rainbow glory, or to glow, if I may so express it, in the glory of God."[139]

[pg 254]
The most characteristic of all the elements of the conversion crisis, and the last one of which I shall speak, is the ecstasy of happiness produced. We have already heard several accounts of it, but I will add a couple more. President Finney's is so vivid that I give it at length:—

"All my feelings seemed to rise and flow out; and the utterance of my heart was, 'I want to pour my whole soul out to God.' The rising of my soul was so great that I rushed into the back room of the front office, to pray. There was no fire and no light in the room; nevertheless it appeared to me as if it were perfectly light. As I went in and shut the door after me, it seemed as if I met the Lord Jesus Christ face to face. It did not occur to me then, nor did it for some time afterwards, that it was wholly a mental state. On the contrary, it seemed to me that I saw him as I would see any other man. He said nothing, but looked at me in such a manner as to break me [pg 255]right down at his feet. I have always since regarded this as a most remarkable state of mind; for it seemed to me a reality that he stood before me, and I fell down at his feet and poured out my soul to him. I wept aloud like a child, and made such confessions as I could with my choked utterance. It seemed to me that I bathed his feet with my tears; and yet I had no distinct impression that I touched him, that I recollect. I must have continued in this state for a good while; but my mind was too much absorbed with the interview to recollect anything that I said. But I know, as soon as my mind became calm enough to break off from the interview, I returned to the front office, and found that the fire that I had made of large wood was nearly burned out. But as I turned and was about to take a seat by the fire, I received a mighty baptism of the Holy Ghost. Without any expectation of it, without ever having the thought in my mind that there was any such thing for me, without any recollection that I had ever heard the thing mentioned by any person in the world, the Holy Spirit descended upon me in a manner that seemed to go through me, body and soul. I could feel the impression, like a wave of electricity, going through and through me. Indeed, it seemed to come in waves and waves of liquid love; for I could not express it in any other way. It seemed like the very breath of God. I can recollect distinctly that it seemed to fan me, like immense wings.

"No words can express the wonderful love that was shed abroad in my heart. I wept aloud with joy and love; and I do not know but I should say I literally bellowed out the unutterable gushings of my heart. These waves came over me, and over me, and over me, one after the other, until I recollect I cried out, 'I shall die if these waves continue to pass over me.' I said, 'Lord, I cannot bear any more;' yet I had no fear of death.

"How long I continued in this state, with this baptism continuing to roll over me and go through me, I do not know. But I know it was late in the evening when a member of my choir—for I was the leader of the choir—came into the office to see me. He was a member of the church. He found me [pg 256]in this state of loud weeping, and said to me, 'Mr. Finney, what ails you?' I could make him no answer for some time. He then said, 'Are you in pain?' I gathered myself up as best I could, and replied, 'No, but so happy that I cannot live.' "

I just now quoted Billy Bray; I cannot do better than give his own brief account of his post-conversion feelings:—

"I can't help praising the Lord. As I go along the street, I lift up one foot, and it seems to say 'Glory'; and I lift up the other, and it seems to say 'Amen'; and so they keep up like that all the time I am walking."[140]

One word, before I close this lecture, on the question of the transiency or permanence of these abrupt conversions. Some of you, I feel sure, knowing that numerous [pg 257] backslidings and relapses take place, make of these their apperceiving mass for interpreting the whole subject, and dismiss it with a pitying smile at so much "hysterics." Psychologically, as well as religiously, however, this is shallow. It misses the point of serious interest, which is not so much the duration as the nature and quality of these shiftings of character to higher levels. Men lapse from every level—we need no statistics to tell us that. Love is, for instance, well known not to be irrevocable, yet, constant or inconstant, it reveals new flights and reaches of ideality while it lasts. These revelations form its significance to men and women, whatever be its duration. So with the conversion experience: that it should for even a short time show a human being what the high-water mark of his spiritual capacity is, this is what constitutes its importance,—an importance which backsliding cannot diminish, although persistence might increase it. As a matter of fact, all the more striking instances of conversion, all those, for instance, which I have quoted, *have* been permanent. The case of which there might be most doubt, on account of its suggesting so strongly an epileptoid seizure, was the case of M. Ratisbonne. Yet I am informed that Ratisbonne's whole future was shaped by those few minutes. He gave up his project of marriage, became a priest, founded at Jerusalem, where he went to dwell, a mission of nuns for the conversion of the Jews, showed no tendency to use for egotistic purposes the notoriety given him by the peculiar circumstances of his conversion,—which, for the rest, he could seldom refer to without tears,—and in short remained an exemplary son of the Church until he died, late in the 80's, if I remember rightly.

The only statistics I know of, on the subject of the duration of conversions, are those collected for Professor [pg 258] Starbuck by Miss Johnston. They embrace only a hundred persons, evangelical church-members, more than half being Methodists. According to the statement of the subjects themselves, there had been backsliding of some sort in nearly all the cases, 93 per cent. of the women, 77 per cent. of the men. Discussing the returns more minutely, Starbuck finds that only 6 per cent. are relapses from the religious faith which the conversion confirmed, and that the backsliding complained of is in most only a fluctuation in the ardor of sentiment. Only six of the hundred cases report a change of faith. Starbuck's conclusion is that the effect of conversion is to bring with it "a changed attitude towards life, which is fairly constant and permanent, although the feelings fluctuate.... In other words, the persons who have passed through conversion, having once taken a stand for the religious life, tend to feel themselves identified with it, no matter how much their religious enthusiasm declines."[141]

[pg 259]

Lectures XI, XII, And XIII. Saintliness.

The last lecture left us in a state of expectancy. What may the practical fruits for life have been, of such movingly happy conversions as those we heard of? With this question the really important part of our task opens, for you remember that we began all this empirical inquiry not merely to open a curious chapter in the natural history of human consciousness, but rather to attain a spiritual judgment as to the total value and positive meaning of all the religious trouble and happiness which we have seen. We must, therefore, first describe the fruits of the religious life, and then we must judge them. This divides our inquiry into two distinct parts. Let us without further preamble proceed to the descriptive task.

It ought to be the pleasantest portion of our business in these lectures. Some small pieces of it, it is true, may be painful, or may show human nature in a pathetic light, but it will be mainly pleasant, because the best fruits of religious experience are the best things that history has to show. They have always been esteemed so; here if anywhere is the genuinely strenuous life; and to call to mind a succession of such examples as I have lately had to wander through, though it has been only in the reading of them, is to feel encouraged and uplifted and washed in better moral air.

The highest flights of charity, devotion, trust, patience, bravery to which the wings of human nature have spread [pg 260] themselves have been flown for religious ideals. I can do no better than quote, as to this, some remarks which Sainte-Beuve in his History of Port-Royal makes on the results of conversion or the state of grace.

"Even from the purely human point of view," Sainte-Beuve says, "the phenomenon of grace must still appear sufficiently extraordinary, eminent, and rare, both in its nature and in its effects, to deserve a closer study. For the soul arrives thereby at a certain fixed and invincible state, a state which is genuinely heroic, and from out of which the greatest deeds which it ever performs are executed. Through all the different forms of communion, and all the diversity of the means which help to produce this state, whether it be reached by a jubilee, by a general confession, by a solitary prayer and effusion, whatever in short be the place and the occasion, it is easy to recognize that it is fundamentally one state in spirit and in fruits. Penetrate a little beneath the diversity of circumstances, and it becomes evident that in Christians of different epochs it is always one and the same modification by which they are affected: there is veritably a single fundamental and identical spirit of piety and charity, common to those who have received grace; an inner state which before all things is one of love and humility, of infinite confidence in God, and of severity for one's self, accompanied with tenderness for others. The fruits peculiar to this condition of the soul have the same savor in all, under distant suns and in different surroundings, in Saint Teresa of Avila just as in any Moravian brother of Herrnhut."[142]

Sainte-Beuve has here only the more eminent instances of regeneration in mind, and these are of course the instructive ones for us also to consider. These devotees [pg 261] have often laid their course so differently from other men that, judging them by worldly law, we might be tempted to call them monstrous aberrations from the path of nature. I begin, therefore, by asking a general psychological question as to what the inner conditions are which may make one human character differ so extremely from another.

I reply at once that where the character, as something distinguished from the intellect, is concerned, the causes of human diversity lie chiefly in our *differing susceptibilities of emotional excitement,* and in the *different impulses and inhibitions* which these bring in their train. Let me make this more clear.

Speaking generally, our moral and practical attitude, at any given time, is always a resultant of two sets of forces within us, impulses pushing us one way and obstructions and inhibitions holding us back. "Yes! yes!" say the impulses; "No! no!" say the inhibitions. Few people who have not expressly reflected on the matter realize how constantly this factor of inhibition is upon us, how it contains and moulds us by its restrictive pressure almost as if we were fluids pent within the cavity of a jar. The influence is so incessant that it becomes subconscious. All of you, for example, sit here with a certain constraint at this moment, and entirely without express consciousness of the fact, because of the influence of the occasion. If left alone in the room, each of you would probably involuntarily rearrange himself, and make his attitude more "free and easy." But proprieties and their inhibitions snap like cobwebs if any great emotional excitement supervenes. I have seen a dandy appear in the street with his face covered with shaving-lather because a house across the way was on fire; and a woman will run among strangers in her nightgown if [pg 262] it be a question of saving her baby's life or her own. Take a self-indulgent woman's life in general. She will yield to every inhibition set by her disagreeable sensations, lie late in bed, live upon tea or bromides, keep indoors from the cold. Every difficulty finds her obedient to its "no." But make a mother of her, and what have you? Possessed by maternal excitement, she now confronts wakefulness, weariness, and toil without an instant of hesitation or a word of complaint. The inhibitive power of pain over her is extinguished wherever the baby's interests are at stake. The inconveniences which this creature occasions have become, as James Hinton says, the glowing heart of a great joy, and indeed are now the very conditions whereby the joy becomes most deep.

This is an example of what you have already heard of as the "expulsive power of a higher affection." But be the affection high or low, it makes no difference, so long as the excitement it brings be strong enough. In one of Henry Drummond's discourses he tells of an inundation in India where an eminence with a bungalow upon it remained unsubmerged, and became the refuge of a number of wild animals and reptiles in addition to the human beings who were there. At a certain moment a royal Bengal tiger appeared swimming towards it, reached it, and lay panting like a dog upon the ground in the midst of the people, still possessed by such an agony of terror that one of the Englishmen could calmly step up with a rifle and blow out its brains. The tiger's habitual ferocity was temporarily quelled by the emotion of fear, which became sovereign, and formed a new centre for his character.

Sometimes no emotional state is sovereign, but many contrary ones are mixed together. In that case one hears [pg 263] both "yeses" and "noes," and the "will" is called on then to solve the conflict. Take a soldier, for example, with his dread of cowardice impelling him to advance, his fears impelling him to run, and his propensities to imitation pushing him towards various courses if his comrades offer various examples. His person becomes the seat of a mass of interferences; and he may for a time simply waver, because no one emotion prevails. There is a pitch of intensity, though, which, if any emotion reach it, enthrones that one as alone effective and sweeps its antagonists and all their inhibitions away. The fury of his comrades' charge, once entered on, will give this pitch of courage to the soldier; the panic of their rout will give this pitch of fear. In these sovereign excitements, things ordinarily impossible grow natural because the inhibitions are annulled. Their "no! no!" not only is not heard, it does not exist. Obstacles are then like tissue-paper hoops to the circus rider—no impediment; the flood is higher than the dam they make. "Lass sie betteln gehn wenn sie hungrig sind!" cries the grenadier, frantic over his Emperor's capture, when his wife and babes are suggested; and men pent into a burning theatre have been known to cut their way through the crowd with knives.[143]

[pg 264]
One mode of emotional excitability is exceedingly important in the composition of the energetic character, from its peculiarly destructive power over inhibitions. I mean what in its lower form is mere irascibility, susceptibility to wrath, the fighting temper; and what in subtler ways manifests itself as impatience, grimness, earnestness, severity of character. Earnestness means willingness to live with energy, though energy bring pain. The pain may be pain to other people or pain to one's self—it makes little difference; for when the strenuous mood is on one, the aim is to break something, no matter whose or what. Nothing annihilates an inhibition as irresistibly as anger does it; for, as Moltke says of war, destruction pure and simple is its essence. This is what makes it so invaluable an ally of every other passion. The sweetest delights are trampled on with a ferocious pleasure the moment they offer themselves as checks to a cause by which our higher indignations are elicited. It costs then nothing to drop friendships, to renounce long-rooted privileges and possessions, to break

with social ties. Rather do we take a stern joy in the astringency and desolation; and what is called weakness of character seems in most cases to consist in the inaptitude for these sacrificial moods, of which one's own inferior self and its pet softnesses must often be the targets and the victims.[144]

[pg 265]
So far I have spoken of temporary alterations produced by shifting excitements in the same person. But the relatively fixed differences of character of different persons are explained in a precisely similar way. In a man with a liability to a special sort of emotion, whole ranges of inhibition habitually vanish, which in other men remain effective, and other sorts of inhibition take their place. When a person has an inborn genius for certain emotions, his life differs strangely from that of ordinary people, for none of their usual deterrents check him. Your mere aspirant to a type of character, on the contrary, only shows, when your natural lover, fighter, or reformer, with whom the passion is a gift of nature, comes along, the hopeless inferiority of voluntary to instinctive action. He has deliberately to overcome his inhibitions; the genius with the inborn passion seems not to feel them at all; he is free of all that inner friction and nervous waste. To a Fox, a Garibaldi, a General Booth, a John Brown, a Louise Michel, a Bradlaugh, the obstacles omnipotent over those around them are as if non-existent. Could the rest of us so disregard them, there might be many such heroes, for many have the wish to live for similar ideals, and only the adequate degree of inhibition-quenching fury is lacking.[145]

[pg 266]
The difference between willing and merely wishing, between having ideals that are creative and ideals that are but pinings and regrets, thus depends solely either on the amount of steam-pressure chronically driving the character in the ideal direction, or on the amount of ideal excitement transiently acquired. Given a certain amount of love, indignation, generosity, magnanimity, admiration, loyalty, or enthusiasm of self-surrender, the result is always the same. That whole raft of cowardly obstructions, which in tame persons and dull moods are sovereign impediments to action, sinks away at once. Our conventionality,[146] our shyness, laziness, and stinginess, our demands for precedent and

permission, for guarantee and surety, our small suspicions, timidities, despairs, where are they now? Severed like cobwebs, broken like bubbles in the sun—

> "Wo sind die Sorge nun und Noth
> Die mich noch gestern wollt' erschlaffen?
> Ich schäm' mich dess' im Morgenroth."

The flood we are borne on rolls them so lightly under that their very contact is unfelt. Set free of them, we float and soar and sing. This auroral openness and [pg 267] uplift gives to all creative ideal levels a bright and caroling quality, which is nowhere more marked than where the controlling emotion is religious. "The true monk," writes an Italian mystic, "takes nothing with him but his lyre."

We may now turn from these psychological generalities to those fruits of the religious state which form the special subject of our present lecture. The man who lives in his religious centre of personal energy, and is actuated by spiritual enthusiasms, differs from his previous carnal self in perfectly definite ways. The new ardor which burns in his breast consumes in its glow the lower "noes" which formerly beset him, and keeps him immune against infection from the entire groveling portion of his nature. Magnanimities once impossible are now easy; paltry conventionalities and mean incentives once tyrannical hold no sway. The stone wall inside of him has fallen, the hardness in his heart has broken down. The rest of us can, I think, imagine this by recalling our state of feeling in those temporary "melting moods" into which either the trials of real life, or the theatre, or a novel sometimes throw us. Especially if we weep! For it is then as if our tears broke through an inveterate inner dam, and let all sorts of ancient peccancies and moral stagnancies drain away, leaving us now washed and soft of heart and open to every nobler leading. With most of us the customary hardness quickly returns, but not so with saintly persons. Many saints, even as energetic ones as Teresa and Loyola, have possessed what the church traditionally reveres as a special grace, the so-called gift of tears.

In these persons the melting mood seems to have held almost uninterrupted control. And as it is with tears and melting moods, so it is with [pg 268] other exalted affections. Their reign may come by gradual growth or by a crisis; but in either case it may have "come to stay."

At the end of the last lecture we saw this permanence to be true of the general paramountcy of the higher insight, even though in the ebbs of emotional excitement meaner motives might temporarily prevail and backsliding might occur. But that lower temptations may remain completely annulled, apart from transient emotion and as if by alteration of the man's habitual nature, is also proved by documentary evidence in certain cases. Before embarking on the general natural history of the regenerate character, let me convince you of this curious fact by one or two examples. The most numerous are those of reformed drunkards. You recollect the case of Mr. Hadley in the last lecture; the Jerry McAuley Water Street Mission abounds in similar instances.[147] You also remember the graduate of Oxford, converted at three in the afternoon, and getting drunk in the hay-field the next day, but after that permanently cured of his appetite. "From that hour drink has had no terrors for me: I never touch it, never want it. The same thing occurred with my pipe, ... the desire for it went at once and has never returned. So with every known sin, the deliverance in each case being permanent and complete. I have had no temptations since conversion."

Here is an analogous case from Starbuck's manuscript collection:—

> "I went into the old Adelphi Theatre, where there was a Holiness meeting, ... and I began saying, 'Lord, Lord, I must have this blessing.' Then what was to me an audible voice said: 'Are you willing to give up everything to the [pg 269]Lord?' and question after question kept coming up, to all of which I said: 'Yes, Lord; yes, Lord!' until this came: 'Why do you not accept it *now*?' and I said: 'I do, Lord.'—I felt no particular joy, only a trust. Just then the meeting closed, and, as I went out on the street, I met a gentleman smoking a fine cigar, and a cloud of smoke came into my face, and I took a long, deep breath of it, and praise the Lord, all my appetite for it was gone. Then as I walked along the street, passing saloons where the fumes of liquor came out, I found that all my taste and longing for that accursed stuff was gone. Glory to God! ... [But] for ten or eleven long years [after that] I was in the wilderness with its ups and downs. My appetite for liquor never came back."

The classic case of Colonel Gardiner is that of a man cured of sexual temptation in a single hour. To Mr. Spears the colonel said, "I was effectually cured of all inclination to that sin I was so strongly addicted to that I thought nothing but shooting me through the head could have cured me of it; and all desire and inclination to it was removed, as entirely as if I had been a sucking child; nor did the temptation return to this day." Mr. Webster's words on the same subject are these: "One thing I have heard the colonel frequently say, that he was much addicted to impurity before his acquaintance with religion; but that, so soon as he was enlightened from above, he felt the power of the Holy Ghost changing his nature so wonderfully that his sanctification in this respect seemed more remarkable than in any other."[148]

Such rapid abolition of ancient impulses and propensities reminds us so strongly of what has been observed as the result of hypnotic suggestion that it is difficult not to believe that subliminal influences play the decisive [pg 270] part in these abrupt changes of heart, just as they do in hypnotism.[149] Suggestive therapeutics abound in records of cure, after a few sittings, of inveterate bad habits with which the patient, left to ordinary moral and physical influences, had struggled in vain. Both drunkenness and sexual vice have been cured in this way, action through the subliminal seeming thus in many individuals to have the prerogative of inducing relatively stable change. If the grace of God miraculously operates, it probably operates through the subliminal door, then. But just *how* anything operates in this region is still unexplained, and we shall do well now to say good-by to the *process* of transformation altogether,—leaving it, if you like, a good deal of a psychological or theological mystery,—and to turn our attention to the fruits of the religious condition, no matter in what way they may have been produced.[150]

[pg 271]
The collective name for the ripe fruits of religion in a character is Saintliness.[151] The saintly character is the character for which spiritual emotions are the habitual centre of the personal energy; and there is a certain composite photograph of universal saintliness, the same in all religions, of which the features can easily be traced.[152]

[pg 272]
They are these:—

1. A feeling of being in a wider life than that of this world's selfish little interests; and a conviction, not merely intellectual, but as it were sensible, of the existence of an Ideal Power. In Christian saintliness this power is always personified as God; but abstract moral ideals, civic or patriotic utopias, or inner visions of holiness or right may also be felt as the true lords and enlargers of our life, in ways which I described in the lecture on the Reality of the Unseen.[153]

[pg 273]
2. A sense of the friendly continuity of the ideal power with our own life, and a willing self-surrender to its control.

3. An immense elation and freedom, as the outlines of the confining selfhood melt down.

4. A shifting of the emotional centre towards loving and harmonious affections, towards "yes, yes" and away from "no," where the claims of the non-ego are concerned.

These fundamental inner conditions have characteristic practical consequences, as follows:—

a. Asceticism.—The self-surrender may become so passionate as to turn into self-immolation. It may then so overrule the ordinary inhibitions of the flesh that the saint finds positive pleasure in sacrifice and asceticism, measuring and expressing as they do the degree of his loyalty to the higher power.

b. Strength of Soul.—The sense of enlargement of life may be so uplifting that personal motives and inhibitions, commonly omnipotent, become too insignificant for notice, and new reaches of patience and fortitude open out. Fears and anxieties go, and blissful equanimity takes their place. Come heaven, come hell, it makes no difference now!

> "We forbid ourselves all seeking after popularity, all ambition to appear important. We pledge ourselves to abstain from falsehood, in all its degrees. We promise not to create or encourage illusions as to what is possible, by what we say or write. We promise to one another active sincerity, which strives to see truth clearly, and which never fears to declare what it sees.
>
> "We promise deliberate resistance to the tidal waves of fashion, to the 'booms' and panics of the public mind, to all the forms of weakness and of fear.
>
> "We forbid ourselves the use of sarcasm. Of serious things we will speak seriously and unsmilingly, without banter and without the appearance of banter;—and even so of all things, for there are serious ways of being light of heart.
>
> "We will put ourselves forward always for what we are, simply and without false humility, as well as without pedantry, affectation, or pride."

[pg 274]
c. Purity.—The shifting of the emotional centre brings with it, first, increase of purity. The sensitiveness to spiritual discords is enhanced, and the cleansing of existence from brutal and sensual elements becomes imperative. Occasions of contact with such elements are avoided: the saintly life must deepen its spiritual consistency and keep unspotted from the world. In some temperaments this need of purity of spirit takes an ascetic turn, and weaknesses of the flesh are treated with relentless severity.

d. Charity.—The shifting of the emotional centre brings, secondly, increase of charity, tenderness for fellow-creatures. The ordinary motives to antipathy, which usually set such close bounds to tenderness among human beings, are inhibited. The saint loves his enemies, and treats loathsome beggars as his brothers.

I now have to give some concrete illustrations of these fruits of the spiritual tree. The only difficulty is to choose, for they are so abundant.

Since the sense of Presence of a higher and friendly Power seems to be the fundamental feature in the spiritual life, I will begin with that.

In our narratives of conversion we saw how the world might look shining and transfigured to the convert,[154] and, apart from anything acutely religious, we all have moments when the universal life seems to wrap us round with friendliness. In youth and health, in summer, in the woods or on the mountains, there come days when the weather seems all whispering with peace, hours when the goodness and beauty of existence enfold us like a dry warm climate, or chime through us as if our inner ears were subtly ringing with the world's security. Thoreau writes:—

[pg 275]

> "Once, a few weeks after I came to the woods, for an hour I doubted whether the near neighborhood of man was not essential to a serene and healthy life. To be alone was somewhat unpleasant. But, in the midst of a gentle rain, while these thoughts prevailed, I was suddenly sensible of such sweet and beneficent society in Nature, in the very pattering of the drops, and in every sight and sound around my house, an infinite and unaccountable friendliness all at once, like an atmosphere, sustaining me, as made the fancied advantages of human neighborhood insignificant, and I have never thought of them since. Every little pine-needle expanded and swelled with sympathy and befriended me. I was so distinctly made aware of the presence of something kindred to me, that I thought no place could ever be strange to me again."[155]

In the Christian consciousness this sense of the enveloping friendliness becomes most personal and definite. "The compensation," writes a German author, "for the loss of that sense of personal independence which man so unwillingly gives up, is the disappearance of all *fear* from one's life, the quite indescribable and inexplicable feeling of an inner *security*, which one can only experience, but which, once it has been experienced, one can never forget."[156]

I find an excellent description of this state of mind in a sermon by Mr. Voysey:—

> "It is the experience of myriads of trustful souls, that this sense of God's unfailing presence with them in their going out and in their coming in, and by night and day, is a source of absolute repose and confident calmness. It drives away all fear of what may befall them. That nearness of God is a constant security against terror and anxiety. It is not that they are at all assured of

physical safety, or deem themselves protected by a love which is denied to others, but that they are in a state of mind equally ready to be safe or to meet with injury. If injury [pg 276]befall them, they will be content to bear it because the Lord is their keeper, and nothing can befall them without his will. If it be his will, then injury is for them a blessing and no calamity at all. Thus and thus only is the trustful man protected and shielded from harm. And I for one—by no means a thick-skinned or hard-nerved man—am absolutely satisfied with this arrangement, and do not wish for any other kind of immunity from danger and catastrophe. Quite as sensitive to pain as the most highly strung organism, I yet feel that the worst of it is conquered, and the sting taken out of it altogether, by the thought that God is our loving and sleepless keeper, and that nothing can hurt us without his will."[157]

More excited expressions of this condition are abundant in religious literature. I could easily weary you with their monotony. Here is an account from Mrs. Jonathan Edwards:—

"Last night," Mrs. Edwards writes, "was the sweetest night I ever had in my life. I never before, for so long a time together, enjoyed so much of the light and rest and sweetness of heaven in my soul, but without the least agitation of body during the whole time. Part of the night I lay awake, sometimes asleep, and sometimes between sleeping and waking. But all night I continued in a constant, clear, and lively sense of the heavenly sweetness of Christ's excellent love, of his nearness to me, and of my dearness to him; with an inexpressibly sweet calmness of soul in an entire rest in him. I seemed to myself to perceive a glow of divine love come down from the heart of Christ in heaven into my heart in a constant stream, like a stream or pencil of sweet light. At the same time my heart and soul all flowed out in love to Christ, so that there seemed to be a constant flowing and reflowing of heavenly love, and I appeared to myself to float or swim, in these bright, sweet beams, like the motes swimming in the beams of the sun, or the streams of his light which come in at the window. I think that what I felt each minute was worth more than all the outward comfort and pleasure which I had enjoyed in my whole life put [pg 277]together. It was pleasure, without the least sting, or any interruption. It was a sweetness, which my soul was lost in; it seemed to be all that my feeble frame could sustain. There was but little difference, whether I was asleep or awake, but if there was any difference, the sweetness was greatest while I was asleep.[158] As I awoke early the next morning, it seemed to me that I had entirely done with myself. I felt that the opinions of the world concerning me were nothing, and that I had no more to do with any outward interest of my own than with that of a person whom I never saw. The glory of God seemed to swallow up every wish and desire of my heart.... After retiring to rest and sleeping a little while, I awoke, and was led to reflect on God's mercy to me, in giving me, for many years, a willingness to die; and after that, in making me willing to live, that I might do and suffer whatever he called me to here. I also thought how God had graciously given me an entire resignation to his will, with respect to the kind and manner of death that I should die; having been made willing to die on the rack, or at the stake, and if it were God's will, to die in darkness. But now it occurred to me, I used to think of living no longer than to the ordinary age of man. Upon this I was led to ask myself, whether I was not willing to be kept out of heaven even longer; and my whole heart seemed immediately to reply: Yes, a thousand years, and a thousand in horror, if it be most for the honor of God, the torment of my body being so great, awful, and overwhelming that none could bear to live in the country where the spectacle was seen, and the torment of my mind being vastly greater. And it seemed to me that I found a perfect willingness, quietness, and alacrity of soul in [pg 278]consenting that it should be so, if it were most for the glory of God, so that there was no hesitation, doubt, or darkness in my mind. The glory of God seemed to overcome me and swallow me up, and every conceivable suffering, and everything that was terrible to my nature, seemed to shrink to nothing before it. This resignation continued in its clearness and brightness the rest of the night, and all the next day, and the night following, and on Monday in the forenoon, without interruption or abatement."[159]

The annals of Catholic saintship abound in records as ecstatic or more ecstatic than this. "Often the assaults of the divine love," it is said of the Sister Séraphique de la Martinière, "reduced her almost to the point of death. She used tenderly to complain of this to God. 'I cannot support it,' she used to say. 'Bear gently with my weakness, or I shall expire under the violence of your love.' "[160]

Let me pass next to the Charity and Brotherly Love which are a usual fruit of saintliness, and have always been reckoned essential theological virtues, however limited may have been the kinds of service which the particular theology enjoined. Brotherly love would follow logically from the assurance of God's friendly presence, the notion of our brotherhood as men being an immediate inference from that of God's fatherhood of us all. When Christ utters the precepts: "Love your enemies, bless them that curse you, do good to them that hate you, and pray for them which despitefully use you, and persecute you," he gives for a reason: "That ye may be the children of your Father which is in heaven: for he maketh his sun to rise on the evil and on the good, and sendeth rain on the just and on the unjust."

One might therefore [pg 279] be tempted to explain both the humility as to one's self and the charity towards others which characterize spiritual excitement, as results of the all-leveling character of theistic belief. But these affections are certainly not mere derivatives of theism. We find them in Stoicism, in Hinduism, and in Buddhism in the highest possible degree. They harmonize with paternal theism beautifully; but they *harmonize* with all reflection whatever upon the dependence of mankind on general causes; and we must, I think, consider them not subordinate but coördinate parts of that great complex excitement in the study of which we are engaged. Religious rapture, moral enthusiasm, ontological wonder, cosmic emotion, are all unifying states of mind, in which the sand and grit of the selfhood incline to disappear, and tenderness to rule. The best thing is to describe the condition integrally as a characteristic affection to which our nature is liable, a region in which we find ourselves at home, a sea in which we swim; but not to pretend to explain its parts by deriving them too cleverly from one another. Like love or fear, the faith-state is a natural psychic complex, and carries charity with it by organic consequence. Jubilation is an expansive affection, and all expansive affections are self-forgetful and kindly so long as they endure.

We find this the case even when they are pathological in origin. In his instructive work, la Tristesse et la Joie,[161] M. Georges Dumas compares together the melancholy and the joyous phase of circular insanity, and shows that, while selfishness characterizes the one, the other is marked by altruistic impulses. No human being so stingy and useless as was Marie in her melancholy period! But the moment the happy period begins, "sympathy and kindness become her characteristic sentiments. She displays [pg 280] a universal goodwill, not only of intention, but in act.... She becomes solicitous of the health of other patients, interested in getting them out, desirous to procure wool to knit socks for some of them. Never since she has been under my observation have I heard her in her joyous period utter any but charitable opinions."[162] And later, Dr. Dumas says of all such joyous conditions that "unselfish sentiments and tender emotions are the only affective states to be found in them. The subject's mind is closed against envy, hatred, and vindictiveness, and wholly transformed into benevolence, indulgence, and mercy."[163]

There is thus an organic affinity between joyousness and tenderness, and their companionship in the saintly life need in no way occasion surprise. Along with the happiness, this increase of tenderness is often noted in narratives of conversion. "I began to work for others";—"I had more tender feeling for my family and friends";—"I spoke at once to a person with whom I had been angry";—"I felt for every one, and loved my friends better";—"I felt every one to be my friend";—these are so many expressions from the records collected by Professor Starbuck.[164]

> "When," says Mrs. Edwards, continuing the narrative from which I made quotation a moment ago, "I arose on the morning of the Sabbath, I felt a love to all mankind, wholly peculiar in its strength and sweetness, far beyond all that I had ever felt before. The power of that love seemed inexpressible. I thought, if I were surrounded by enemies, who were venting their malice and cruelty upon me, in tormenting me, it would still be impossible that I should cherish any feelings towards them but those of love, and pity, and ardent desires for their happiness. I never before felt so far from a disposition to judge and censure others, as I did that morning. I realized also, in [pg 281]an unusual and very lively manner, how great a part of Christianity lies in the performance of our social and relative duties to one another. The same joyful sense continued throughout the day—a sweet love to God and all mankind."

Whatever be the explanation of the charity, it may efface all usual human barriers.[165]

Here, for instance, is an example of Christian non-resistance from Richard Weaver's autobiography. Weaver was a collier, a semi-professional pugilist in his younger days, who became a much beloved evangelist. Fighting, after drinking, seems to have been the sin to which he originally felt his flesh most perversely inclined. After his first conversion he had a backsliding, which consisted in pounding a man who had insulted a girl. Feeling that, having once fallen, he might as well be hanged for a sheep as for a lamb, he got drunk and went and broke the jaw of another man who had lately challenged him to fight and taunted him with cowardice for refusing as a Christian man;—I mention these incidents to show how genuine a change of heart is implied in the later conduct which he describes as follows:—

[pg 282]

"I went down the drift and found the boy crying because a fellow-workman was trying to take the wagon from him by force. I said to him:—

" 'Tom, you mustn't take that wagon.'

"He swore at me, and called me a Methodist devil. I told him that God did not tell me to let him rob me. He cursed again, and said he would push the wagon over me.

" 'Well,' I said, 'let us see whether the devil and thee are stronger than the Lord and me.'

"And the Lord and I proving stronger than the devil and he, he had to get out of the way, or the wagon would have gone over him. So I gave the wagon to the boy. Then said Tom:—

" 'I've a good mind to smack thee on the face.'

" 'Well,' I said, 'if that will do thee any good, thou canst do it.' So he struck me on the face.

"I turned the other cheek to him, and said, 'Strike again.'

"He struck again and again, till he had struck me five times. I turned my cheek for the sixth stroke; but he turned away cursing. I shouted after him: 'The Lord forgive thee, for I do, and the Lord save thee.'

"This was on a Saturday; and when I went home from the coal-pit my wife saw my face was swollen, and asked what was the matter with it. I said: 'I've been fighting, and I've given a man a good thrashing.'

"She burst out weeping, and said, 'O Richard, what made you fight?' Then I told her all about it; and she thanked the Lord I had not struck back.

"But the Lord had struck, and his blows have more effect than man's. Monday came. The devil began to tempt me, saying: 'The other men will laugh at thee for allowing Tom to treat thee as he did on Saturday.' I cried, 'Get thee behind me, Satan;'—and went on my way to the coal-pit.

"Tom was the first man I saw. I said 'Good-morning,' but got no reply.

"He went down first. When I got down, I was surprised to see him sitting on the wagon-road waiting for me. When I came to him he burst into tears and said: 'Richard, will you forgive me for striking you?'

[pg 283]
"'I have forgiven thee,' said I; 'ask God to forgive thee. The Lord bless thee.' I gave him my hand, and we went each to his work."[166]

"Love your enemies!" Mark you, not simply those who happen not to be your friends, but your *enemies*, your positive and active enemies. Either this is a mere Oriental hyperbole, a bit of verbal extravagance, meaning only that we should, as far as we can, abate our animosities, or else it is sincere and literal. Outside of certain cases of intimate individual relation, it seldom has been taken literally. Yet it makes one ask the question: Can there in general be a level of emotion so unifying, so obliterative of differences between man and man, that even enmity may come to be an irrelevant circumstance and fail to inhibit the friendlier interests aroused? If positive well-wishing could attain so supreme a degree of excitement, those who were swayed by it might well seem superhuman beings. Their life would be morally discrete from the life of other men, and there is no saying, in the absence of positive experience of an authentic kind,—for there are few active examples in our scriptures, and the Buddhistic examples are legendary,[167]—what the effects might be: they might conceivably transform the world.

Psychologically and in principle, the precept "Love your enemies" is not self-contradictory. It is merely the extreme limit of a kind of magnanimity with which, in the shape of pitying tolerance of our oppressors, we are fairly familiar. Yet if radically followed, it would involve such a breach with our instinctive springs of action as a whole, and with the present world's arrangements, [pg 284] that a critical point would practically be passed, and we should be born into another kingdom of being. Religious emotion makes us feel that other kingdom to be close at hand, within our reach.

The inhibition of instinctive repugnance is proved not only by the showing of love to enemies, but by the showing of it to any one who is personally loathsome. In the annals of saintliness we find a curious mixture of motives impelling in this direction. Asceticism plays its part; and along with charity pure and simple, we find humility or the desire to disclaim distinction and to grovel on the common level before God. Certainly all three principles were at work when Francis of Assisi and Ignatius Loyola exchanged their garments with those of filthy beggars. All three are at work when religious persons consecrate their lives to the care of leprosy or other peculiarly unpleasant diseases. The nursing of the sick is a function to which the religious seem strongly drawn, even apart from the fact that church traditions set that way. But in the annals of this sort of charity we find fantastic excesses of devotion recorded which are only explicable by the frenzy of self-immolation simultaneously aroused. Francis of Assisi kisses his lepers; Margaret Mary Alacoque, Francis Xavier, St. John of God, and others are said to have cleansed the sores and ulcers of their patients with their respective tongues; and the lives of such saints as Elizabeth of Hungary and Madame de Chantal are full of a sort of reveling in hospital purulence, disagreeable to read of, and which makes us admire and shudder at the same time.

So much for the human love aroused by the faith-state. Let me next speak of the Equanimity, Resignation, Fortitude, and Patience which it brings.

[pg 285]
"A paradise of inward tranquillity" seems to be faith's usual result; and it is easy, even without being religious one's self, to understand this. A moment back, in treating of the sense of God's presence, I spoke of the unaccountable feeling of safety which one may then have. And, indeed, how can it possibly fail to steady the nerves, to cool the fever, and appease the fret, if one be sensibly conscious that, no matter what one's difficulties for the moment may appear to be, one's life as a whole is in the keeping of a power whom one can absolutely trust? In deeply religious men the abandonment of self to this power is passionate. Whoever not only says, but *feels*, "God's will be done," is mailed against every weakness; and the whole historic array of martyrs, missionaries, and religious reformers is there to prove the tranquil-mindedness, under naturally agitating or distressing circumstances, which self-surrender brings.

The temper of the tranquil-mindedness differs, of course, according as the person is of a constitutionally sombre or of a constitutionally cheerful cast of mind. In the sombre it partakes more of resignation and submission; in the cheerful it is a joyous consent. As an example of the former temper, I quote part of a letter from Professor Lagneau, a venerated teacher of philosophy who lately died, a great invalid, at Paris:—

> "My life, for the success of which you send good wishes, will be what it is able to be. I ask nothing from it, I expect nothing from it. For long years now I exist, think, and act, and am worth what I am worth, only through the despair which is my sole strength and my sole foundation. May it preserve for me, even in these last trials to which I am coming, the courage to do without the desire of deliverance. I ask nothing more from the Source whence all strength cometh, and if that is granted, your wishes will have been accomplished."[168]

[pg 286]
There is something pathetic and fatalistic about this, but the power of such a tone as a protection against outward shocks is manifest. Pascal is another Frenchman of pessimistic natural temperament. He expresses still more amply the temper of self-surrendering submissiveness:—

> "Deliver me, Lord," he writes in his prayers, "from the sadness at my proper suffering which self-love might give, but put into me a sadness like your own. Let my sufferings appease your choler. Make them an occasion for my conversion and salvation. I ask you neither for health nor for sickness, for life nor for death; but that you may dispose of my health and my sickness, my life and my death, for your glory, for my salvation, and for the use of the Church and of your saints, of whom I would by your grace be one. You alone know what is expedient for me; you are the sovereign master; do with me according to your will. Give to me, or take away from me, only conform my will to yours. I know but one thing, Lord, that it is good to follow you, and bad to offend you. Apart from that, I know not what is good or bad in anything. I know not which is most profitable to me, health or sickness, wealth or poverty, nor anything else in the world. That discernment is beyond the power of men or angels, and is hidden among the secrets of your Providence, which I adore, but do not seek to fathom."[169]

When we reach more optimistic temperaments, the resignation grows less passive. Examples are sown so broadcast throughout history that I might well pass on without citation. As it is, I snatch at the first that occurs to my mind. Madame Guyon, a frail creature physically, was yet of a happy native disposition. She went through many perils with admirable serenity of soul. After being sent to prison for heresy,—

> "Some of my friends," she writes, "wept bitterly at the hearing of it, but such was my state of acquiescence and resignation [pg 287]that it failed to draw any tears from me.... There appeared to be in me then, as I find it to be in me now, such an entire loss of what regards myself, that any of my own interests gave me little pain or pleasure; ever wanting to will or wish for myself only the very thing which God does." In another place she writes: "We all of us came near perishing in a river which we found it necessary to pass. The carriage sank in the quicksand. Others who were with us threw themselves out in excessive fright. But I found my thoughts so much taken up with God that I had no distinct sense of danger. It is true that the thought of being drowned passed across my mind, but it cost no other sensation or reflection in me than this—that I felt quite contented and willing it were so, if it were my heavenly Father's choice." Sailing from Nice to Genoa, a storm keeps her eleven days at sea. "As the irritated waves dashed round us," she writes, "I could not help experiencing a certain degree of satisfaction in my mind. I pleased myself with thinking that those mutinous billows, under the command of Him who does all things rightly, might probably furnish me with a watery grave. Perhaps I carried the point too far, in the pleasure which I took in thus seeing myself beaten and bandied by the swelling waters. Those who were with me took notice of my intrepidity."[170]

The contempt of danger which religious enthusiasm produces may be even more buoyant still. I take an example from that charming recent autobiography, "With Christ at Sea," by Frank Bullen. A couple of days after he went through the conversion on shipboard of which he there gives an account,—

> "It was blowing stiffly," he writes, "and we were carrying a press of canvas to get north out of the bad weather. Shortly after four bells we hauled down the flying-jib, and I sprang out astride the boom to furl it. I was sitting astride the boom when suddenly it gave way with me. The sail slipped through my fingers, and I fell backwards, hanging head downwards [pg 288]over the seething tumult of shining foam under the ship's bows, suspended by one foot. But I felt only high exultation in my certainty of eternal life. Although death was divided from me by a hair's breadth, and I was acutely conscious of the fact, it gave me no sensation but joy. I suppose I could have hung there

no longer than five seconds, but in that time I lived a whole age of delight. But my body asserted itself, and with a desperate gymnastic effort I regained the boom. How I furled the sail I don't know, but I sang at the utmost pitch of my voice praises to God that went pealing out over the dark waste of waters."[171]

The annals of martyrdom are of course the signal field of triumph for religious imperturbability. Let me cite as an example the statement of a humble sufferer, persecuted as a Huguenot under Louis XIV.:—

"They shut all the doors," Blanche Gamond writes, "and I saw six women, each with a bunch of willow rods as thick as the hand could hold, and a yard long. He gave me the order, 'Undress yourself,' which I did. He said, 'You are leaving on your shift; you must take it off.' They had so little patience that they took it off themselves, and I was naked from the waist up. They brought a cord with which they tied me to a beam in the kitchen. They drew the cord tight with all their strength and asked me, 'Does it hurt you?' and then they discharged their fury upon me, exclaiming as they struck me, 'Pray now to your God.' It was the Roulette woman who held this language. But at this moment I received the greatest consolation that I can ever receive in my life, since I had the honor of being whipped for the name of Christ, and in addition of being crowned with his mercy and his consolations. Why can I not write down the inconceivable influences, consolations, and peace which I felt interiorly? To understand them one must have passed by the same trial; they were so great that I was ravished, for there where afflictions abound grace is given superabundantly. In vain the women cried, 'We must double our blows; she does not feel them, for she neither speaks nor [pg 289]cries.' And how should I have cried, since I was swooning with happiness within?"[172]

The transition from tenseness, self-responsibility, and worry, to equanimity, receptivity, and peace, is the most wonderful of all those shiftings of inner equilibrium, those changes of the personal centre of energy, which I have analyzed so often; and the chief wonder of it is that it so often comes about, not by doing, but by simply relaxing and throwing the burden down. This abandonment of self-responsibility seems to be the fundamental act in specifically religious, as distinguished from moral practice. It antedates theologies and is independent of philosophies. Mind-cure, theosophy, stoicism, ordinary neurological hygiene, insist on it as emphatically as

Christianity does, and it is capable of entering into closest marriage with every speculative creed.[173] Christians who have it strongly live in what is called "recollection," and are never anxious about the future, nor worry over the outcome of the day. Of Saint Catharine of Genoa it is said that "she took cognizance of things, only as they were presented to her in succession, *moment by moment.*" To her holy soul, "the divine moment was the present moment,... and when the present moment was estimated in itself and in its relations, and when the duty that was involved in it was accomplished, it was permitted to pass away as if it had never been, and to give way to the facts and duties of the moment which came after."[174]

[pg 290]
Hinduism, mind-cure, and theosophy all lay great emphasis upon this concentration of the consciousness upon the moment at hand.

The next religious symptom which I will note is what I have called Purity of Life. The saintly person becomes exceedingly sensitive to inner inconsistency or discord, and mixture and confusion grow intolerable. All the mind's objects and occupations must be ordered with reference to the special spiritual excitement which is now its keynote. Whatever is unspiritual taints the pure water of the soul and is repugnant. Mixed with this exaltation of the moral sensibilities there is also an ardor of sacrifice, for the beloved deity's sake, of everything unworthy of him. Sometimes the spiritual ardor is so sovereign that purity is achieved at a stroke—we have seen examples. Usually it is a more gradual conquest. Billy Bray's account of his abandonment of tobacco is a good example of the latter form of achievement.

> "I had been a smoker as well as a drunkard, and I used to love my tobacco as much as I loved my meat, and I would rather go down into the mine without my dinner than without my pipe. In the days of old, the Lord spoke by the mouths of his servants, the prophets; now he speaks to us by the spirit of his Son. I had not only the feeling part of religion, but I could hear the small, still voice within speaking to me. When I took the pipe to smoke, it would be applied within, 'It is an idol, a lust; worship the Lord with clean lips.' So, I felt it was not right to smoke. The Lord also sent a woman to convince me. I

was one day in a house, and I took out my pipe to light it at the fire, and Mary Hawke—for that was the woman's name—said, 'Do you not feel it is wrong to smoke?' I said that I felt something inside telling me that it was an idol, a lust, and she said that was the Lord. Then I said, 'Now, I must give it up, for the Lord is telling me of it inside, and the woman outside, [pg 291]so the tobacco must go, love it as I may.' There and then I took the tobacco out of my pocket, and threw it into the fire, and put the pipe under my foot, 'ashes to ashes, dust to dust.' And I have not smoked since. I found it hard to break off old habits, but I cried to the Lord for help, and he gave me strength, for he has said, 'Call upon me in the day of trouble, and I will deliver thee.' The day after I gave up smoking I had the toothache so bad that I did not know what to do. I thought this was owing to giving up the pipe, but I said I would never smoke again, if I lost every tooth in my head. I said, 'Lord, thou hast told us My yoke is easy and my burden is light,' and when I said that, all the pain left me. Sometimes the thought of the pipe would come back to me very strong; but the Lord strengthened me against the habit, and, bless his name, I have not smoked since."

Bray's biographer writes that after he had given up smoking, he thought that he would chew a little, but he conquered this dirty habit, too. "On one occasion," Bray said, "when at a prayer-meeting at Hicks Mill, I heard the Lord say to me, 'Worship me with clean lips.' So, when we got up from our knees, I took the quid out of my mouth and 'whipped 'en'[threw it] under the form. But, when we got on our knees again, I put another quid into my mouth. Then the Lord said to me again, 'Worship me with clean lips.' So I took the quid out of my mouth, and whipped 'en under the form again, and said, 'Yes, Lord, I will.' From that time I gave up chewing as well as smoking, and have been a free man."

The ascetic forms which the impulse for veracity and purity of life may take are often pathetic enough. The early Quakers, for example, had hard battles to wage against the worldliness and insincerity of the ecclesiastical Christianity of their time. Yet the battle that cost them most wounds was probably that which they fought in defense of their own right to social veracity and sincerity in their thee-ing and thou-ing, in not doffing the hat or giving titles of respect. It was laid on George Fox [pg 292] that these conventional customs were a lie and a sham, and the whole body of his followers thereupon renounced them, as a sacrifice to truth, and so that their acts and the spirit they professed might be more in accord.

"When the Lord sent me into the world," says Fox in his Journal, "he forbade me to put off my hat to any, high or low: and I was required to 'thee' and 'thou' all men and women, without any respect to rich or poor, great or small. And as I traveled up and down, I was not to bid people Good-morning, or Good-evening, neither might I bow or scrape with my leg to any one. This made the sects and professions rage. Oh! the rage that was in the priests, magistrates, professors, and people of all sorts: and especially in priests and professors: for though 'thou' to a single person was according to their accidence and grammar rules, and according to the Bible, yet they could not bear to hear it: and because I could not put off my hat to them, it set them all into a rage.... Oh! the scorn, heat, and fury that arose! Oh! the blows, punchings, beatings, and imprisonments that we underwent for not putting off our hats to men! Some had their hats violently plucked off and thrown away, so that they quite lost them. The bad language and evil usage we received on this account is hard to be expressed, besides the danger we were sometimes in of losing our lives for this matter, and that by the great professors of Christianity, who thereby discovered they were not true believers. And though it was but a small thing in the eye of man, yet a wonderful confusion it brought among all professors and priests: but, blessed be the Lord, many came to see the vanity of that custom of putting off hats to men, and felt the weight of Truth's testimony against it."

In the autobiography of Thomas Elwood, an early Quaker, who at one time was secretary to John Milton, we find an exquisitely quaint and candid account of the trials he underwent both at home and abroad, in following Fox's canons of sincerity. The anecdotes are too lengthy for citation; but Elwood sets down his manner of feeling [pg 293] about these things in a shorter passage, which I will quote as a characteristic utterance of spiritual sensibility:—

"By this divine light, then," says Elwood, "I saw that though I had not the evil of the common uncleanliness, debauchery, profaneness, and pollutions of the world to put away, because I had, through the great goodness of God and a civil education, been preserved out of those grosser evils, yet I had many other evils to put away and to cease from; some of which were not by the world, which lies in wickedness (1 John v. 19), accounted evils, but by the light of Christ were made manifest to me to be evils, and as such condemned in me.

"As particularly those fruits and effects of pride that discover themselves in the vanity and superfluity of apparel; which I took too much delight in. This evil of my doings I was required to put away and cease from; and judgment lay upon me till I did so.

"I took off from my apparel those unnecessary trimmings of lace, ribbons, and useless buttons, which had no real service, but were set on only for that which was by mistake called ornament; and I ceased to wear rings.

"Again, the giving of flattering titles to men between whom and me there was not any relation to which such titles could be pretended to belong. This was an evil I had been much addicted to, and was accounted a ready artist in; therefore this evil also was I required to put away and cease from. So that thenceforward I durst not say, Sir, Master, My Lord, Madam (or My Dame); or say Your Servant to any one to whom I did not stand in the real relation of a servant, which I had never done to any.

"Again, respect of persons, in uncovering the head and bowing the knee or body in salutation, was a practice I had been much in the use of; and this, being one of the vain customs of the world, introduced by the spirit of the world, instead of the true honor which this is a false representation of, and used in deceit as a token of respect by persons one to another, who bear no real respect one to another; and besides this, being a [pg 294]type and a proper emblem of that divine honor which all ought to pay to Almighty God, and which all of all sorts, who take upon them the Christian name, appear in when they offer their prayers to him, and therefore should not be given to men;—I found this to be one of those evils which I had been too long doing; therefore I was now required to put it away and cease from it.

"Again, the corrupt and unsound form of speaking in the plural number to a single person, *you* to one, instead of *thou*, contrary to the pure, plain, and single language of truth, *thou* to one, and *you* to more than one, which had always been used by God to men, and men to God, as well as one to another, from the oldest record of time till corrupt men, for corrupt ends, in later and corrupt times, to flatter, fawn, and work upon the corrupt nature in men, brought in that false and senseless way of speaking *you* to one, which has since corrupted the modern languages, and hath greatly debased the spirits and depraved the manners of men;—this evil custom I had been as forward in as others, and this I was now called out of and required to cease from.

"These and many more evil customs which had sprung up in the night of darkness and general apostasy from the truth and true religion were now, by the inshining of this pure ray of divine light in my conscience, gradually discovered to me to be what I ought to cease from, shun, and stand a witness against."[175]

These early Quakers were Puritans indeed. The slightest inconsistency between profession and deed jarred some of them to active protest. John Woolman writes in his diary:—

"In these journeys I have been where much cloth hath been dyed; and have at sundry times walked over ground where much of their dyestuffs has drained away. This hath produced a longing in my mind that people might come into cleanness of spirit, cleanness of person, and cleanness about their houses [pg 295]and garments. Dyes being invented partly to please the eye, and partly to hide dirt, I have felt in this weak state, when traveling in dirtiness, and affected with unwholesome scents, a strong desire that the nature of dyeing cloth to hide dirt may be more fully considered.

"Washing our garments to keep them sweet is cleanly, but it is the opposite to real cleanliness to hide dirt in them. Through giving way to hiding dirt in our garments a spirit which would conceal that which is disagreeable is strengthened. Real cleanliness becometh a holy people; but hiding that which is not clean by coloring our garments seems contrary to the sweetness of sincerity. Through some sorts of dyes cloth is rendered less useful. And if the value of dyestuffs, and expense of dyeing, and the damage done to cloth, were all added together, and that cost applied to keeping all sweet and clean, how much more would real cleanliness prevail.

"Thinking often on these things, the use of hats and garments dyed with a dye hurtful to them, and wearing more clothes in summer than are useful, grew more uneasy to me; believing them to be customs which have not their foundation in pure wisdom. The apprehension of being singular from my beloved friends was a strait upon me; and thus I continued in the use of some things, contrary to my judgment, about nine months. Then I thought of getting a hat the natural color of the fur, but the apprehension of being looked upon as one affecting singularity felt uneasy to me. On this account I was under close exercise of mind in the time of our general spring meeting in 1762, greatly desiring to be rightly directed; when, being deeply bowed in spirit before the Lord, I was made willing to submit to what I apprehended was required of me; and when I returned home, got a hat of the natural color of the fur.

"In attending meetings, this singularity was a trial to me, and more especially at this time, as white hats were used by some who were fond of following the changeable modes of dress, and as some friends, who knew not from what motives I wore it, grew shy of me, I felt my way for a time shut up in the exercise of the ministry. Some friends were apprehensive that my wearing such a hat savored of an affected singularity: [pg 296]those who spoke with me in a friendly way, I generally informed in a few words, that I believed my wearing it was not in my own will."

When the craving for moral consistency and purity is developed to this degree, the subject may well find the outer world too full of shocks to dwell in, and can unify his life and keep his soul unspotted only by withdrawing from it. That law which impels the artist to achieve harmony in his composition by simply dropping out whatever jars, or suggests a discord, rules also in the spiritual life. To omit, says Stevenson, is the one art in literature: "If I knew how to omit, I should ask no other knowledge." And life, when full of disorder and slackness and vague superfluity, can no more have what we call character than literature can have it under similar conditions. So monasteries and communities of sympathetic devotees open their doors, and in their changeless order, characterized by omissions quite as much as constituted of actions, the holy-minded person finds that inner smoothness and cleanness which it is torture to him to feel violated at every turn by the discordancy and brutality of secular existence.

That the scrupulosity of purity may be carried to a fantastic extreme must be admitted. In this it resembles Asceticism, to which further symptom of saintliness we had better turn next. The adjective "ascetic" is applied to conduct originating on diverse psychological levels, which I might as well begin by distinguishing from one another.

>1. Asceticism may be a mere expression of organic hardihood, disgusted with too much ease.
>
>2. Temperance in meat and drink, simplicity of apparel, [pg 297]chastity, and non-pampering of the body generally, may be fruits of the love of purity, shocked by whatever savors of the sensual.
>
>3. They may also be fruits of love, that is, they may appeal to the subject in the light of sacrifices which he is happy in making to the Deity whom he acknowledges.
>
>4. Again, ascetic mortifications and torments may be due to pessimistic feelings about the self, combined with theological beliefs concerning expiation. The devotee may feel that he is buying himself free, or escaping worse sufferings hereafter, by doing penance now.
>
>5. In psychopathic persons, mortifications may be entered on irrationally, by a sort of obsession or fixed idea which comes as a challenge and must be worked off, because only thus does the subject get his interior consciousness feeling right again.
>
>6. Finally, ascetic exercises may in rarer instances be prompted by genuine perversions of the bodily sensibility, in consequence of which normally pain-giving stimuli are actually felt as pleasures.

I will try to give an instance under each of these heads in turn; but it is not easy to get them pure, for in cases pronounced enough to be immediately classed as ascetic, several of the assigned motives usually work together. Moreover, before citing any examples at all, I must invite you to some general psychological considerations which apply to all of them alike.

A strange moral transformation has within the past century swept over our Western world. We no longer think that we are called on to face physical pain with equanimity. It is not expected of a man that he should either endure it or inflict much of it, and to listen to the recital of cases of it makes our flesh creep morally as well as physically. The way in which our ancestors [pg 298] looked upon pain as an eternal ingredient of the world's order, and both caused and suffered it as a matter-of-course portion of their day's work, fills us with amazement. We wonder that any human beings could have been so callous. The result of this historic alteration is that even in the Mother Church herself, where ascetic discipline has such a fixed traditional prestige as a factor of merit, it has largely come into desuetude, if not discredit. A believer who flagellates or "macerates" himself to-day arouses more wonder and fear than emulation. Many Catholic writers who admit that the times have changed in this respect do so resignedly; and even add that perhaps it is as well not to waste feelings in regretting the matter, for to return to the heroic corporeal discipline of ancient days might be an extravagance.

Where to seek the easy and the pleasant seems instinctive—and instinctive it appears to be in man; any deliberate tendency to pursue the hard and painful as such and for their own sakes might well strike one as purely abnormal. Nevertheless, in moderate degrees it is natural and even usual to human nature to court the arduous. It is only the extreme manifestations of the tendency that can be regarded as a paradox.

The psychological reasons for this lie near the surface. When we drop abstractions and take what we call our will in the act, we see that it is a very complex function. It involves both stimulations and inhibitions; it follows generalized habits; it is escorted by reflective criticisms; and it leaves a good or a bad taste of itself behind, according to the manner of the performance. The result is that, quite apart from the immediate pleasure which any sensible experience may give us, our own general moral attitude in procuring or undergoing the experience brings with it a secondary satisfaction or distaste. Some [pg 299] men and women, indeed, there are who can live on smiles and the word "yes" forever. But for others (indeed for most), this is too tepid and relaxed a moral climate. Passive happiness is slack and insipid, and soon grows mawkish and intolerable. Some austerity and wintry negativity, some roughness, danger, stringency, and effort, some "no! no!" must be mixed in, to produce the sense of an existence with character and texture and power. The range of individual differences in this respect is enormous; but whatever the mixture of yeses and noes may be, the person is infallibly aware when he has struck it in the right proportion *for him*. This, he feels, is my proper vocation, this is the *optimum*, the law, the life for me to live. Here I find the degree of equilibrium, safety, calm, and leisure which I need, or here I find the challenge, passion, fight, and hardship without which my soul's energy expires.

Every individual soul, in short, like every individual machine or organism, has its own best conditions of efficiency. A given machine will run best under a certain steam-pressure, a certain amperage; an organism under a certain diet, weight, or exercise. You seem to do best, I heard a doctor say to a patient, at about 140 millimeters of arterial tension. And it is just so with our sundry souls: some are happiest in calm weather; some need the sense of tension, of strong volition, to make them feel alive and well. For these latter souls, whatever is gained from day to day must be paid for by sacrifice and inhibition, or else it comes too cheap and has no zest.

Now when characters of this latter sort become religious, they are apt to turn the edge of their need of effort and negativity against their natural self; and the ascetic life gets evolved as a consequence.

When Professor Tyndall in one of his lectures tells us [pg 300] that Thomas Carlyle put him into his bath-tub every morning of a freezing Berlin winter, he proclaimed one of the lowest grades of asceticism. Even without Carlyle, most of us find it necessary to our soul's health to start the day with a rather cool immersion. A little farther along the scale we get such statements as this, from one of my correspondents, an agnostic:—

> "Often at night in my warm bed I would feel ashamed to depend so on the warmth, and whenever the thought would come over me I would have to get up, no matter what time of night it was, and stand for a minute in the cold, just so as to prove my manhood."

Such cases as these belong simply to our head 1. In the next case we probably have a mixture of heads 2 and 3—the asceticism becomes far more systematic and pronounced. The writer is a Protestant, whose sense of moral energy could doubtless be gratified on no lower terms, and I take his case from Starbuck's manuscript collection.

> "I practiced fasting and mortification of the flesh. I secretly made burlap shirts, and put the burrs next the skin, and wore pebbles in my shoes. I would spend nights flat on my back on the floor without any covering."

The Roman Church has organized and codified all this sort of thing, and given it a market-value in the shape of "merit." But we see the cultivation of hardship cropping out under every sky and in every faith, as a spontaneous need of character. Thus we read of Channing, when first settled as a Unitarian minister, that—

> "He was now more simple than ever, and seemed to have become incapable of any form of self-indulgence. He took the smallest room in the house for his study, though he might easily have commanded one more light, airy, and in every way more suitable; and chose for his sleeping chamber an attic which he [pg 301]shared with a younger brother. The furniture of the latter might have answered for the cell of an anchorite, and consisted of a hard mattress on a cot-bedstead, plain wooden chairs and table, with matting on the floor. It was without fire, and to cold he was throughout life extremely sensitive; but he never complained or appeared in any way to be conscious of inconvenience. 'I recollect,' says his brother, 'after one most severe night, that in the morning he sportively thus alluded to his suffering: "If my bed were my country, I should be somewhat like Bonaparte: I have no control except over the part which I occupy; the instant I move, frost takes

possession."' In sickness only would he change for the time his apartment and accept a few comforts. The dress too that he habitually adopted was of most inferior quality; and garments were constantly worn which the world would call mean, though an almost feminine neatness preserved him from the least appearance of neglect."[176]

Channing's asceticism, such as it was, was evidently a compound of hardihood and love of purity. The democracy which is an offshoot of the enthusiasm of humanity, and of which I will speak later under the head of the cult of poverty, doubtless bore also a share. Certainly there was no pessimistic element in his case. In the next case we have a strongly pessimistic element, so that it belongs under head 4. John Cennick was Methodism's first lay preacher. In 1735 he was convicted of sin, while walking in Cheapside,—

> "And at once left off song-singing, card-playing, and attending theatres. Sometimes he wished to go to a popish monastery, to spend his life in devout retirement. At other times he longed to live in a cave, sleeping on fallen leaves, and feeding on forest fruits. He fasted long and often, and prayed nine times a day.... Fancying dry bread too great an indulgence for so great a sinner as himself, he began to feed on potatoes, acorns, crabs, and grass; and often wished that he could live on roots [pg 302]and herbs. At length, in 1737, he found peace with God, and went on his way rejoicing."[177]

In this poor man we have morbid melancholy and fear, and the sacrifices made are to purge out sin, and to buy safety. The hopelessness of Christian theology in respect of the flesh and the natural man generally has, in systematizing fear, made of it one tremendous incentive to self-mortification. It would be quite unfair, however, in spite of the fact that this incentive has often been worked in a mercenary way for hortatory purposes, to call it a mercenary incentive. The impulse to expiate and do penance is, in its first intention, far too immediate and spontaneous an expression of self-despair and anxiety to be obnoxious to any such reproach. In the form of loving sacrifice, of spending all we have to show our devotion, ascetic discipline of the severest sort may be the fruit of highly optimistic religious feeling.

M. Vianney, the curé of Ars, was a French country priest, whose holiness was exemplary. We read in his life the following account of his inner need of sacrifice:—

> " 'On this path,' M. Vianney said, 'it is only the first step that costs. There is in mortification a balm and a savor without which one cannot live when once one has made their acquaintance. There is but one way in which to give one's self to God,—that is, to give one's self entirely, and to keep nothing for one's self. The little that one keeps is only good to double one and make one suffer.' Accordingly he imposed it on himself that he should never smell a flower, never drink when parched with thirst, never drive away a fly, never show disgust before a repugnant object, never complain of anything that had to do with his personal comfort, never sit down, never lean upon his elbows when he was kneeling. The Curé of Ars was very sensitive to cold, but he would never take means to protect [pg 303]himself against it. During a very severe winter, one of his missionaries contrived a false floor to his confessional and placed a metal case of hot water beneath. The trick succeeded, and the Saint was deceived: 'God is very good,' he said with emotion. 'This year, through all the cold, my feet have always been warm.' "[178]

In this case the spontaneous impulse to make sacrifices for the pure love of God was probably the uppermost conscious motive. We may class it, then, under our head 3. Some authors think that the impulse to sacrifice is the main religious phenomenon. It is a prominent, a universal phenomenon certainly, and lies deeper than any special creed. Here, for instance, is what seems to be a spontaneous example of it, simply expressing what seemed right at the time between the individual and his Maker. Cotton Mather, the New England Puritan divine, is generally reputed a rather grotesque pedant; yet what is more touchingly simple than his relation of what happened when his wife came to die?

> "When I saw to what a point of resignation I was now called of the Lord," he says, "I resolved, with his help, therein to glorify him. So, two hours before my lovely consort expired, I kneeled by her bedside, and I took into my two hands a dear hand, the dearest in the world. With her thus in my hands, I solemnly and sincerely gave her up unto the Lord: and in token of my real *Resignation*, I gently put her out of my hands, and laid away a most lovely hand, resolving that I would never touch it more. This was the hardest, and perhaps the bravest action that ever I did. She ... told me that she signed and

sealed my act of resignation. And though before that she called for me continually, she after this never asked for me any more."[179]

[pg 304]
Father Vianney's asceticism taken in its totality was simply the result of a permanent flood of high spiritual enthusiasm, longing to make proof of itself. The Roman Church has, in its incomparable fashion, collected all the motives towards asceticism together, and so codified them that any one wishing to pursue Christian perfection may find a practical system mapped out for him in any one of a number of ready-made manuals.[180] The dominant Church notion of perfection is of course the negative one of avoidance of sin. Sin proceeds from concupiscence, and concupiscence from our carnal passions and temptations, chief of which are pride, sensuality in all its forms, and the loves of worldly excitement and possession. All these sources of sin must be resisted; and discipline and austerities are a most efficacious mode of meeting them. Hence there are always in these books chapters on self-mortification. But whenever a procedure is codified, the more delicate spirit of it evaporates, and if we wish the undiluted ascetic spirit,—the passion of self-contempt wreaking itself on the poor flesh, the divine irrationality of devotion making a sacrificial gift of all it has (its sensibilities, namely) to the object of its adoration,—we must go to autobiographies, or other individual documents.

Saint John of the Cross, a Spanish mystic who flourished—or rather who existed, for there was little that suggested flourishing about him—in the sixteenth century, will supply a passage suitable for our purpose.

> "First of all, carefully excite in yourself an habitual affectionate will in all things to imitate Jesus Christ. If anything agreeable offers itself to your senses, yet does not at the same [pg 305]time tend purely to the honor and glory of God, renounce it and separate yourself from it for the love of Christ, who all his life long had no other taste or wish than to do the will of his Father whom he called his meat and nourishment. For example, you take satisfaction in *hearing* of things in which the glory of God bears no part. Deny yourself this satisfaction, mortify your wish to listen. You take pleasure in *seeing* objects which do not raise your mind to God: refuse yourself this pleasure, and turn away your eyes. The same with conversations and all other things. Act similarly, so far as you are able, with all the operations of the senses, striving to make yourself free from their yokes.

"The radical remedy lies in the mortification of the four great natural passions, joy, hope, fear, and grief. You must seek to deprive these of every satisfaction and leave them as it were in darkness and the void. Let your soul therefore turn always:

"Not to what is most easy, but to what is hardest;

"Not to what tastes best, but to what is most distasteful;

"Not to what most pleases, but to what disgusts;

"Not to matter of consolation, but to matter for desolation rather;

"Not to rest, but to labor;

"Not to desire the more, but the less;

"Not to aspire to what is highest and most precious, but to what is lowest and most contemptible;

"Not to will anything, but to will nothing;

"Not to seek the best in everything, but to seek the worst, so that you may enter for the love of Christ into a complete destitution, a perfect poverty of spirit, and an absolute renunciation of everything in this world.

"Embrace these practices with all the energy of your soul and you will find in a short time great delights and unspeakable consolations.

"Despise yourself, and wish that others should despise you.

"Speak to your own disadvantage, and desire others to do the same;

"Conceive a low opinion of yourself, and find it good when others hold the same;

[pg 306]
"To enjoy the taste of all things, have no taste for anything.

"To know all things, learn to know nothing.

"To possess all things, resolve to possess nothing.

"To be all things, be willing to be nothing.

"To get to where you have no taste for anything, go through whatever experiences you have no taste for.

"To learn to know nothing, go whither you are ignorant.

> "To reach what you possess not, go whithersoever you own nothing.
>
> "To be what you are not, experience what you are not."

These later verses play with that vertigo of self-contradiction which is so dear to mysticism. Those that come next are completely mystical, for in them Saint John passes from God to the more metaphysical notion of the All.

> "When you stop at one thing, you cease to open yourself to the All.
>
> "For to come to the All you must give up the All.
>
> "And if you should attain to owning the All, you must own it, desiring Nothing.
>
> "In this spoliation, the soul finds its tranquillity and rest. Profoundly established in the centre of its own nothingness, it can be assailed by naught that comes from below; and since it no longer desires anything, what comes from above cannot depress it; for its desires alone are the causes of its woes."[181]

And now, as a more concrete example of heads 4 and 5, in fact of all our heads together, and of the irrational extreme to which a psychopathic individual may go in the line of bodily austerity, I will quote the sincere Suso's account of his own self-tortures. Suso, you will remember, was one of the fourteenth century German mystics; his autobiography, written in the third person, is a classic religious document.

[pg 307]

> "He was in his youth of a temperament full of fire and life; and when this began to make itself felt, it was very grievous to him; and he sought by many devices how he might bring his body into subjection. He wore for a long time a hair shirt and an iron chain, until the blood ran from him, so that he was obliged to leave them off. He secretly caused an undergarment to be made for him; and in the undergarment he had strips of leather fixed, into which a hundred and fifty brass nails, pointed and filed sharp, were driven, and the points of the nails were always turned towards the flesh. He had this garment made very tight, and so arranged as to go round him and fasten in front, in order that it might fit the closer to his body, and the pointed nails might be

driven into his flesh; and it was high enough to reach upwards to his navel. In this he used to sleep at night. Now in summer, when it was hot, and he was very tired and ill from his journeyings, or when he held the office of lecturer, he would sometimes, as he lay thus in bonds, and oppressed with toil, and tormented also by noxious insects, cry aloud and give way to fretfulness, and twist round and round in agony, as a worm does when run through with a pointed needle. It often seemed to him as if he were lying upon an ant-hill, from the torture caused by the insects; for if he wished to sleep, or when he had fallen asleep, they vied with one another.[182] Sometimes he cried to Almighty God in the fullness of his heart: Alas! Gentle God, what a dying is this! When a man is killed by murderers or strong beasts of prey it is soon over; but I lie dying here under the cruel insects, and yet cannot die. The nights in winter were never so long, nor was the summer so hot, as to make him leave off this exercise. On the contrary, he devised something farther—two leathern loops into which he put his hands, and fastened one on each side his throat, and made the fastenings so secure that even if his cell had been

[pg 308]on fire about him, he could not have helped himself. This he continued until his hands and arms had become almost tremulous with the strain, and then he devised something else: two leather gloves; and he caused a brazier to fit them all over with sharp-pointed brass tacks, and he used to put them on at night, in order that if he should try while asleep to throw off the hair undergarment, or relieve himself from the gnawings of the vile insects, the tacks might then stick into his body. And so it came to pass. If ever he sought to help himself with his hands in his sleep, he drove the sharp tacks into his breast, and tore himself, so that his flesh festered. When after many weeks the wounds had healed, he tore himself again and made fresh wounds.

"He continued this tormenting exercise for about sixteen years. At the end of this time, when his blood was now chilled, and the fire of his temperament destroyed, there appeared to him in a vision on Whitsunday, a messenger from heaven, who told him that God required this of him no longer. Whereupon he discontinued it, and threw all these things away into a running stream."

Suso then tells how, to emulate the sorrows of his crucified Lord, he made himself a cross with thirty protruding iron needles and nails. This he bore on his bare back between his shoulders day and night. "The first time that he stretched out this cross upon his back his tender frame was struck with terror at it, and blunted the sharp nails slightly against a stone. But soon, repenting of this womanly cowardice, he pointed them all again with a file, and placed once more the cross upon him. It made his back, where the bones are, bloody and seared. Whenever he sat down or stood up, it was as if a hedgehog-skin were on him. If any one touched him unawares, or pushed against his clothes, it tore him."

Suso next tells of his penitences by means of striking this cross and forcing the nails deeper into the flesh, and likewise of his self-scourgings,—a dreadful story,—and then goes on as follows: "At this same period the

Servitor procured an old castaway door, and he used to lie upon it at night without any bedclothes to make him comfortable, except that he took off [pg 309]his shoes and wrapped a thick cloak round him. He thus secured for himself a most miserable bed; for hard pea-stalks lay in humps under his head, the cross with the sharp nails stuck into his back, his arms were locked fast in bonds, the horsehair undergarment was round his loins, and the cloak too was heavy and the door hard. Thus he lay in wretchedness, afraid to stir, just like a log, and he would send up many a sigh to God.

"In winter he suffered very much from the frost. If he stretched out his feet they lay bare on the floor and froze, if he gathered them up the blood became all on fire in his legs, and this was great pain. His feet were full of sores, his legs dropsical, his knees bloody and seared, his loins covered with scars from the horsehair, his body wasted, his mouth parched with intense thirst, and his hands tremulous from weakness. Amid these torments he spent his nights and days; and he endured them all out of the greatness of the love which he bore in his heart to the Divine and Eternal Wisdom, our Lord Jesus Christ, whose agonizing sufferings he sought to imitate. After a time he gave up this penitential exercise of the door, and instead of it he took up his abode in a very small cell, and used the bench, which was so narrow and short that he could not stretch himself upon it, as his bed. In this hole, or upon the door, he lay at night in his usual bonds, for about eight years. It was also his custom, during the space of twenty-five years, provided he was staying in the convent, never to go after compline in winter into any warm room, or to the convent stove to warm himself, no matter how cold it might be, unless he was obliged to do so for other reasons. Throughout all these years he never took a bath, either a water or a sweating bath; and this he did in order to mortify his comfort-seeking body. He practiced during a long time such rigid poverty that he would neither receive nor touch a penny, either with leave or without it. For a considerable time he strove to attain such a high degree of purity that he would neither scratch nor touch any part of his body, save only his hands and feet."[183]

[pg 310]
I spare you the recital of poor Suso's self-inflicted tortures from thirst. It is pleasant to know that after his fortieth year, God showed him by a series of visions that he had sufficiently broken down the natural man, and that he might leave these exercises off. His case is distinctly pathological, but he does not seem to have had the alleviation, which some ascetics have enjoyed, of an alteration of sensibility capable of actually turning torment into a perverse kind of pleasure. Of the founder of the Sacred Heart order, for example, we read that

> "Her love of pain and suffering was insatiable.... She said that she could cheerfully live till the day of judgment, provided she might always have matter for suffering for God; but that to live a single day without suffering would be intolerable. She said again that she was devoured with two unassuageable fevers, one for the holy communion, the other for suffering, humiliation, and annihilation. 'Nothing but pain,' she continually said in her letters, 'makes my life supportable.' "[184]

So much for the phenomena to which the ascetic impulse will in certain persons give rise. In the ecclesiastically consecrated character three minor branches of self-mortification have been recognized as indispensable pathways to perfection. I refer to the chastity, obedience, and poverty which the monk vows to observe; and upon the heads of obedience and poverty I will make a few remarks.

First, of Obedience. The secular life of our twentieth century opens with this virtue held in no high esteem. The duty of the individual to determine his own conduct and profit or suffer by the consequences seems, on the [pg 311] contrary, to be one of our best rooted contemporary Protestant social ideals. So much so that it is difficult even imaginatively to comprehend how men possessed of an inner life of their own could ever have come to think the subjection of its will to that of other finite creatures recommendable. I confess that to myself it seems something of a mystery. Yet it evidently corresponds to a profound interior need of many persons, and we must do our best to understand it.

On the lowest possible plane, one sees how the expediency of obedience in a firm ecclesiastical organization must have led to its being viewed as meritorious. Next, experience shows that there are times in every one's life when one can be better counseled by others than by one's self. Inability to decide is one of the commonest symptoms of fatigued nerves; friends who see our troubles more broadly, often see them more wisely than we do; so it is frequently an act of excellent virtue to consult and obey a doctor, a partner, or a wife. But, leaving these lower prudential regions, we find, in the nature of some of the spiritual excitements which we have been studying, good reasons for idealizing obedience. Obedience may spring from the general religious phenomenon of inner softening and self-surrender and throwing one's self on higher powers. So saving are these attitudes felt to be that in themselves, apart from utility, they become ideally consecrated; and in obeying a man whose fallibility we see through thoroughly, we, nevertheless, may feel much as we do when we resign our will to that of infinite wisdom. Add self-despair and the passion of self-crucifixion to this, and obedience becomes an ascetic sacrifice, agreeable quite irrespective of whatever prudential uses it might have.

It is as a sacrifice, a mode of "mortification," that [pg 312] obedience is primarily conceived by Catholic writers, a "sacrifice which man offers to God, and of which he is himself both the priest and the victim. By poverty he immolates his exterior possessions; by chastity he immolates his body; by obedience he completes the sacrifice, and gives to God all that he yet holds as his own, his two most precious goods, his intellect and his will. The sacrifice is then complete and unreserved, a genuine holocaust, for the entire victim is now consumed for the honor of God."[185] Accordingly, in Catholic discipline, we obey our superior not as mere man, but as the representative of Christ. Obeying God in him by our intention, obedience is easy. But when the text-book theologians marshal collectively all their reasons for recommending it, the mixture sounds to our ears rather odd.

> "One of the great consolations of the monastic life," says a Jesuit authority, "is the assurance we have that in obeying we can commit no fault. The Superior may commit a fault in commanding you to do this thing or that, but you are certain that you commit no fault so long as you obey, because God will only ask you if you have duly performed what orders you received, and if you can furnish a clear account in that respect, you are absolved entirely. Whether the things you did were opportune, or whether there were not something better that might have been done, these are questions not asked of you, but rather of your Superior. The moment what you did was done obediently, God wipes it out of your account, and charges it to the Superior. So that Saint Jerome well exclaimed, in celebrating the advantages of obedience, 'Oh, sovereign liberty! Oh, holy and blessed security by which one becomes almost impeccable!'
>
> "Saint John Climachus is of the same sentiment when he calls obedience an excuse before God. In fact, when God asks why you have done this or that, and you reply, it is because I [pg 313] was so ordered by my Superiors, God will ask for no other excuse. As a passenger in a good vessel with a

good pilot need give himself no farther concern, but may go to sleep in peace, because the pilot has charge over all, and 'watches for him'; so a religious person who lives under the yoke of obedience goes to heaven as if while sleeping, that is, while leaning entirely on the conduct of his Superiors, who are the pilots of his vessel, and keep watch for him continually. It is no small thing, of a truth, to be able to cross the stormy sea of life on the shoulders and in the arms of another, yet that is just the grace which God accords to those who live under the yoke of obedience. Their Superior bears all their burdens.... A certain grave doctor said that he would rather spend his life in picking up straws by obedience, than by his own responsible choice busy himself with the loftiest works of charity, because one is certain of following the will of God in whatever one may do from obedience, but never certain in the same degree of anything which we may do of our own proper movement."[186]

One should read the letters in which Ignatius Loyola recommends obedience as the backbone of his order, if one would gain insight into the full spirit of its cult.[187] They are too long to quote; but Ignatius's belief is so vividly expressed in a couple of sayings reported by companions that, though they have been so often cited, I will ask your permission to copy them once more:—

"I ought," an early biographer reports him as saying, "on entering religion, and thereafter, to place myself entirely in the hands of God, and of him who takes His place by His authority. I ought to desire that my Superior should oblige me to give up my own judgment, and conquer my own mind. I ought to set up no difference between one Superior and another, ... but recognize them all as equal before God, whose place they fill. For if I distinguish persons, I weaken the spirit of obedience. [pg 314]In the hands of my Superior, I must be a soft wax, a thing, from which he is to require whatever pleases him, be it to write or receive letters, to speak or not to speak to such a person, or the like; and I must put all my fervor in executing zealously and exactly what I am ordered. I must consider myself as a corpse which has neither intelligence nor will; be like a mass of matter which without resistance lets itself be placed wherever it may please any one; like a stick in the hand of an old man, who uses it according to his needs and places it where it suits him. So must I be under the hands of the Order, to serve it in the way it judges most useful.

"I must never ask of the Superior to be sent to a particular place, to be employed in a particular duty.... I must consider nothing as belonging to me personally, and as regards the things I use, be like a statue which lets itself be stripped and never opposes resistance."[188]

The other saying is reported by Rodriguez in the chapter from which I a moment ago made quotations. When speaking of the Pope's authority, Rodriguez writes:—

> "Saint Ignatius said, when general of his company, that if the Holy Father were to order him to set sail in the first bark which he might find in the port of Ostia, near Rome, and to abandon himself to the sea, without a mast, without sails, without oars or rudder or any of the things that are needful for navigation or subsistence, he would obey not only with alacrity, but without anxiety or repugnance, and even with a great internal satisfaction."[189]

With a solitary concrete example of the extravagance to which the virtue we are considering has been carried, I will pass to the topic next in order.

> "Sister Marie Claire [of Port Royal] had been greatly imbued with the holiness and excellence of M. de Langres. This prelate, soon after he came to Port Royal, said to her one day, seeing her so tenderly attached to Mother Angélique, that it [pg 315] would perhaps be better not to speak to her again. Marie Claire, greedy of obedience, took this inconsiderate word for an oracle of God, and from that day forward remained for several years without once speaking to her sister."[190]

Our next topic shall be Poverty, felt at all times and under all creeds as one adornment of a saintly life. Since the instinct of ownership is fundamental in man's nature, this is one more example of the ascetic paradox. Yet it appears no paradox at all, but perfectly reasonable, the moment one recollects how easily higher excitements hold lower cupidities in check. Having just quoted the Jesuit Rodriguez on the subject of obedience, I will, to give immediately a concrete turn to our discussion of poverty, also read you a page from his chapter on this latter virtue. You must remember that he is writing instructions for monks of his own order, and bases them all on the text, "Blessed are the poor in spirit."

> "If any one of you," he says, "will know whether or not he is really poor in spirit, let him consider whether he loves the ordinary consequences and effects of poverty, which are hunger, thirst, cold, fatigue, and the denudation of all conveniences. See if you are glad to wear a worn-out habit full of patches. See if you are glad when something is lacking to your meal, when

you are passed by in serving it, when what you receive is distasteful to you, when your cell is out of repair. If you are not glad of these things, if instead of loving them you avoid them, then there is proof that you have not attained the perfection of poverty of spirit." Rodriguez then goes on to describe the practice of poverty in more detail. "The first point is that which Saint Ignatius proposes in his constitutions, when he says, 'Let no one use anything as if it were his private possession.' 'A religious person,' he says, 'ought in respect to all the things that he uses, to be like a statue which one may drape with clothing, but which feels no grief and makes no resistance when one [pg 316]strips it again. It is in this way that you should feel towards your clothes, your books, your cell, and everything else that you make use of; if ordered to quit them, or to exchange them for others, have no more sorrow than if you were a statue being uncovered. In this way you will avoid using them as if they were your private possession. But if, when you give up your cell, or yield possession of this or that object or exchange it for another, you feel repugnance and are not like a statue, that shows that you view these things as if they were your private property.'

"And this is why our holy founder wished the superiors to test their monks somewhat as God tested Abraham, and to put their poverty and their obedience to trial, that by this means they may become acquainted with the degree of their virtue, and gain a chance to make ever farther progress in perfection, ... making the one move out of his room when he finds it comfortable and is attached to it; taking away from another a book of which he is fond; or obliging a third to exchange his garment for a worse one. Otherwise we should end by acquiring a species of property in all these several objects, and little by little the wall of poverty that surrounds us and constitutes our principal defense would be thrown down. The ancient fathers of the desert used often thus to treat their companions.... Saint Dositheus, being sick-nurse, desired a certain knife, and asked Saint Dorotheus for it, not for his private use, but for employment in the infirmary of which he had charge. Whereupon Saint Dorotheus answered him: 'Ha! Dositheus, so that knife pleases you so much! Will you be the slave of a knife or the slave of Jesus Christ? Do you not blush with shame at wishing that a knife should be your master? I will not let you touch it.' Which reproach and refusal had such an effect upon the holy disciple that since that time he never touched the knife again." ...

"Therefore, in our rooms," Father Rodriguez continues, "there must be no other furniture than a bed, a table, a bench, and a candlestick, things purely necessary, and nothing more. It is not allowed among us that our cells should be ornamented with pictures or aught else, neither armchairs, carpets, curtains, [pg 317]nor any sort of cabinet or bureau of any elegance. Neither is it allowed us to keep anything to eat, either for ourselves or for those who may come to visit us. We must ask permission to go to the refectory even for a glass of water; and finally we may not keep a book in which we can write a line, or which we may take away with us. One cannot deny that thus we are in great poverty. But this poverty is at the same time a great repose and a great perfection. For it would be inevitable, in case a religious person were allowed to own superfluous possessions, that these things would greatly occupy his mind, be it to acquire them, to preserve them, or to increase them; so that in not permitting us at all to own them, all these inconveniences are remedied. Among the various good reasons why the company forbids secular persons to enter our cells, the principal one is that thus we may the easier be kept in poverty. After all, we are all men, and if we were to receive people of the world into our rooms, we should not have the strength to remain within the bounds prescribed, but should at least wish to adorn them with some books to give the visitors a better opinion of our scholarship."[191]

Since Hindu fakirs, Buddhist monks, and Mohammedan dervishes unite with Jesuits and Franciscans in idealizing poverty as the loftiest individual state, it is worth while to examine into the spiritual grounds for such a seemingly unnatural opinion. And first, of those which lie closest to common human nature.

The opposition between the men who *have* and the men who *are* is immemorial. Though the gentleman, in the old-fashioned sense of the man who is well born, has usually in point of fact been predaceous and reveled in lands and goods, yet he has never identified his essence with these possessions, but rather with the personal superiorities, the courage, generosity, and pride supposed to be his birthright. To certain huckstering kinds of [pg 318] consideration he thanked God he was forever inaccessible, and if in life's vicissitudes he should become destitute through their lack, he was glad to think that with his sheer valor he was all the freer to work out his salvation. "Wer nur selbst was hätte," says Lessing's Tempelherr, in Nathan the Wise, "mein Gott, mein Gott, ich habe nichts!" This ideal of the well-born man without possessions was embodied in knight-errantry and templardom; and, hideously corrupted as it has always been, it still dominates sentimentally, if not practically, the military and aristocratic view of life. We glorify the soldier as the man absolutely unencumbered. Owning nothing but his bare life, and willing to toss that up at any moment when the cause commands him, he is the representative of unhampered freedom in ideal directions. The laborer who pays with his person day by day, and has no rights invested in the future, offers also much of this ideal detachment. Like the savage, he may make his bed wherever his right arm can support him, and from his simple and athletic attitude of observation, the property-owner seems buried and smothered in ignoble externalities and trammels, "wading in straw and rubbish to his knees." The claims which *things* make are corrupters of manhood, mortgages on the soul, and a drag anchor on our progress towards the empyrean.

"Everything I meet with," writes Whitefield, "seems to carry this voice with it,—'Go thou and preach the Gospel; be a pilgrim on earth; have no party or certain dwelling place.' My heart echoes back, 'Lord Jesus, help me to do or suffer thy will. When thou seest me in danger of *nestling*,—in pity—in tender pity,—put a *thorn* in my nest to prevent me from it.'"[192]

[pg 319]
The loathing of "capital" with which our laboring classes to-day are growing more and more infected seems largely composed of this sound sentiment of antipathy for lives based on mere having. As an anarchist poet writes:—

"Not by accumulating riches, but by giving away that which you have,

"Shall you become beautiful;

"You must undo the wrappings, not case yourself in fresh ones;

"Not by multiplying clothes shall you make your body sound and healthy, but rather by discarding them ...

"For a soldier who is going on a campaign does not seek what fresh furniture he can carry on his back, but rather what he can leave behind;

"Knowing well that every additional thing which he cannot freely use and handle is an impediment."[193]

In short, lives based on having are less free than lives based either on doing or on being, and in the interest of action people subject to spiritual excitement throw away possessions as so many clogs. Only those who have no private interests can follow an ideal straight away. Sloth and cowardice creep in with every dollar or guinea we have to guard. When a brother novice came to Saint Francis, saying: "Father, it would be a great consolation to me to own a psalter, but even supposing that our general should concede to me this indulgence, still I should like also to have your consent," Francis put him off with the examples of Charlemagne, Roland, and Oliver, pursuing the infidels in sweat and labor, and finally dying on the field of battle. "So care not," he said, "for owning books and knowledge, but care rather for works of goodness." And when some weeks later the novice came [pg 320] again to talk of his craving for the psalter, Francis said: "After you have got your psalter you will crave a breviary; and after you have got your breviary you will sit in your stall like a grand prelate, and will say to your brother: 'Hand me my breviary.' ... And thenceforward he denied all such requests, saying: 'A man possesses of learning only so much as comes out of him in action, and a monk is a good preacher only so far as his deeds proclaim him such, for every tree is known by its fruits.' "[194]

But beyond this more worthily athletic attitude involved in doing and being, there is, in the desire of not having, something profounder still, something related to that fundamental mystery of religious experience, the satisfaction found in absolute surrender to the larger power. So long as any secular safeguard is retained, so long as any residual prudential guarantee is clung to, so long the surrender is incomplete, the vital crisis is not passed, fear still stands sentinel, and mistrust of the divine obtains: we hold by two anchors, looking to God, it is true, after a fashion, but also holding by our proper machinations. In certain medical experiences we have the same critical point to overcome. A drunkard, or a morphine or cocaine maniac, offers himself to be cured. He appeals to the doctor to wean him from his enemy, but he dares not face blank abstinence. The tyrannical drug is still an anchor to windward: he hides supplies of it among his clothing; arranges secretly to have it smuggled in in case of need. Even so an incompletely regenerate man still trusts in his own expedients. His money is like the sleeping potion which the chronically wakeful patient keeps beside his bed; he throws himself on God, but *if* he should need the other help, there it [pg 321] will be also. Every one knows cases of this incomplete and ineffective desire for reform,—drunkards whom, with all their self-reproaches and resolves, one perceives to be quite unwilling seriously to contemplate *never* being drunk again! Really to give up anything on which we have relied, to give it up definitively, "for good and all" and forever, signifies one of those radical alterations of character which came under our notice in the lectures on conversion. In it the inner man rolls over into an entirely different position of equilibrium, lives in a new centre of energy from this time on, and the turning-point and hinge of all such operations seems usually to involve the sincere acceptance of certain nakednesses and destitutions.

Accordingly, throughout the annals of the saintly life, we find this ever-recurring note: Fling yourself upon God's providence without making any reserve whatever,—take no thought for the morrow,—sell all you have and give it to the poor,—only when the sacrifice is ruthless and reckless will the higher safety really arrive. As a concrete example let me read a page from the biography of Antoinette Bourignon, a good woman, much persecuted in her day by both Protestants and Catholics, because she would not take her religion at second hand. When a young girl, in her father's house,—

> "She spent whole nights in prayer, oft repeating: *Lord, what wilt thou have me to do?* And being one night in a most profound penitence, she said from the bottom of her heart: 'O my Lord! What must I do to please thee? For I have nobody to teach me. Speak to my soul and it will hear thee.' At that instant she heard, as if another had spoke within her: *Forsake all earthly things. Separate thyself from the love of the creatures. Deny thyself.* She was quite astonished, not understanding this language, and mused long on these three points, thinking how she could fulfill them. She thought she could not live without earthly things, nor without loving the creatures, [pg 322]nor without loving herself. Yet she said, 'By thy Grace I will do it, Lord!' But when she would perform her promise, she knew not where to begin. Having thought on the religious in monasteries, that they forsook all earthly things by being shut up in a cloister, and the love of themselves by subjecting of their wills, she asked leave of her father to enter into a cloister of the barefoot Carmelites, but he would not permit it, saying he would rather see her laid in her grave. This seemed to her a great cruelty, for she thought to find in the cloister the true Christians she had been seeking, but she found afterwards that he knew the cloisters better than she; for after he had forbidden her, and told her he would never permit her to be a religious, nor give her any money to enter there, yet she went to Father Laurens, the Director, and offered to serve in the monastery and work hard for her bread, and be content with little, if he would receive her. At which he smiled and said: *That cannot be. We must have money to build; we take no maids without money; you must find the way to get it, else there is no entry here.*
>
> "This astonished her greatly, and she was thereby undeceived as to the cloisters, resolving to forsake all company and live alone till it should please God to show her what she ought to do and whither to go. She asked always earnestly, 'When shall I be perfectly thine, O my God?' And she thought he

still answered her, *When thou shalt no longer possess anything, and shalt die to thyself*. 'And where shall I do that, Lord?' He answered her, *In the desert*. This made so strong an impression on her soul that she aspired after this; but being a maid of eighteen years only, she was afraid of unlucky chances, and was never used to travel, and knew no way. She laid aside all these doubts and said, 'Lord, thou wilt guide me how and where it shall please thee. It is for thee that I do it. I will lay aside my habit of a maid, and will take that of a hermit that I may pass unknown.' Having then secretly made ready this habit, while her parents thought to have married her, her father having promised her to a rich French merchant, she prevented the time, and on Easter evening, having cut her hair, put on the habit, and slept a little, she went out of her chamber [pg 323]about four in the morning, taking nothing but one penny to buy bread for that day. And it being said to her in the going out, *Where is thy faith? in a penny?* she threw it away, begging pardon of God for her fault, and saying, 'No, Lord, my faith is not in a penny, but in thee alone.' Thus she went away wholly delivered from the heavy burthen of the cares and good things of this world, and found her soul so satisfied that she no longer wished for anything upon earth, resting entirely upon God, with this only fear lest she should be discovered and be obliged to return home; for she felt already more content in this poverty than she had done for all her life in all the delights of the world."[195]

The penny was a small financial safeguard, but an effective spiritual obstacle. Not till it was thrown away could the character settle into the new equilibrium completely.

Over and above the mystery of self-surrender, there are in the cult of poverty other religious mysteries. There is [pg 324] the mystery of veracity: "Naked came I into the world," etc.,—whoever first said that, possessed this mystery. My own bare entity must fight the battle—shams cannot save me. There is also the mystery of democracy, or sentiment of the equality before God of all his creatures. This sentiment (which seems in general to have been more widespread in Mohammedan than in Christian lands) tends to nullify man's usual acquisitiveness. Those who have it spurn dignities and honors, privileges and advantages, preferring, as I said in a former lecture, to grovel on the common level before the face of God. It is not exactly the sentiment of humility, though it comes so close to it in practice. It is *humanity,* rather, refusing to enjoy anything that others do not share. A profound moralist, writing of Christ's saying, "Sell all thou hast and follow me," proceeds as follows:—

> "Christ may have meant: If you love mankind absolutely you will as a result not care for any possessions whatever, and this seems a very likely proposition. But it is one thing to believe that a proposition is probably true; it is another thing to see it as a fact. If you loved mankind as Christ loved them, you would see his conclusion as a fact. It would be obvious. You would sell your goods, and they would be no loss to you. These truths, while literal to Christ, and to any mind that has Christ's love for mankind, become parables to lesser natures. There are in every generation people who, beginning innocently, with no predetermined intention of becoming saints, find themselves drawn into the vortex by their interest in helping mankind, and by the understanding that comes from actually doing it. The abandonment of their old mode of life is like dust in the balance. It is done gradually, incidentally, imperceptibly. Thus the whole question of the abandonment of luxury is no question at all, but a mere incident to another question, namely, the degree to which we abandon ourselves to the remorseless logic of our love for others."[196]

[pg 325]
But in all these matters of sentiment one must have "been there" one's self in order to understand them. No American can ever attain to understanding the loyalty of a Briton towards his king, of a German towards his emperor; nor can a Briton or German ever understand the peace of heart of an American in having no king, no Kaiser, no spurious nonsense, between him and the common God of all. If sentiments as simple as these are mysteries which one must receive as gifts of birth, how much more is this the case with those subtler religious sentiments which we have been considering! One can never fathom an emotion or divine its dictates by standing outside of it. In the glowing hour of excitement, however, all incomprehensibilities are solved, and what was so enigmatical from without becomes transparently obvious. Each emotion obeys a logic of its own, and makes deductions which no other logic can draw. Piety and charity live in a different universe from worldly lusts and fears, and form another centre of energy altogether. As in a supreme sorrow lesser vexations may become a consolation; as a supreme love may turn minor sacrifices into gain; so a supreme trust may render common safeguards odious, and in certain glows of generous excitement it may appear unspeakably mean to retain one's hold

of personal possessions. The only sound plan, if we are ourselves outside the pale of such emotions, is to observe as well as we are able those who feel them, and to record faithfully what we observe; and this, I need hardly say, is what I have striven to do in these last two descriptive lectures, which I now hope will have covered the ground sufficiently for our present needs.

[pg 326]

Lectures XIV And XV. The Value Of Saintliness.

We have now passed in review the more important of the phenomena which are regarded as fruits of genuine religion and characteristics of men who are devout. To-day we have to change our attitude from that of description to that of appreciation; we have to ask whether the fruits in question can help us to judge the absolute value of what religion adds to human life. Were I to parody Kant, I should say that a "Critique of pure Saintliness" must be our theme.

If, in turning to this theme, we could descend upon our subject from above like Catholic theologians, with our fixed definitions of man and man's perfection and our positive dogmas about God, we should have an easy time of it. Man's perfection would be the fulfillment of his end; and his end would be union with his Maker. That union could be pursued by him along three paths, active, purgative, and contemplative, respectively; and progress along either path would be a simple matter to measure by the application of a limited number of theological and moral conceptions and definitions. The absolute significance and value of any bit of religious experience we might hear of would thus be given almost mathematically into our hands.

If convenience were everything, we ought now to grieve at finding ourselves cut off from so admirably convenient a method as this. But we did cut ourselves off from it deliberately in those remarks which you remember we [pg 327] made, in our first lecture, about the empirical method; and it must be confessed that after that act of renunciation we can never hope for clean-cut and scholastic results. *We* cannot divide man sharply into an animal and a rational part. *We* cannot distinguish natural from supernatural effects; nor among the latter know which are favors of God, and which are counterfeit operations of the demon. We have merely to collect things together without any special *a priori* theological system, and out of an aggregate of piecemeal judgments as to the value of this and that experience—judgments in which our general philosophic prejudices, our instincts, and our common sense are our only guides—decide that *on the whole* one type of religion is approved by its fruits, and another type condemned. "On the whole,"—I fear we shall never escape complicity with that qualification, so dear to your practical man, so repugnant to your systematizer!

I also fear that as I make this frank confession, I may seem to some of you to throw our compass overboard, and to adopt caprice as our pilot. Skepticism or wayward choice, you may think, can be the only results of such a formless method as I have taken up. A few remarks in deprecation of such an opinion, and in farther explanation of the empiricist principles which I profess, may therefore appear at this point to be in place.

Abstractly, it would seem illogical to try to measure the worth of a religion's fruits in merely human terms of value. How *can* you measure their worth without considering whether the God really exists who is supposed to inspire them? If he really exists, then all the conduct instituted by men to meet his wants must necessarily be a reasonable fruit of his religion,—it would be [pg 328] unreasonable only in case he did not exist. If, for instance, you were to condemn a religion of human or animal sacrifices by virtue of your subjective sentiments, and if all the while a deity were really there demanding such sacrifices, you would be making a theoretical mistake by tacitly assuming that the deity must be non-existent; you would be setting up a theology of your own as much as if you were a scholastic philosopher.

To this extent, to the extent of disbelieving peremptorily in certain types of deity, I frankly confess that we must be theologians. If disbeliefs can be said to constitute a theology, then the prejudices, instincts, and common sense which I chose as our guides make theological partisans of us whenever they make certain beliefs abhorrent.

But such common-sense prejudices and instincts are themselves the fruit of an empirical evolution. Nothing is more striking than the secular alteration that goes on in the moral and religious tone of men, as their insight into nature and their social arrangements progressively develop. After an interval of a few generations the mental climate proves unfavorable to notions of the deity which at an earlier date were perfectly satisfactory: the older gods have fallen below the common secular level, and can no longer be believed in. To-day a deity who should require bleeding sacrifices to placate him would be too sanguinary to be taken seriously. Even if powerful historical credentials were put forward in his favor, we would not look at them. Once, on the contrary, his cruel appetites were of themselves credentials. They positively recommended him to men's imaginations in ages when such coarse signs of power were respected and no others could be understood. Such deities then were worshiped because such fruits were relished.

[pg 329]
Doubtless historic accidents always played some later part, but the original factor in fixing the figure of the gods must always have been psychological. The deity to whom the prophets, seers, and devotees who founded the particular cult bore witness was worth something to them personally. They could use him. He guided their imagination, warranted their hopes, and controlled their will,—or else they required him as a safeguard against the demon and a curber of other people's crimes. In any case, they chose him for the value of the fruits he seemed to them to yield. So soon as the fruits began to seem quite worthless; so soon as they conflicted with indispensable human ideals, or thwarted too extensively other values; so soon as they appeared childish, contemptible, or immoral when reflected on, the deity grew discredited, and was erelong neglected and forgotten. It was in this way that the Greek and Roman gods ceased to be believed in by educated pagans; it is thus that we ourselves judge of the Hindu, Buddhist, and Mohammedan theologies; Protestants have so dealt with the Catholic notions of deity, and liberal Protestants with older Protestant notions; it is thus that Chinamen judge of us, and that all of us now living will be judged by our descendants. When we cease to admire or approve what the definition of a deity implies, we end by deeming that deity incredible.

Few historic changes are more curious than these mutations of theological opinion. The monarchical type of sovereignty was, for example, so ineradicably planted in the mind of our own forefathers that a dose of cruelty and arbitrariness in their deity seems positively to have been required by their imagination. They called the cruelty "retributive justice," and a God without it would certainly have struck them as not "sovereign" enough. But [pg 330] to-day we abhor the very notion of eternal suffering inflicted; and that arbitrary dealing-out of salvation and damnation to selected individuals, of which Jonathan Edwards could persuade himself that he had not only a conviction, but a "delightful conviction," as of a doctrine "exceeding pleasant, bright, and sweet," appears to us, if sovereignly anything, sovereignly irrational and mean. Not only the cruelty, but the paltriness of character of the gods believed in by earlier centuries also strikes later centuries with surprise. We shall see examples of it from the annals of Catholic saintship which make us rub our Protestant eyes. Ritual worship in general appears to the modern transcendentalist, as well as to the ultra-puritanic type of mind, as if addressed to a deity of an almost absurdly childish character, taking delight in toy-shop furniture, tapers and tinsel, costume and mumbling and mummery, and finding his "glory" incomprehensibly enhanced thereby;—just as on the other hand the formless spaciousness of pantheism appears quite empty to ritualistic natures, and the gaunt theism of evangelical sects seems intolerably bald and chalky and bleak. Luther, says Emerson, would have cut off his right hand rather than nail his theses to the door at Wittenberg, if he had supposed that they were destined to lead to the pale negations of Boston Unitarianism.

So far, then, although we are compelled, whatever may be our pretensions to empiricism, to employ some sort of a standard of theological probability of our own whenever we assume to estimate the fruits of other men's religion, yet this very standard has been begotten out of the drift of common life. It is the voice of human experience within us, judging and condemning all gods that stand athwart the pathway along which it feels itself to be advancing. Experience, if we take it in the largest sense, is [pg 331] thus the parent of those disbeliefs which, it was charged, were inconsistent with the experiential method. The inconsistency, you see, is immaterial, and the charge may be neglected.

If we pass from disbeliefs to positive beliefs, it seems to me that there is not even a formal inconsistency to be laid against our method. The gods we stand by are the gods we need and can use, the gods whose demands on us are reinforcements of our demands on ourselves and on one another. What I then propose to do is, briefly stated, to test saintliness by common sense, to use human standards to help us decide how far the religious life commends itself as an ideal kind of human activity. If it commends itself, then any theological beliefs that may inspire it, in so far forth will stand accredited. If not, then they will be discredited, and all without reference to anything but human working principles. It is but the elimination of the humanly unfit, and the survival of the humanly fittest, applied to religious beliefs; and if we look at history candidly and without prejudice, we have to admit that no religion has ever in the long run established or proved itself in any other way. Religions have *approved* themselves; they have ministered to sundry vital needs which they found reigning. When they violated other needs too strongly, or when other faiths came which served the same needs better, the first religions were supplanted.

The needs were always many, and the tests were never sharp. So the reproach of vagueness and subjectivity and "on the whole"-ness, which can with perfect legitimacy be addressed to the empirical method as we are forced to use it, is after all a reproach to which the entire life of man in dealing with these matters is obnoxious. No religion has ever yet owed its prevalence to "apodictic [pg 332] certainty." In a later lecture I will ask whether objective certainty can ever be added by theological reasoning to a religion that already empirically prevails.

One word, also, about the reproach that in following this sort of an empirical method we are handing ourselves over to systematic skepticism.

Since it is impossible to deny secular alterations in our sentiments and needs, it would be absurd to affirm that one's own age of the world can be beyond correction by the next age. Skepticism cannot, therefore, be ruled out by any set of thinkers as a possibility against which their conclusions are secure; and no empiricist ought to claim exemption from this universal liability. But to admit one's liability to correction is one thing, and to embark upon a sea of wanton doubt is another. Of willfully playing into the hands of skepticism we cannot be accused. He who acknowledges the imperfectness of his instrument, and makes allowance for it in discussing his observations, is in a much better position for gaining truth than if he claimed his instrument to be infallible. Or is dogmatic or scholastic theology less doubted in point of fact for claiming, as it does, to be in point of right undoubtable? And if not, what command over truth would this kind of theology really lose if, instead of absolute certainty, she only claimed reasonable probability for her conclusions? If *we* claim only reasonable probability, it will be as much as men who love the truth can ever at any given moment hope to have within their grasp. Pretty surely it will be more than we could have had, if we were unconscious of our liability to err.

Nevertheless, dogmatism will doubtless continue to condemn us for this confession. The mere outward form of [pg 333] inalterable certainty is so precious to some minds that to renounce it explicitly is for them out of the question. They will claim it even where the facts most patently pronounce its folly. But the safe thing is surely to recognize that all the insights of creatures of a day like ourselves must be provisional. The wisest of critics is an altering being, subject to the better insight of the morrow, and right at any moment, only "up to date" and "on the whole." When larger ranges of truth open, it is surely best to be able to open ourselves to their reception, unfettered by our previous pretensions. "Heartily know, when half-gods go, the gods arrive."

The fact of diverse judgments about religious phenomena is therefore entirely unescapable, whatever may be one's own desire to attain the irreversible. But apart from that fact, a more fundamental question awaits us, the question whether men's opinions ought to be expected to be absolutely uniform in this field. Ought all men to have the same religion? Ought they to approve the same fruits and follow the same leadings? Are they so like in their inner needs that, for hard and soft, for proud and humble, for strenuous and lazy, for healthy-minded and despairing, exactly the same religious incentives are required? Or are different functions in the organism of humanity allotted to different types of man, so that some may really be the better for a religion of consolation and reassurance, whilst others are better for one of terror and reproof? It might conceivably be so; and we shall, I think, more and more suspect it to be so as we go on. And if it be so, how can any possible judge or critic help being biased in favor of the religion by which his own needs are best met? He aspires to impartiality; but he is too close to the struggle not to be to some degree a participant, and he is sure to approve [pg 334] most warmly those fruits of piety in others which taste most good and prove most nourishing to *him*.

I am well aware of how anarchic much of what I say may sound. Expressing myself thus abstractly and briefly, I may seem to despair of the very notion of truth. But I beseech you to reserve your judgment until we see it applied to the details which lie before us. I do indeed disbelieve that we or any other mortal men can attain on a given day to absolutely incorrigible and unimprovable truth about such matters of fact as those with which religions deal. But I reject this dogmatic ideal not out of a perverse delight in intellectual instability. I am no lover of disorder and doubt as such. Rather do I fear to lose truth by this pretension to possess it already wholly. That we can gain more and more of it by moving always in the right direction, I believe as much as any one, and I hope to bring you all to my way of thinking before the termination of these lectures. Till then, do not, I pray you, harden your minds irrevocably against the empiricism which I profess.

I will waste no more words, then, in abstract justification of my method, but seek immediately to use it upon the facts.

In critically judging of the value of religious phenomena, it is very important to insist on the distinction between religion as an individual personal function, and religion as an institutional, corporate, or tribal product. I drew this distinction, you may remember, in my second lecture. The word "religion," as ordinarily used, is equivocal. A survey of history shows us that, as a rule, religious geniuses attract disciples, and produce groups of sympathizers. When these groups get strong enough to "organize" themselves, they become ecclesiastical institutions [pg 335] with corporate ambitions of their own. The spirit of politics and the lust of dogmatic rule are then apt to enter and to contaminate the originally innocent thing; so that when we hear the word "religion" nowadays, we think inevitably of some "church" or other; and to some persons the word "church" suggests so much hypocrisy and tyranny and meanness and tenacity of superstition that in a wholesale undiscerning way they glory in saying that they are "down" on religion altogether. Even we who belong to churches do not exempt other churches than our own from the general condemnation.

But in this course of lectures ecclesiastical institutions hardly concern us at all. The religious experience which we are studying is that which lives itself out within the private breast. First-hand individual experience of this kind has always appeared as a heretical sort of innovation to those who witnessed its birth. Naked comes it into the world and lonely; and it has always, for a time at least, driven him who had it into the wilderness, often into the literal wilderness out of doors, where the Buddha, Jesus, Mohammed, St. Francis, George Fox, and so many others had to go. George Fox expresses well this isolation; and I can do no better at this point than read to you a page from his Journal, referring to the period of his youth when religion began to ferment within him seriously.

> "I fasted much," Fox says, "walked abroad in solitary places many days, and often took my Bible, and sat in hollow trees and lonesome places until night came on; and frequently in the night walked mournfully about by myself; for I was a man of sorrows in the time of the first workings of the Lord in me.
>
> "During all this time I was never joined in profession of religion with any, but gave up myself to the Lord, having forsaken [pg 336]all evil company, taking leave of father and mother, and all other relations, and traveled up and down as a stranger on the earth, which way the Lord inclined my heart; taking a chamber to myself in the town where I came, and tarrying sometimes more, sometimes less in a place: for I durst not stay long in a place, being afraid both of professor and profane, lest, being a tender young man, I should be hurt by conversing much with either. For which reason I kept much as a stranger, seeking heavenly wisdom and getting knowledge from the Lord; and was brought off from outward things, to rely on the Lord alone. As I had forsaken the priests, so I left the separate preachers also, and those called the most experienced people; for I saw there was none among them all that could speak to my condition. And when all my hopes in them and in all men were gone so that I had nothing outwardly to help me, nor could tell what to do; then, oh then, I heard a voice which said, 'There is one, even Jesus Christ, that can speak to thy condition.' When I heard it, my heart did leap for joy. Then the Lord let me see why there was none upon the earth

that could speak to my condition. I had not fellowship with any people, priests, nor professors, nor any sort of separated people. I was afraid of all carnal talk and talkers, for I could see nothing but corruptions. When I was in the deep, under all shut up, I could not believe that I should ever overcome; my troubles, my sorrows, and my temptations were so great that I often thought I should have despaired, I was so tempted. But when Christ opened to me how he was tempted by the same devil, and had overcome him, and had bruised his head; and that through him and his power, life, grace, and spirit, I should overcome also, I had confidence in him. If I had had a king's diet, palace, and attendance, all would have been as nothing; for nothing gave me comfort but the Lord by his power. I saw professors, priests, and people were whole and at ease in that condition which was my misery, and they loved that which I would have been rid of. But the Lord did stay my desires upon himself, and my care was cast upon him alone."[197]

[pg 337]
A genuine first-hand religious experience like this is bound to be a heterodoxy to its witnesses, the prophet appearing as a mere lonely madman. If his doctrine prove contagious enough to spread to any others, it becomes a definite and labeled heresy. But if it then still prove contagious enough to triumph over persecution, it becomes itself an orthodoxy; and when a religion has become an orthodoxy, its day of inwardness is over: the spring is dry; the faithful live at second hand exclusively and stone the prophets in their turn. The new church, in spite of whatever human goodness it may foster, can be henceforth counted on as a staunch ally in every attempt to stifle the spontaneous religious spirit, and to stop all later bubblings of the fountain from which in purer days it drew its own supply of inspiration. Unless, indeed, by adopting new movements of the spirit it can make capital out of them and use them for its selfish corporate designs! Of protective action of this politic sort, promptly or tardily decided on, the dealings of the Roman ecclesiasticism with many individual saints and prophets yield examples enough for our instruction.

The plain fact is that men's minds are built, as has been often said, in water-tight compartments. Religious after a fashion, they yet have many other things in them beside their religion, and unholy entanglements and associations inevitably obtain. The basenesses so commonly charged to religion's account are thus, almost all of them, not chargeable at all to religion proper, but rather to religion's wicked practical partner, the spirit of corporate dominion. And the bigotries are most of them in their turn chargeable to religion's wicked intellectual partner, the spirit of dogmatic dominion, the passion for laying down the law in the form of an absolutely closed-in theoretic system. The ecclesiastical spirit in general is the [pg 338] sum of these two spirits of dominion; and I beseech you never to confound the phenomena of mere tribal or corporate psychology which it presents with those manifestations of the purely interior life which are the exclusive object of our study. The baiting of Jews, the hunting of Albigenses and Waldenses, the stoning of Quakers and ducking of Methodists, the murdering of Mormons and the massacring of Armenians, express much rather that aboriginal human neophobia, that pugnacity of which we all share the vestiges, and that inborn hatred of the alien and of eccentric and non-conforming men as aliens, than they express the positive piety of the various perpetrators. Piety is the mask, the inner force is tribal instinct. You believe as little as I do, in spite of the Christian unction with which the German emperor addressed his troops upon their way to China, that the conduct which he suggested, and in which other Christian armies went beyond them, had anything whatever to do with the interior religious life of those concerned in the performance.

Well, no more for past atrocities than for this atrocity should we make piety responsible. At most we may blame piety for not availing to check our natural passions, and sometimes for supplying them with hypocritical pretexts. But hypocrisy also imposes obligations, and with the pretext usually couples some restriction; and when the passion gust is over, the piety may bring a reaction of repentance which the irreligious natural man would not have shown.

For many of the historic aberrations which have been laid to her charge, religion as such, then, is not to blame. Yet of the charge that over-zealousness or fanaticism is one of her liabilities we cannot wholly acquit her, so I will next make a remark upon that point. But I will [pg 339] preface it by a preliminary remark which connects itself with much that follows.

Our survey of the phenomena of saintliness has unquestionably produced in your minds an impression of extravagance. Is it necessary, some of you have asked, as one example after another came before us, to be quite so fantastically good as that? We who have no vocation for the extremer ranges of sanctity will surely be let off at the last day if our humility, asceticism, and devoutness prove of a less convulsive sort. This practically amounts to saying that much that it is legitimate to admire in this field need nevertheless not be imitated, and that religious phenomena, like all other human phenomena, are subject to the law of the golden mean. Political reformers accomplish their successive tasks in the history of nations by being blind for the time to other causes. Great schools of art work out the effects which it is their mission to reveal, at the cost of a one-sidedness for which other schools must make amends. We accept a John Howard, a Mazzini, a Botticelli, a Michael Angelo, with a kind of indulgence. We are glad they existed to show us that way, but we are glad there are also other ways of seeing and taking life. So of many of the saints whom we have looked at. We are proud of a human nature that could be so passionately extreme, but we shrink from advising others to follow the example. The conduct we blame ourselves for not following lies nearer to the middle line of human effort. It is less dependent on particular beliefs and doctrines. It is such as wears well in different ages, such as under different skies all judges are able to commend.

The fruits of religion, in other words, are, like all human products, liable to corruption by excess. Common [pg 340] sense must judge them. It need not blame the votary; but it may be able to praise him only conditionally, as one who acts faithfully according to his lights. He shows us heroism in one way, but the unconditionally good way is that for which no indulgence need be asked.

We find that error by excess is exemplified by every saintly virtue. Excess, in human faculties, means usually one-sidedness or want of balance; for it is hard to imagine an essential faculty too strong, if only other faculties equally strong be there to coöperate with it in action. Strong affections need a strong will; strong active powers need a strong intellect; strong intellect needs strong sympathies, to keep life steady. If the balance exist, no one faculty can possibly be too strong—we only get the stronger all-round character. In the life of saints, technically so called, the spiritual faculties are strong, but what gives the impression of extravagance proves usually on examination to be a relative deficiency of intellect. Spiritual excitement takes pathological forms whenever other interests are too few and the intellect too narrow. We find this exemplified by all the saintly attributes in turn—devout love of God, purity, charity, asceticism, all may lead astray. I will run over these virtues in succession.

First of all let us take Devoutness. When unbalanced, one of its vices is called Fanaticism. Fanaticism (when not a mere expression of ecclesiastical ambition) is only loyalty carried to a convulsive extreme. When an intensely loyal and narrow mind is once grasped by the feeling that a certain superhuman person is worthy of its exclusive devotion, one of the first things that happens is that it idealizes the devotion itself. To adequately realize the merits of the idol gets to be considered the [pg 341] one great merit of the worshiper; and the sacrifices and servilities by which savage tribesmen have from time immemorial exhibited their faithfulness to chieftains are now outbid in favor of the deity. Vocabularies are exhausted and languages altered in the attempt to praise him enough; death is looked on as gain if it attract his grateful notice; and the personal attitude of being his devotee becomes what one might almost call a new and exalted kind of professional specialty within the tribe.[198] The legends that gather round the lives of holy persons are fruits of this impulse to celebrate and glorify. The Buddha[199] and Mohammed[200] and their companions and many Christian saints are incrusted with a heavy jewelry [pg 342] of anecdotes which are meant to be honorific, but are simply *abgeschmackt* and silly, and form a touching expression of man's misguided propensity to praise.

An immediate consequence of this condition of mind is jealousy for the deity's honor. How can the devotee show his loyalty better than by sensitiveness in this regard? The slightest affront or neglect must be resented, the deity's enemies must be put to shame. In exceedingly narrow minds and active wills, such a care may become an engrossing preoccupation; and crusades have been preached and massacres instigated for no other reason than to remove a fancied slight upon the God.

Theologies representing the gods as mindful of their glory, and churches with imperialistic policies, have conspired to fan this temper to a glow, so that intolerance and persecution have come to be vices associated by some of us inseparably with the saintly mind. They are unquestionably its besetting sins. The saintly temper is a moral temper, and a moral temper has often to be cruel. It is a partisan temper, and that is cruel. Between his own and Jehovah's enemies a David knows no difference; a Catherine of Siena, panting to stop the warfare among Christians which was the scandal of her epoch, can think of no better method of union among them than a crusade to massacre the Turks; Luther finds no word of protest or regret over the atrocious tortures with which the Anabaptist leaders were put to death; and a Cromwell praises the Lord for delivering his enemies into his hands for "execution." Politics come in in all such cases; but piety finds the partnership not quite unnatural. So, when "freethinkers" tell us that religion and fanaticism are twins, we cannot make an unqualified denial of the charge.

Fanaticism must then be inscribed on the wrong side [pg 343] of religion's account, so long as the religious person's intellect is on the stage which the despotic kind of God satisfies. But as soon as the God is represented as less intent on his own honor and glory, it ceases to be a danger.

Fanaticism is found only where the character is masterful and aggressive. In gentle characters, where devoutness is intense and the intellect feeble, we have an imaginative absorption in the love of God to the exclusion of all practical human interests, which, though innocent enough, is too one-sided to be admirable. A mind too narrow has room but for one kind of affection. When the love of God takes possession of such a mind, it expels all human loves and human uses. There is no English name for such a sweet excess of devotion, so I will refer to it as a *theopathic* condition.

The blessed Margaret Mary Alacoque may serve as an example.

> "To be loved here upon the earth," her recent biographer exclaims: "to be loved by a noble, elevated, distinguished being; to be loved with fidelity, with devotion,—what enchantment! But to be loved by God! and loved by him to distraction [aimé jusqù'à la folie]!—Margaret melted away with love at the thought of such a thing. Like Saint Philip of Neri in former times, or

like Saint Francis Xavier, she said to God: 'Hold back, O my God, these torrents which overwhelm me, or else enlarge my capacity for their reception.' "[201]

The most signal proofs of God's love which Margaret Mary received were her hallucinations of sight, touch, and hearing, and the most signal in turn of these were the revelations of Christ's sacred heart, "surrounded with rays more brilliant than the Sun, and transparent like a crystal. The wound which he received on the cross visibly appeared upon it. There [pg 344]was a crown of thorns round about this divine Heart, and a cross above it." At the same time Christ's voice told her that, unable longer to contain the flames of his love for mankind, he had chosen her by a miracle to spread the knowledge of them. He thereupon took out her mortal heart, placed it inside of his own and inflamed it, and then replaced it in her breast, adding: "Hitherto thou hast taken the name of my slave, hereafter thou shalt be called the well-beloved disciple of my Sacred Heart."

In a later vision the Saviour revealed to her in detail the "great design" which he wished to establish through her instrumentality. "I ask of thee to bring it about that every first Friday after the week of holy Sacrament shall be made into a special holy day for honoring my Heart by a general communion and by services intended to make honorable amends for the indignities which it has received. And I promise thee that my Heart will dilate to shed with abundance the influences of its love upon all those who pay to it these honors, or who bring it about that others do the same."

"This revelation," says Mgr. Bougaud, "is unquestionably the most important of all the revelations which have illumined the Church since that of the Incarnation and of the Lord's Supper.... After the Eucharist, the supreme effort of the Sacred Heart."[202] Well, what were its good fruits for Margaret Mary's life? Apparently little else but sufferings and prayers and absences of mind and swoons and ecstasies. She became increasingly useless about the convent, her absorption in Christ's love,—

"which grew upon her daily, rendering her more and more incapable of attending to external duties. They tried her in the infirmary, but without much success, although her kindness, zeal, and devotion were without bounds, and her charity rose to acts of such a heroism that our readers would not bear the recital [pg 345]of them. They tried her in the kitchen, but were forced to give it up as hopeless—everything dropped out of her hands. The admirable humility with which she made amends for her clumsiness could not prevent this from being prejudicial to the order and regularity which must always reign in a community. They put her in the school, where the little girls

> cherished her, and cut pieces out of her clothes [for relics] as if she were already a saint, but where she was too absorbed inwardly to pay the necessary attention. Poor dear sister, even less after her visions than before them was she a denizen of earth, and they had to leave her in her heaven."[203]

Poor dear sister, indeed! Amiable and good, but so feeble of intellectual outlook that it would be too much to ask of us, with our Protestant and modern education, to feel anything but indulgent pity for the kind of saintship which she embodies. A lower example still of theopathic saintliness is that of Saint Gertrude, a Benedictine nun of the thirteenth century, whose "Revelations," a well-known mystical authority, consist mainly of proofs of Christ's partiality for her undeserving person. Assurances of his love, intimacies and caresses and compliments of the most absurd and puerile sort, addressed by Christ to Gertrude as an individual, form the tissue of this paltry-minded recital.[204] In reading such a narrative, [pg 346] we realize the gap between the thirteenth and the twentieth century, and we feel that saintliness of character may yield almost absolutely worthless fruits if it be associated with such inferior intellectual sympathies. What with science, idealism, and democracy, our own imagination has grown to need a God of an entirely different temperament from that Being interested exclusively in dealing out personal favors, with whom our ancestors were so contented. Smitten as we are with the vision of social righteousness, a God indifferent to everything but adulation, and full of partiality for his individual favorites, lacks an essential element of largeness; and even the best professional sainthood of former centuries, pent in as it is to such a conception, seems to us curiously shallow and unedifying.

Take Saint Teresa, for example, one of the ablest women, in many respects, of whose life we have the record. She had a powerful intellect of the practical order. She wrote admirable descriptive psychology, possessed a will equal to any emergency, great talent for politics and business, a buoyant disposition, and a first-rate literary style. She was tenaciously aspiring, and put her whole life at the service of her religious ideals. Yet so paltry were these, according to our present way of thinking, that (although I know that others have been moved differently) I confess that my only feeling in [pg 347] reading her has been pity that so much vitality of soul should have found such poor employment.

In spite of the sufferings which she endured, there is a curious flavor of superficiality about her genius. A Birmingham anthropologist, Dr. Jordan, has divided the human race into two types, whom he calls "shrews" and "non-shrews" respectively.[205] The shrew-type is defined as possessing an "active unimpassioned temperament." In other words, shrews are the "motors," rather than the "sensories,"[206] and their expressions are as a rule more energetic than the feelings which appear to prompt them. Saint Teresa, paradoxical as such a judgment may sound, was a typical shrew, in this sense of the term. The bustle of her style, as well as of her life, proves it. Not only must she receive unheard-of personal favors and spiritual graces from her Saviour, but she must immediately write about them and *exploiter* them professionally, and use her expertness to give instruction to those less privileged. Her voluble egotism; her sense, not of radical bad being, as the really contrite have it, but of her "faults" and "imperfections" in the plural; her stereotyped humility and return upon herself, as covered with "confusion" at each new manifestation of God's singular partiality for a person so unworthy, are typical of shrewdom: a paramountly feeling nature would be objectively lost in gratitude, and silent. She had some public instincts, it is true; she hated the Lutherans, and longed for the church's triumph over them; but in the main her idea of religion seems to have been that of an endless amatory flirtation—if one may say so without irreverence—between [pg 348] the devotee and the deity; and apart from helping younger nuns to go in this direction by the inspiration of her example and instruction, there is absolutely no human use in her, or sign of any general human interest. Yet the spirit of her age, far from rebuking her, exalted her as superhuman.

We have to pass a similar judgment on the whole notion of saintship based on merits. Any God who, on the one hand, can care to keep a pedantically minute account of individual shortcomings, and on the other can feel such partialities, and load particular creatures with such insipid marks of favor, is too small-minded a God for our credence. When Luther, in his immense manly way, swept off by a stroke of his hand the very notion of a debit and credit account kept with individuals by the Almighty, he stretched the soul's imagination and saved theology from puerility.

So much for mere devotion, divorced from the intellectual conceptions which might guide it towards bearing useful human fruit.

The next saintly virtue in which we find excess is Purity. In theopathic characters, like those whom we have just considered, the love of God must not be mixed with any other love. Father and mother, sisters, brothers, and friends are felt as interfering distractions; for sensitiveness and narrowness, when they occur together, as they often do, require above all things a simplified world to dwell in. Variety and confusion are too much for their powers of comfortable adaptation. But whereas your aggressive pietist reaches his unity objectively, by forcibly stamping disorder and divergence out, your retiring pietist reaches his subjectively, leaving disorder in the world at large, but making a smaller world in which he dwells [pg 349] himself and from which he eliminates it altogether. Thus, alongside of the church militant with its prisons, dragonnades, and inquisition methods, we have the church *fugient,* as one might call it, with its hermitages, monasteries, and sectarian organizations, both churches pursuing the same object—to unify the life,[207] and simplify the spectacle presented to the soul. A mind extremely sensitive to inner discords will drop one external relation after another, as interfering with the absorption of consciousness in spiritual things. Amusements must go first, then conventional "society," then business, then family duties, until at last seclusion, with a subdivision of the day into hours for stated religious acts, is the only thing that can be borne. The lives of saints are a history of successive renunciations of complication, one form of contact with the outer life being dropped after another, to save the purity of inner tone.[208] "Is it not better," a young sister [pg 350] asks her Superior, "that I should not speak at all during the hour of recreation, so as not to run the risk, by speaking, of falling into some sin of which I might not be conscious?"[209] If the life remains a social one at all, those who take part in it must follow one identical rule. Embosomed in this monotony, the zealot for purity feels clean and free once more. The minuteness of uniformity maintained in certain sectarian communities, whether monastic or not, is something almost inconceivable to a man of the world. Costume, phraseology, hours, and habits are absolutely stereotyped, and there is no doubt that some persons are so made as to find in this stability an incomparable kind of mental rest.

We have no time to multiply examples, so I will let the case of Saint Louis of Gonzaga serve as a type of excess in purification. I think you will agree that this youth carried the elimination of the external and discordant to a point which we cannot unreservedly admire. At the age of ten, his biographer says:—

"The inspiration came to him to consecrate to the Mother of God his own virginity—that being to her the most agreeable of possible presents. Without delay, then, and with all the fervor there was in him, joyous of heart, and burning with love, he made his vow of perpetual chastity. Mary accepted the offering of his innocent heart, and obtained for him from God, as a recompense, the extraordinary grace of never feeling during his entire life the slightest touch of temptation against the virtue of purity. This was an altogether exceptional favor, rarely accorded even to Saints themselves, and all the more marvelous in that Louis dwelt always in courts and among great folks, where danger and opportunity are so unusually frequent. It is true that Louis from his earliest childhood had shown a natural repugnance for whatever might be impure or [pg 351]unvirginal, and even for relations of any sort whatever between persons of opposite sex. But this made it all the more surprising that he should, especially since this vow, feel it necessary to have recourse to such a number of expedients for protecting against even the shadow of danger the virginity which he had thus consecrated. One might suppose that if any one could have contented himself with the ordinary precautions, prescribed for all Christians, it would assuredly have been he. But no! In the use of preservatives and means of defense, in flight from the most insignificant occasions, from every possibility of peril, just as in the mortification of his flesh, he went farther than the majority of saints. He, who by an extraordinary protection of God's grace was never tempted, measured all his steps as if he were threatened on every side by particular dangers. Thenceforward he never raised his eyes, either when walking in the streets, or when in society. Not only did he avoid all business with females even more scrupulously than before, but he renounced all conversation and every kind of social recreation with them, although his father tried to make him take part; and he commenced only too early to deliver his innocent body to austerities of every kind."[210]

At the age of twelve, we read of this young man that "if by chance his mother sent one of her maids of honor to him with a message, he never allowed her to come in, but listened to her through the barely opened door, and dismissed her immediately. He did not like to be alone with his own mother, whether at table or in conversation; and when the rest of the company withdrew, he sought also a pretext for retiring.... Several great ladies, relatives of his, he avoided learning to know even by sight; and he made a sort of treaty with his father, engaging promptly and readily to accede to all his wishes, if he might only be excused from all visits to ladies." (Ibid., p. 71.)

[pg 352]
When he was seventeen years old Louis joined the Jesuit order[211] against his father's passionate entreaties, for he was heir of a princely house; and when a year later the father died, he took the loss as a "particular attention" to himself on God's part, and wrote letters of stilted good advice, as from a spiritual superior, to his grieving mother. He soon became so good a monk that if any one asked him the number of his brothers and sisters, he had to reflect and count them over before replying. A Father asked him one day if he were never troubled by the thought of his family, to which, "I never think of them except when praying for them," was his only answer. Never was he seen to hold in his hand a flower or anything perfumed, that he might take pleasure in it. On the contrary, in the hospital, he used to seek for whatever was most disgusting, and eagerly snatch the bandages of ulcers, etc., from the hands of his companions. He avoided worldly talk, and immediately tried to turn every conversation on to pious subjects, or else he remained silent. He systematically refused to notice his surroundings. Being ordered one day to bring a book from the rector's seat in the refectory, he had to ask where the rector sat, for in the three months he had eaten bread there, so carefully did he guard his eyes that he had not noticed the place. One day, during recess, having looked by chance on one of his companions, he reproached himself as for a grave sin against modesty. He cultivated silence, as preserving from sins of the tongue; and his greatest penance was the limit which his superiors set to his bodily penances. He sought after [pg 353] false accusations and unjust reprimands as opportunities of humility; and such was his obedience that, when a room-mate, having no more paper, asked him for a sheet, he did not feel free to give it to him without first obtaining the permission of the superior, who, as such, stood in the place of God, and transmitted his orders.

I can find no other sorts of fruit than these of Louis's saintship. He died in 1591, in his twenty-ninth year, and is known in the Church as the patron of all young people. On his festival, the altar in the chapel devoted to him in a certain church in Rome "is embosomed in flowers, arranged with exquisite taste; and a pile of letters may be seen at its foot, written to the Saint by young men and women, and directed to 'Paradiso.' They are supposed to be burnt unread except by San Luigi, who must find singular petitions in these pretty little missives, tied up now with a green ribbon, expressive of hope, now with a red one, emblematic of love," etc.[212]

[pg 354]
Our final judgment of the worth of such a life as this will depend largely on our conception of God, and of the sort of conduct he is best pleased with in his creatures. The Catholicism of the sixteenth century paid little heed to social righteousness; and to leave the world to the devil whilst saving one's own soul was then accounted no discreditable scheme. To-day, rightly or wrongly, helpfulness in general human affairs is, in consequence of one of those secular mutations in moral sentiment of which I spoke, deemed an essential element of worth in character; and to be of some public or private use is also reckoned as a species of divine service. Other early Jesuits, especially the missionaries among them, the Xaviers, Brébeufs, Jogues, were objective minds, and fought in their way for the world's welfare; so their lives to-day inspire us. But when the intellect, as in this Louis, is originally no larger than a pin's head, and cherishes ideas of God of corresponding smallness, the result, notwithstanding the heroism put forth, is on the whole repulsive. Purity, we see in the object-lesson, is *not* the one thing needful; and it is better that a life should contract many a dirt-mark, than forfeit usefulness in its efforts to remain unspotted.

[pg 355]
Proceeding onwards in our search of religious extravagance, we next come upon excesses of Tenderness and Charity. Here saintliness has to face the charge of preserving the unfit, and breeding parasites and beggars. "Resist not evil," "Love your enemies," these are saintly maxims of which men of this world find it hard to speak without impatience. Are the men of this world right, or are the saints in possession of the deeper range of truth?

No simple answer is possible. Here, if anywhere, one feels the complexity of the moral life, and the mysteriousness of the way in which facts and ideals are interwoven.

Perfect conduct is a relation between three terms: the actor, the objects for which he acts, and the recipients of the action. In order that conduct should be abstractly perfect, all three terms, intention, execution, and reception, should be suited to one another. The best intention will fail if it either work by false means or address itself to the wrong recipient. Thus no critic or estimator of the value of conduct can confine himself to the actor's animus alone, apart from the other elements of the performance. As there is no worse lie than a truth misunderstood by those who hear it, so reasonable arguments, challenges to magnanimity, and appeals to sympathy or justice, are folly when we are dealing with human crocodiles and boa-constrictors. The saint may simply give the universe into the hands of the enemy by his trustfulness. He may by non-resistance cut off his own survival.

Herbert Spencer tells us that the perfect man's conduct will appear perfect only when the environment is perfect: to no inferior environment is it suitably adapted. We may paraphrase this by cordially admitting that [pg 356] saintly conduct would be the most perfect conduct conceivable in an environment where all were saints already; but by adding that in an environment where few are saints, and many the exact reverse of saints, it must be ill adapted. We must frankly confess, then, using our empirical common sense and ordinary practical prejudices, that in the world that actually is, the virtues of sympathy, charity, and non-resistance may be, and often have been, manifested in excess. The powers of darkness have systematically taken advantage of them. The whole modern scientific organization of charity is a consequence of the failure of simply giving alms. The whole history of constitutional government is a commentary on the excellence of resisting evil, and when one cheek is smitten, of smiting back and not turning the other cheek also.

You will agree to this in general, for in spite of the Gospel, in spite of Quakerism, in spite of Tolstoi, you believe in fighting fire with fire, in shooting down usurpers, locking up thieves, and freezing out vagabonds and swindlers.

And yet you are sure, as I am sure, that were the world confined to these hard-headed, hard-hearted, and hard-fisted methods exclusively, were there no one prompt to help a brother first, and find out afterwards whether he were worthy; no one willing to drown his private wrongs in pity for the wronger's person; no one ready to be duped many a time rather than live always on suspicion; no one glad to treat individuals passionately and impulsively rather than by general rules of prudence; the world would be an infinitely worse place than it is now to live in. The tender grace, not of a day that is dead, but of a day yet to be born somehow, with the golden rule grown natural, would be cut out from the perspective of our imaginations.

[pg 357]
The saints, existing in this way, may, with their extravagances of human tenderness, be prophetic. Nay, innumerable times they have proved themselves prophetic. Treating those whom they met, in spite of the past, in spite of all appearances, as worthy, they have stimulated them to *be* worthy, miraculously transformed them by their radiant example and by the challenge of their expectation.

From this point of view we may admit the human charity which we find in all saints, and the great excess of it which we find in some saints, to be a genuinely creative social force, tending to make real a degree of virtue which it alone is ready to assume as possible. The saints are authors, *auctores*, increasers, of goodness. The potentialities of development in human souls are unfathomable. So many who seemed irretrievably hardened have in point of fact been softened, converted, regenerated, in ways that amazed the subjects even more than they surprised the spectators, that we never can be sure in advance of any man that his salvation by the way of love is hopeless. We have no right to speak of human crocodiles and boa-constrictors as of fixedly incurable beings. We know not the complexities of personality, the smouldering emotional fires, the other facets of the character-polyhedron, the resources of the subliminal region. St. Paul long ago made our ancestors familiar with the idea that every soul is virtually sacred. Since Christ died for us all without exception, St. Paul said, we must despair of no one. This belief in the essential sacredness of every one expresses itself to-day in all sorts of humane customs and reformatory institutions, and in a growing aversion to the death penalty and to brutality in punishment. The saints, with their extravagance of human tenderness, are the great torch-bearers of this [pg 358] belief, the tip of the wedge, the clearers of the darkness. Like the single drops which sparkle in the sun as they are flung far ahead of the advancing edge of a wave-crest or of a flood, they show the way and are forerunners. The world is not yet with them, so they often seem in the midst of the world's affairs to be preposterous. Yet they are impregnators of the world, vivifiers and animaters of potentialities of goodness which but for them would lie forever dormant. It is not possible to be quite as mean as we naturally are, when they have passed before us. One fire kindles another; and without that over-trust in human worth which they show, the rest of us would lie in spiritual stagnancy.

Momentarily considered, then, the saint may waste his tenderness and be the dupe and victim of his charitable fever, but the general function of his charity in social evolution is vital and essential. If things are ever to move upward, some one must be ready to take the first step, and assume the risk of it. No one who is not willing to try charity, to try non-resistance as the saint is always willing, can tell whether these methods will or will not succeed. When they do succeed, they are far more powerfully successful than force or worldly prudence. Force destroys enemies; and the best that can be said of prudence is that it keeps what we already have in safety. But non-resistance, when successful, turns enemies into friends; and charity regenerates its objects. These saintly methods are, as I said, creative energies; and genuine saints find in the elevated excitement with which their faith endows them an authority and impressiveness which makes them irresistible in situations where men of shallower nature cannot get on at all without the use of worldly prudence. This practical proof that worldly wisdom may be safely transcended is the saint's [pg 359] magic gift to mankind.[213] Not only does his vision of a better world console us for the generally prevailing prose [pg 360] and barrenness; but even when on the whole we have to confess him ill adapted, he makes some converts, and the environment gets better for his ministry. He is an effective ferment of goodness, a slow transmuter of the earthly into a more heavenly order.

In this respect the Utopian dreams of social justice in which many contemporary socialists and anarchists indulge are, in spite of their impracticability and non-adaptation to present environmental conditions, analogous to the saint's belief in an existent kingdom of heaven. They help to break the edge of the general reign of hardness, and are slow leavens of a better order.

The next topic in order is Asceticism, which I fancy you are all ready to consider without argument a virtue liable to extravagance and excess. The optimism and refinement of the modern imagination has, as I have already said elsewhere, changed the attitude of the church towards corporeal mortification, and a Suso or a Saint Peter of Alcantara[214] appear to us to-day rather in the [pg 361] light of tragic mountebanks than of sane men inspiring us with respect. If the inner dispositions are right, we ask, what need of all this torment, this violation of the outer nature? It keeps the outer nature too important. Any one who is genuinely emancipated from the flesh will look on pleasures and pains, abundance and privation, as alike irrelevant and indifferent. He can engage in actions and experience enjoyments without fear of corruption or enslavement. As the Bhagavad-Gita says, only those need renounce worldly actions who are still inwardly attached thereto. If one be really unattached to the fruits of action, one may mix in the world with equanimity. I quoted in a former lecture Saint Augustine's antinomian saying: If you only love God enough, you may safely follow all your inclinations. "He needs no devotional practices," is one of Ramakrishna's maxims, "whose heart is moved to tears at the mere mention of the name of Hari."[215] And the Buddha, in pointing out what he called "the middle way" to his disciples, told them to abstain from both extremes, excessive mortification being as unreal and unworthy as mere desire and pleasure. The only perfect life, he said, is that of inner wisdom, which makes one thing as indifferent to [pg 362] us as another, and thus leads to rest, to peace, and to Nirvâna.[216]

We find accordingly that as ascetic saints have grown older, and directors of conscience more experienced, they usually have shown a tendency to lay less stress on special bodily mortifications. Catholic teachers have always professed the rule that, since health is needed for efficiency in God's service, health must not be sacrificed to mortification. The general optimism and healthy-mindedness of liberal Protestant circles to-day makes mortification for mortification's sake repugnant to us. We can no longer sympathize with cruel deities, and the notion that God can take delight in the spectacle of sufferings self-inflicted in his honor is abhorrent. In consequence of all these motives you probably are disposed, unless some special utility can be shown in some individual's discipline, to treat the general tendency to asceticism as pathological.

Yet I believe that a more careful consideration of the whole matter, distinguishing between the general good intention of asceticism and the uselessness of some of the particular acts of which it may be guilty, ought to rehabilitate it in our esteem. For in its spiritual meaning asceticism stands for nothing less than for the essence of the twice-born philosophy. It symbolizes, lamely enough no doubt, but sincerely, the belief that there is an element of real wrongness in this world, which is neither to be ignored nor evaded, but which must be squarely met and overcome by an appeal to the soul's heroic resources, and neutralized and cleansed away by suffering. As against this view, the ultra-optimistic form of the once-born philosophy thinks we may treat evil by the method of ignoring. Let a man who, by fortunate health and circumstances, [pg 363] escapes the suffering of any great amount of evil in his own person, also close his eyes to it as it exists in the wider universe outside his private experience, and he will be quit of it altogether, and can sail through life happily on a healthy-minded basis. But we saw in our lectures on melancholy how precarious this attempt necessarily is. Moreover it is but for the individual; and leaves the evil outside of him, unredeemed and unprovided for in his philosophy.

No such attempt can be a *general* solution of the problem; and to minds of sombre tinge, who naturally feel life as a tragic mystery, such optimism is a shallow dodge or mean evasion. It accepts, in lieu of a real deliverance, what is a lucky personal accident merely, a cranny to escape by. It leaves the general world unhelped and still in the clutch of Satan. The real deliverance, the twice-born folk insist, must be of universal application. Pain and wrong and death must be fairly met and overcome in higher excitement, or else their sting remains essentially unbroken. If one has ever taken the fact of the prevalence of tragic death in this world's history fairly into his mind,—freezing, drowning, entombment alive, wild beasts, worse men, and hideous diseases,—he can with difficulty, it seems to me, continue his own career of worldly prosperity without suspecting that he may all the while not be really inside the game, that he may lack the great initiation.

Well, this is exactly what asceticism thinks; and it voluntarily takes the initiation. Life is neither farce nor genteel comedy, it says, but something we must sit at in mourning garments, hoping its bitter taste will purge us of our folly. The wild and the heroic are indeed such rooted parts of it that healthy-mindedness pure and simple, with its sentimental optimism, can hardly be regarded [pg 364] by any thinking man as a serious solution. Phrases of neatness, cosiness, and comfort can never be an answer to the sphinx's riddle.

In these remarks I am leaning only upon mankind's common instinct for reality, which in point of fact has always held the world to be essentially a theatre for heroism. In heroism, we feel, life's supreme mystery is hidden. We tolerate no one who has no capacity whatever for it in any direction. On the other hand, no matter what a man's frailties otherwise may be, if he be willing to risk death, and still more if he suffer it heroically, in the service he has chosen, the fact consecrates him forever. Inferior to ourselves in this or that way, if yet we cling to life, and he is able "to fling it away like a flower" as caring nothing for it, we account him in the deepest way our born superior. Each of us in his own person feels that a high-hearted indifference to life would expiate all his shortcomings.

The metaphysical mystery, thus recognized by common sense, that he who feeds on death that feeds on men possesses life supereminently and excellently, and meets best the secret demands of the universe, is the truth of which asceticism has been the faithful champion. The folly of the cross, so inexplicable by the intellect, has yet its indestructible vital meaning.

Representatively, then, and symbolically, and apart from the vagaries into which the unenlightened intellect of former times may have let it wander, asceticism must, I believe, be acknowledged to go with the profounder way of handling the gift of existence. Naturalistic optimism is mere syllabub and flattery and sponge-cake in comparison. The practical course of action for us, as religious men, would therefore, it seems to me, not be simply to turn our backs upon the ascetic impulse, as most of us to-day [pg 365] turn them, but rather to discover some outlet for it of which the fruits in the way of privation and hardship might be objectively useful. The older monastic asceticism occupied itself with pathetic futilities, or terminated in the mere egotism of the individual, increasing his own perfection.[217] But is it not possible for us to discard most of these older forms of mortification, and yet find saner channels for the heroism which inspired them?

Does not, for example, the worship of material luxury and wealth, which constitutes so large a portion of the "spirit" of our age, make somewhat for effeminacy and unmanliness? Is not the exclusively sympathetic and facetious way in which most children are brought up to-day—so different from the education of a hundred years ago, especially in evangelical circles—in danger, in spite of its many advantages, of developing a certain trashiness of fibre? Are there not hereabouts some points of application for a renovated and revised ascetic discipline?

Many of you would recognize such dangers, but would point to athletics, militarism, and individual and national enterprise and adventure as the remedies. These contemporary ideals are quite as remarkable for the energy with which they make for heroic standards of life, as contemporary religion is remarkable for the way in which it neglects them.[218] War and adventure assuredly keep all who engage in them from treating themselves too tenderly. They demand such incredible efforts, depth [pg 366] beyond depth of exertion, both in degree and in duration, that the whole scale of motivation alters. Discomfort and annoyance, hunger and wet, pain and cold, squalor and filth, cease to have any deterrent operation whatever. Death turns into a commonplace matter, and its usual power to check our action vanishes. With the annulling of these customary inhibitions, ranges of new energy are set free, and life seems cast upon a higher plane of power.

The beauty of war in this respect is that it is so congruous with ordinary human nature. Ancestral evolution has made us all potential warriors; so the most insignificant individual, when thrown into an army in the field, is weaned from whatever excess of tenderness towards his precious person he may bring with him, and may easily develop into a monster of insensibility.

But when we compare the military type of self-severity with that of the ascetic saint, we find a world-wide difference in all their spiritual concomitants.

" 'Live and let live,' " writes a clear-headed Austrian officer, "is no device for an army. Contempt for one's own comrades, for the troops of the enemy, and, above all, fierce contempt for one's own person, are what war demands of every one. Far better is it for an army to be too savage, too cruel, too barbarous, than to possess too much sentimentality and human reasonableness. If the soldier is to be good for anything as a soldier, he must be exactly the opposite of a reasoning and thinking man. The measure of goodness in him is his possible use in war. War, and even peace, require of the soldier absolutely peculiar standards of morality. The recruit brings with him common moral notions, of which he must seek immediately to get rid. For him victory, success, must be *everything*. The most barbaric tendencies [pg 367] in men come to life again in war, and for war's uses they are incommensurably good."[219]

These words are of course literally true. The immediate aim of the soldier's life is, as Moltke said, destruction, and nothing but destruction; and whatever constructions wars result in are remote and non-military. Consequently the soldier cannot train himself to be too feelingless to all those usual sympathies and respects, whether for persons or for things, that make for conservation. Yet the fact remains that war is a school of strenuous life and heroism; and, being in the line of aboriginal instinct, is the only school that as yet is universally available. But when we gravely ask ourselves whether this wholesale organization of irrationality and crime be our only bulwark against effeminacy, we stand aghast at the thought, and think more kindly of ascetic religion. One hears of the mechanical equivalent of heat. What we now need to discover in the social realm is the moral equivalent of war: something heroic that will speak to men as universally as war does, and yet will be as compatible with their spiritual selves as war has proved itself to be incompatible. I have often thought that in the old monkish poverty-worship, in spite of the pedantry which infested it, there might be something like that moral equivalent of war which we are seeking. May not voluntarily accepted poverty be "the strenuous life," without the need of crushing weaker peoples?

Poverty indeed *is* the strenuous life,—without brass bands or uniforms or hysteric popular applause or lies or circumlocutions; and when one sees the way in which wealth-getting enters as an ideal into the very bone and marrow of our generation, one wonders whether a revival [pg 368] of the belief that poverty is a worthy religious vocation may not be "the transformation of military courage," and the spiritual reform which our time stands most in need of.

Among us English-speaking peoples especially do the praises of poverty need once more to be boldly sung. We have grown literally afraid to be poor. We despise any one who elects to be poor in order to simplify and save his inner life. If he does not join the general scramble and pant with the money-making street, we deem him spiritless and lacking in ambition. We have lost the power even of imagining what the ancient idealization of poverty could have meant: the liberation from material attachments, the unbribed soul, the manlier indifference, the paying our way by what we are or do and not by what we have, the right to fling away our life at any moment irresponsibly,—the more athletic trim, in short, the moral fighting shape. When we of the so-called better classes are scared as men were never scared in history at material ugliness and hardship; when we put off marriage until our house can be artistic, and quake at the thought of having a child without a bank-account and doomed to manual labor, it is time for thinking men to protest against so unmanly and irreligious a state of opinion.

It is true that so far as wealth gives time for ideal ends and exercise to ideal energies, wealth is better than poverty and ought to be chosen. But wealth does this in only a portion of the actual cases. Elsewhere the desire to gain wealth and the fear to lose it are our chief breeders of cowardice and propagators of corruption. There are thousands of conjunctures in which a wealth-bound man must be a slave, whilst a man for whom poverty has no terrors becomes a freeman. Think of the strength which personal indifference to poverty would [pg 369] give us if we were devoted to unpopular causes. We need no longer hold our tongues or fear to vote the revolutionary or reformatory ticket. Our stocks might fall, our hopes of promotion vanish, our salaries stop, our club doors close in our faces; yet, while we lived, we would imperturbably bear witness to the spirit, and our example would help to set free our generation. The cause would need its funds, but we its servants would be potent in proportion as we personally were contented with our poverty.

I recommend this matter to your serious pondering, for it is certain that the prevalent fear of poverty among the educated classes is the worst moral disease from which our civilization suffers.

I have now said all that I can usefully say about the several fruits of religion as they are manifested in saintly lives, so I will make a brief review and pass to my more general conclusions.

Our question, you will remember, is as to whether religion stands approved by its fruits, as these are exhibited in the saintly type of character. Single attributes of saintliness may, it is true, be temperamental endowments, found in non-religious individuals. But the whole group of them forms a combination which, as such, is religious, for it seems to flow from the sense of the divine as from its psychological centre. Whoever possesses strongly this sense comes naturally to think that the smallest details of this world derive infinite significance from their relation to an unseen divine order. The thought of this order yields him a superior denomination of happiness, and a steadfastness of soul with which no other can compare. In social relations his serviceability is exemplary; he abounds in impulses to help. His help is inward [pg 370] as well as outward, for his sympathy reaches souls as well as bodies, and kindles unsuspected faculties therein. Instead of placing happiness where common men place it, in comfort, he places it in a higher kind of inner excitement, which converts discomforts into sources of cheer and annuls unhappiness. So he turns his back upon no duty, however thankless; and when we are in need of assistance, we can count upon the saint lending his hand with more certainty than we can count upon any other person. Finally, his humble-mindedness and his ascetic tendencies save him from the petty personal pretensions which so obstruct our ordinary social intercourse, and his purity gives us in him a clean man for a companion. Felicity, purity, charity, patience, self-severity,—these are splendid excellencies, and the saint of all men shows them in the completest possible measure.

But, as we saw, all these things together do not make saints infallible. When their intellectual outlook is narrow, they fall into all sorts of holy excesses, fanaticism or theopathic absorption, self-torment, prudery, scrupulosity, gullibility, and morbid inability to meet the world. By the very intensity of his fidelity to the paltry ideals with which an inferior intellect may inspire him, a saint can be even more objectionable and damnable than a superficial carnal man would be in the same situation. We must judge him not sentimentally only, and not in isolation, but using our own intellectual standards, placing him in his environment, and estimating his total function.

Now in the matter of intellectual standards, we must bear in mind that it is unfair, where we find narrowness of mind, always to impute it as a vice to the individual, for in religious and theological matters he probably absorbs his narrowness from his generation. Moreover, we [pg 371] must not confound the essentials of saintliness, which are those general passions of which I have spoken, with its accidents, which are the special determinations of these passions at any historical moment. In these determinations the saints will usually be loyal to the temporary idols of their tribe. Taking refuge in monasteries was as much an idol of the tribe in the middle ages, as bearing a hand in the world's work is to-day. Saint Francis or Saint Bernard, were they living to-day, would undoubtedly be leading consecrated lives of some sort, but quite as undoubtedly they would not lead them in retirement. Our animosity to special historic manifestations must not lead us to give away the saintly impulses in their essential nature to the tender mercies of inimical critics.

The most inimical critic of the saintly impulses whom I know is Nietzsche. He contrasts them with the worldly passions as we find these embodied in the predaceous military character, altogether to the advantage of the latter. Your born saint, it must be confessed, has something about him which often makes the gorge of a carnal man rise, so it will be worth while to consider the contrast in question more fully.

Dislike of the saintly nature seems to be a negative result of the biologically useful instinct of welcoming leadership, and glorifying the chief of the tribe. The chief is the potential, if not the actual tyrant, the masterful, overpowering man of prey. We confess our inferiority and grovel before him. We quail under his glance, and are at the same time proud of owning so dangerous a lord. Such instinctive and submissive hero-worship must have been indispensable in primeval tribal life. In the endless wars of those times, leaders were absolutely needed for the tribe's survival. If there were any tribes who owned no leaders, they can have left no [pg 372] issue to narrate their doom. The leaders always had good consciences, for conscience in them coalesced with will, and those who looked on their face were as much smitten with wonder at their freedom from inner restraint as with awe at the energy of their outward performances.

Compared with these beaked and taloned graspers of the world, saints are herbivorous animals, tame and harmless barn-yard poultry. There are saints whose beard you may, if you ever care to, pull with impunity. Such a man excites no thrills of wonder veiled in terror; his conscience is full of scruples and returns; he stuns us neither by his inward freedom nor his outward power; and unless he found within us an altogether different faculty of admiration to appeal to, we should pass him by with contempt.

In point of fact, he does appeal to a different faculty. Reënacted in human nature is the fable of the wind, the sun, and the traveler. The sexes embody the discrepancy. The woman loves the man the more admiringly the stormier he shows himself, and the world deifies its rulers the more for being willful and unaccountable. But the woman in turn subjugates the man by the mystery of gentleness in beauty, and the saint has always charmed the world by something similar. Mankind is susceptible and suggestible in opposite directions, and the rivalry of influences is unsleeping. The saintly and the worldly ideal pursue their feud in literature as much as in real life.

For Nietzsche the saint represents little but sneakingness and slavishness. He is the sophisticated invalid, the degenerate *par excellence,* the man of insufficient vitality. His prevalence would put the human type in danger.

> "The sick are the greatest danger for the well. The weaker, not the stronger, are the strong's undoing. It is not *fear* of our fellow-man, which we should wish to see diminished; for [pg 373]fear rouses those who are strong to become terrible in turn themselves, and preserves the hard-earned and successful type of humanity. What is to be dreaded by us more than any other doom is not fear, but rather the great disgust, not fear, but rather the great pity —disgust and pity for our human fellows.... The *morbid* are our greatest peril —not the 'bad' men, not the predatory beings. Those born wrong, the

> miscarried, the broken—they it is, the *weakest*, who are undermining the vitality of the race, poisoning our trust in life, and putting humanity in question. Every look of them is a sigh,—'Would I were something other! I am sick and tired of what I am.' In this swamp-soil of self-contempt, every poisonous weed flourishes, and all so small, so secret, so dishonest, and so sweetly rotten. Here swarm the worms of sensitiveness and resentment; here the air smells odious with secrecy, with what is not to be acknowledged; here is woven endlessly the net of the meanest of conspiracies, the conspiracy of those who suffer against those who succeed and are victorious; here the very aspect of the victorious is hated—as if health, success, strength, pride, and the sense of power were in themselves things vicious, for which one ought eventually to make bitter expiation. Oh, how these people would themselves like to inflict the expiation, how they thirst to be the hangmen! And all the while their duplicity never confesses their hatred to be hatred."[220]

Poor Nietzsche's antipathy is itself sickly enough, but we all know what he means, and he expresses well the clash between the two ideals. The carnivorous-minded "strong man," the adult male and cannibal, can see nothing but mouldiness and morbidness in the saint's gentleness and self-severity, and regards him with pure loathing. The whole feud revolves essentially upon two pivots: Shall the seen world or the unseen world be our chief sphere of adaptation? and must our means of adaptation in this seen world be aggressiveness or non-resistance?

[pg 374]
The debate is serious. In some sense and to some degree both worlds must be acknowledged and taken account of; and in the seen world both aggressiveness and non-resistance are needful. It is a question of emphasis, of more or less. Is the saint's type or the strong-man's type the more ideal?

It has often been supposed, and even now, I think, it is supposed by most persons, that there can be one intrinsically ideal type of human character. A certain kind of man, it is imagined, must be the best man absolutely and apart from the utility of his function, apart from economical considerations. The saint's type, and the knight's or gentleman's type, have always been rival claimants of this absolute ideality; and in the ideal of military religious orders both types were in a manner blended. According to the empirical philosophy, however, all ideals are matters of relation. It would be absurd, for example, to ask for a definition of "the ideal horse," so long as dragging drays and running races, bearing children, and jogging about with tradesmen's packages all remain as indispensable differentiations of equine function. You may take what you call a general all-round animal as a compromise, but he will be inferior to any horse of a more specialized type, in some one particular direction. We must not forget this now when, in discussing saintliness, we ask if it be an ideal type of manhood. We must test it by its economical relations.

I think that the method which Mr. Spencer uses in his Data of Ethics will help to fix our opinion. Ideality in conduct is altogether a matter of adaptation. A society where all were invariably aggressive would destroy itself by inner friction, and in a society where some are aggressive, others must be non-resistant, if there is to be any kind of order. This is the present constitution of society, [pg 375] and to the mixture we owe many of our blessings. But the aggressive members of society are always tending to become bullies, robbers, and swindlers; and no one believes that such a state of things as we now live in is the millennium. It is meanwhile quite possible to conceive an imaginary society in which there should be no aggressiveness, but only sympathy and fairness,—any small community of true friends now realizes such a society. Abstractly considered, such a society on a large scale would be the millennium, for every good thing might be realized there with no expense of friction. To such a millennial society the saint would be entirely adapted. His peaceful modes of appeal would be efficacious over his companions, and there would be no one extant to take advantage of his non-resistance. The saint is therefore abstractly a higher type of man than the "strong man," because he is adapted to the highest society conceivable, whether that society ever be concretely possible or not. The strong man would immediately tend by his presence to make that society deteriorate. It would become inferior in everything save in a certain kind of bellicose excitement, dear to men as they now are.

But if we turn from the abstract question to the actual situation, we find that the individual saint may be well or ill adapted, according to particular circumstances. There is, in short, no absoluteness in the excellence of sainthood. It must be confessed that as far as this world goes, any one who makes an out-and-out saint of himself does so at his peril. If he is not a large enough man, he may appear more insignificant and contemptible, for all his saintship, than if he had remained a worldling.[221] Accordingly religion has seldom been so radically [pg 376] taken in our Western world that the devotee could not mix it with some worldly temper. It has always found good men who could follow most of its impulses, but who stopped short when it came to non-resistance. Christ himself was fierce upon occasion. Cromwells, Stonewall Jacksons, Gordons, show that Christians can be strong men also.

How is success to be absolutely measured when there are so many environments and so many ways of looking at the adaptation? It cannot be measured absolutely; the verdict will vary according to the point of view adopted. From the biological point of view Saint Paul was a failure, because he was beheaded. Yet he was magnificently adapted to the larger environment of history; and so far as any saint's example is a leaven of righteousness in the world, and draws it in the direction of more prevalent habits of saintliness, he is a success, no matter what his immediate bad fortune may be. The greatest saints, the spiritual heroes whom every one acknowledges, the Francises, Bernards, Luthers, Loyolas, Wesleys, Channings, Moodys, Gratrys, the Phillips Brookses, the Agnes Joneses, Margaret Hallahans, and Dora Pattisons, are successes from the outset. They show themselves, and there is no question; every one perceives their strength and stature. Their sense of mystery in things, their passion, their goodness, irradiate about them and enlarge their outlines while they soften them. They are like pictures with an atmosphere and background; and, placed alongside of them, the strong men of this world and no other seem as dry as sticks, as hard and crude as blocks of stone or brickbats.

[pg 377]
In a general way, then, and "on the whole,"[222] our abandonment of theological criteria, and our testing of religion by practical common sense and the empirical method, leave it in possession of its towering place in history. Economically, the saintly group of qualities is indispensable to the world's welfare. The great saints are immediate successes; the smaller ones are at least heralds and harbingers, and they may be leavens also, of a better mundane order. Let us be saints, then, if we can, whether or not we succeed visibly and temporally. But in our Father's house are many mansions, and each of us must discover for himself the kind of religion and the amount of

saintship which best comports with what he believes to be his powers and feels to be his truest mission and vocation. There are no successes to be guaranteed and no set orders to be given to individuals, so long as we follow the methods of empirical philosophy.

This is my conclusion so far. I know that on some of your minds it leaves a feeling of wonder that such a method should have been applied to such a subject, and this in spite of all those remarks about empiricism which I made at the beginning of Lecture XIII.[223] How, you say, can religion, which believes in two worlds and an invisible order, be estimated by the adaptation of its fruits to this world's order alone? It is its *truth*, not its utility, you insist, upon which our verdict ought to depend. If religion is true, its fruits are good fruits, even though in this world they should prove uniformly ill adapted and full of naught but pathos. It goes back, then, after all, to the question of the truth of theology. The plot inevitably thickens upon us; we cannot escape theoretical considerations. I propose, then, that to some [pg 378] degree we face the responsibility. Religious persons have often, though not uniformly, professed to see truth in a special manner. That manner is known as mysticism. I will consequently now proceed to treat at some length of mystical phenomena, and after that, though more briefly, I will consider religious philosophy.